THE SILKE

The
SILKEN TWINE

A Study of the Works of Michael McLaverty

SOPHIA HILLAN KING

POOLBEG

A Paperback Original
First published 1992 by
Poolbeg Press Ltd
Knocksedan House,
Swords, Co Dublin, Ireland

The publisher gratefully acknowledges the financial assistance
of the Arts Council of Northern Ireland

ISBN 1 85371 173 X

Cover illustration courtesy of Ulster Museum, Belfast
Cover design by Pomphrey Associates
Set by Richard Parfrey in ITC Stone Serif 9.5/15
Printed by The Guernsey Press Company Ltd,
Vale, Guernsey, Channel Islands

ACKNOWLEDGEMENTS

The author wishes to express her grateful appreciation to Michael McLaverty and his family for their unfailing help and support during the preparation of this work; to Professor Seamus Deane, who supervised the project in its initial stages; to Professor Leo Macnamara, Ann Arbor, Michigan, for permission to consult his unpublished study of Michael McLaverty; to Professor John Cronin, who supervised the doctoral thesis from which this book grew, and who has continued to give invaluable help and advice; to Professor RH Buchanan and the staff and members of the Institute of Irish Studies, Queen's University, Belfast, where the work was carried out; and to the staff of the Queen's University, Linenhall and the Central Libraries of Belfast, for their tireless assistance.

For my parents, Edward and Anne Hillan

Man was made for joy and woe,
And when this we rightly know
Through the world we safely go.
Joy and woe are woven fine,
A clothing for the soul divine.
Under every grief and pine
Runs a joy with silken twine.

William Blake
"Auguries of Innocence"

CONTENTS

INTRODUCTION

      The Whole Man   1

SECTION I   VALEDICTION AND LOSS

  1   The Island   29
  2   The City   49
  3   Uprooted   76

SECTION II   QUIET DESPERATION

  4   An Exploration of Charity   109
  5   The Tether of God   138

SECTION III   JOY AND WOE

  6   Sins of the Mind   167
  7   The Choice   194
  8   The Stranger   214

CONCLUSION

      The Silken Twine   240

SELECT BIBLIOGRAPHY   258

INDEX   264

INTRODUCTION

THE WHOLE MAN

> The whole man is one whose knowledge, whose knowing-
> ness, has not outrun his natural wisdom, his intuition of
> the whole. Intimate knowledge of an acre is more valuable
> for the man and the books he may write than a detailed
> knowledge of a national plan for agriculture. The sane
> man builds with Blake's grain of sand.[1]

These words are taken from an article written in 1946 by
the poet Roy McFadden. It was based on a lecture he had
given in 1945 on "Contemporary Ulster Writing," and the
"whole man" of whom he wrote was Michael McLaverty.
Although McLaverty was some seventeen years McFadden's
senior, the two had been friends for several years, since
McLaverty had written to the younger man to praise his
poem "Easter 1942" for its "proud spirit" and "passionate
urgency."[2] To McFadden, McLaverty's work was "the most
important" to have appeared in local writing during the
years of the Second World War.[3] Both men were members
of a loosely-connected group of writers, trying to make
their way in the Forties. One of these, Robert Greacen,
remembers this time in Belfast, and establishes the

prominence of McLaverty:

> In 1939 Belfast was largely a cultural desert. One had
> heard indeed of the Ulster Literary Theatre but those
> Rutherford Mayne days were past. The Opera House was
> devoted largely to West End successes that bore little
> resemblance to the realities of Belfast life. St John Ervine
> in far-off Devon no longer spoke for us in any significant
> way. George Sheils had a good sense of theatre, but was
> superficial. Louis MacNeice, though born in Belfast, usually
> cast a jaundiced eye on his homeland, and at that time
> was largely associated with the Auden group in England.
> Local writers like Tom Carnduff, Denis Ireland, Matt
> Mulcahy and Richard Rowley did not seem particularly
> inspiring to the young men who had just left school. The
> only writers in the city we could really respect were the
> poet John Hewitt and the fiction writer Michael
> McLaverty.[4]

McLaverty was an established writer, published in London
and New York, accessible to and respected by his fellow
authors. Yet, when McFadden addressed the New Ireland
Society in 1945, he found it necessary to defend McLaverty's
writing. Something had happened which would change
the whole direction of McLaverty's work, and which would
cause him to relinquish his place in Belfast's literary society.

By 1945 McLaverty was under attack, most notably by
his fellow-writer, St John Ervine. In a scathing review of
McLaverty's third novel, *In This Thy Day*, Ervine had
attacked the very attention to detail which had made
McLaverty renowned as a craftsman, and had cast doubt

on McLaverty's ability to succeed in the longer form of the novel as he undoubtedly had in the short story.[5] Other critics wondered about this novel, not for its attention to detail, but for its stark and uncompromising ending, in which hero and heroine are parted for ever through the implacable bigotry of the young man's mother. Yet, it was in the writing of this novel that McLaverty believed he had finally found his voice. Indeed, as a consequence of his dedication to it, he preferred to change his publisher rather than his ending. Moreover, he moved further and further from the form in which he had first written, the short story, to improve and refine his vision of the well-written novel. The enigma of McLaverty lies in his dedication to his craft, and his undoubted creative gift, set against an evident divergence of purpose between author and critic from this time onwards, so that by the end of the Forties the author was prepared to turn his back on the general public rather than compromise his deeply held principles.

McLaverty deliberately withdrew because of a finely-tuned moral sense. It did not seem possible to him, by the end of the Forties, to follow the literary path apparently laid out for him, and, as soon as he had clarified in his own mind what it was his conscience would forbid or permit him, he set himself to go his own way, at whatever cost in terms of popularity. When he took this decision to be a moral novelist and, in his own phrase, "turn his back on the short story," he had been publishing his work for only seventeen years. He had, by the beginning of 1950, published four novels and two selections of short stories. In the remainder of his career, he would publish four more novels, a further seven short stories, and see one new anthology and an edition of his collected stories appear.[6] Yet, he would not again feel it necessary to mount a defence of his approach to fiction. His struggle and crisis belong to the troubled decade of the Forties, just as his time of learning and apprenticeship belongs to the Thirties. What he has done since 1950 has been to consolidate his position, to reaffirm—even at the cost of literary popularity—what he believes to be the truth, both in morality and literature. In McLaverty's work, the two cannot be divided. At the heart of his literary craftsmanship is an inviolable moral code: in the midst of unshakable morality is the deeply-felt need to express and transform ideas into poetic form.

From that dual base comes McLaverty's contribution to Irish literature. Yet, he did not write a story until he was almost twenty-eight, and had trained, not as an artist or a writer, but as a scientist. Literature came to him as a delightful surprise when he was already a grown man, and he took to it completely and naturally, bringing his scientific eye for detail to bear on an entirely new range of subjects. Perhaps it is partly from his scientific training that there derives his scrupulous attention to finer points and his unerring accuracy in description.

He was born on 5 July 1904, to Michael and Catherine McLaverty of Magheross, Carrickmacross, Co Monaghan. His father worked as a waiter in a hotel in that town and, later, the family moved to Belfast, where his father worked, again as a waiter, in the Queen's Cafe in Queen's Arcade. In an interview given in 1983, McLaverty recorded his memories of this time:

I was born in Carrickmacross, Co. Monaghan but I left it at about five years of age...I haven't been back to Carrick for about twelve years but I wrote about it in my novel *The Choice*. I don't remember much about it except the death of a baby: I remember the people coming in and a tin of biscuits on the table, the wine bottle and the glasses, and I remember the little cot. It was on the table with a veil over it, that I remember well...This was Gerard who died, and then there was Patrick who was the eldest and then there is myself and we had about five girls.

I went for just one day to the school and I remember it quite well because I never liked it. At lunch time when the boys were running around and shouting and squealing I got very frightened and I started to cry in a corner, and then one of the teaching brothers came over and took my hand and patted it. I remember he had a green girdle...and he brought me inside and gave me a cup of hot cocoa and I'll never forget how good it tasted.

My father was a waiter in the hotel and he came to Belfast with his two brothers as they did not have enough land to support all of them. The two others cleared off and my father opened a pub, but as he trusted people the shopboys robbed him blind so he had to seek another job.

My mother was from Kildare via Dublin. My mother took ill after having her ninth baby. She had married when she was only eighteen and having a baby every year was just too much for her and she died very young.[7]

Despite the absence of his mother, McLaverty remembers his childhood as a happy one. He was especially fond of football, and remembers this part of his life with contentment:

> I next went to St Gall's School off the Springfield Road
> with the De la Salle Brothers and I was very happy there.
> The family lived in Clowney Street off the Falls Road and
> at the back of it was wasteground where we played football
> all day long.[8]

Later, in the Thirties, when McLaverty was beginning to
write his first novel, about a young boy in Belfast, his
working title was *Waste Ground*, and the place was Belfast's
Falls Road. As a boy, however, he had no thought of writing,
though he remembers an inspiring teacher, Father
McCloskey, at his next school, St Malachy's College, who
taught him to love Shakespeare's language.[9]

He entered Queen's University in October 1924, as a
student of Physics, obtaining in July 1927 the degree of
Bachelor of Science with Second Class Honours. In 1928,
after a year at St Mary's, Strawberry Hill, in London, he was
awarded the Higher Diploma in Education, and was
admitted to the degree of Master of Science, again from
Queen's University Belfast, in 1933. Throughout his
university career, he mixed with arts students, and he
remembers his interest in literature growing, helped at a
crucial point by a football injury, which compelled him to
rest. He began to read widely, with growing enthusiasm, so
that when he finished his science degrees, he was in a
position to concentrate his mind on literature. The first
turning of his life had been reached.

The year 1933 was significant in another way, too, for
this was when he married Mary Conroy, formerly Giles, a
young widow and fellow-teacher at St John's Public
Elementary School in Colinward Street in West Belfast,

where McLaverty began his teaching career. He remembers this time vividly:

> I first started teaching in St John's off the Springfield Road. I was teaching boys of fourteen and fifteen years of age, and while I was there I put on a different Shakespearean play every year so that I could learn along with the children. I taught there from 1929 until 1957.
>
> ...I met my wife in St John's Primary School. I had started there on 1 September 1929. She was a childless widow who had been married to a young solicitor. She was also a teacher and started school three weeks after I did...If she were off sick for a while I realised there was something missing in my life. When she came back I was very glad to see her and in that way I suppose love developed...
>
> We were married in 1933. I was a very shy sort of fellow and arranged that we would be married on 13 July when everybody would be in bed after the Twelfth celebrations, and there would be nobody out to see us; and not only that, but we selected a little church, St Joseph's at Hannahstown, way up the mountainside. We were married there and we discovered later that her brother Dr Giles had been married there, and also her mother had been married there, so we must all have been very shy people![10]

His time in St John's was happy and fulfilling, and it was while he was there that he wrote his first five novels and all but four of his short stories. Fifteen short stories were published between 1932 and 1937, when life with his young family must have been at its busiest. His children were born between 1934 and 1944: had he never written a line, Michael McLaverty's life as teacher and father of a family of four[11] would have been an exceedingly full one. He became, after his discovery of literature during his student days, an avid reader not only of fiction but also of history, philosophy, biography and criticism. It may be difficult to imagine how he would have avoided, in such circumstances, putting pen to paper, but the fact remains that he lived a kind of double life, throwing himself into his schoolwork for half the day, and writing well into the evening when he came home. At holiday times, he went with his young family of four children to Killard, in Strangford, to stay in a bungalow which had been for many years in his wife's family. There he involved himself in the outdoor pursuits which were to find their way into his writing. At all times, and in all circumstances, even during the disruptive years of the Second World War, he continued to write stories, novels, and critical articles. In his unfailingly modest way, he acknowledged in a letter to a student in 1960 the difficulties presented by a full, alternative life, but he reaffirmed his dedication to his art at whatever cost to himself:

I am, I suppose, a private sort of person, a bit of a recluse, and so can't offer you anything startlingly adventurous for your Introduction. I have had a happy childhood and recall my schooldays not with contempt but with gratitude for those who taught me...Any letters that I have written to friends and other writers will probably be of no value until I pass out—even then I doubt if many readers would be interested. Like Forrest Reid my books have had little or no sale. But then he had a small private income to sustain him and could devote his whole time and energy to writing. I am not in a position to do that though I wish I were. My only desire in writing is to write well and to have my books make their own way spontaneously and without my striving to boost them. That is my policy; it may seem to lack ambition but there it is and I'm not likely to change now that the unseen arteries are hardening and I look forward to retiring at the first pensionable opportunity and devoting my remaining years to some books that I have still to write. The life I lead now, though it is an interesting and happy one, gives me little energy or time to write in the way I would like to.[12]

When he wrote these words to Mme de Micheaux in 1960, he had left St John's, after the death of his friend and headmaster, Dan Clarke. From 1957 until his early retirement in 1964, he was principal of a large school on the Whiterock Road, St Thomas's Boys' Secondary. There, one year before his early retirement in 1963, he would welcome as a teacher the young Seamus Heaney. Heaney recalls McLaverty's dedication to education in the fullest sense of the word:

He had them in the palm of his hand. They rejoiced in the way his talk heightened their world of football teams and street corners and they were affected by the style of his sincerity.

But Michael was as concerned to educate the taste of this young graduate as he was successful in enlivening the

imaginations of those veteran pupils. "Look for the
intimate thing," he would say, and go on to praise "the
note of exile" in Chekhov, or to exhort me to read Tolstoy's
"Death of Ivan Illych," one of his sacred texts.[13]

This is McLaverty the man; but it is not McFadden's "whole
man." Beneath this apparently calm exterior there lay a
complicated and deeply scrupulous sensibility, for, almost
from the beginning of his literary career, McLaverty was
concerned not only with the style and quality of his writing,
but also with its moral import. Indeed, in his earliest
writings, there can be discerned the seeds of his decision to
withdraw from the public world of letters.

Until the early years of the Forties, McLaverty's work
had followed a definite pattern. He had begun, tentatively,
in 1932, with gentle, sometimes melancholy stories of island
people, in which, through close observation of man's
relation to his element, he had uncovered with delicate
precision fundamental truths concerning the nature of joy
and relief, loneliness and guilt. As the Thirties progressed,
he darkened and sharpened this vision, adding to the
celebration of the people he remembered from his
childhood, Chekhovian studies of the selfishness of
otherwise well-meaning folk. By 1940, his stories of children
on islands and in cities had contributed to his first, very
successful novel, *Call My Brother Back* (1939); and he had
moved on to studies of the plight of the old and
dispossessed. This preoccupation, reinforced as was *Call My
Brother Back* by his own memories of the early part of the
century, resulted in the stories entitled "Stone," "The White
Mare," "The Sea," (later "Look At The Boats,"), "Becalmed,"

(later "The Schooner,"), and his second novel, *Lost Fields*
(1941).[14]

From 1941 onwards, however, the pattern changes.
There was no loss of enthusiasm, no sudden lack of interest
in writing, but from about this time the author's writings
began to take a different turn, so that eight years later, in
1949, he would write to John Pudney, who had asked him
for a contribution to his prestigious journal, *New Writing*:
"I have turned my back on the short story."[15]

From one who had received nothing but acclaim for his
work in the short story form, this seems a surprising statement. Closer examination of the list of his works reveals,
however, a gradual move away from the shorter form from
the beginning of the Forties onwards. In contrast to the
twenty short stories of the initial nine years, he was to
write between 1941 and 1949 only four, while producing,
as before, two novels. Even more surprisingly, although
four more novels have appeared, he has published, in the
forty years since that renunciation, just seven short stories.

It is an ironic fact that in the very last of the stories
published before the author's renunciation of the form,
"Six Weeks On and Two Ashore," he appears to have been
on the verge of a significant change of direction in his
writing. The stories of the middle Forties dealt with those
who, in Thoreau's phrase, "lead lives of quiet desperation,"
and in "Six Weeks On and Two Ashore," McLaverty refined
his observations to a new degree of sensitivity.[16] This story
deals with a lightkeeper and his wife, embittered and soured
towards each other because of their loss of sexual love and
unable to find a way of healing their differences. All is
suggested, never made explicit, and the author reveals in

the tightly controlled, allusive and powerful prose, a new dimension to his understanding. Yet, while seven stories were published after this one, McLaverty would touch only once more—in the late story, "After Forty Years"[17]—on the area of sexual relations. It seemed, in 1948, that he had ceased to believe in the short story.

The key to this renunciation of what had been, in his early writing years, a natural form, seems to lie in the journals which he kept throughout the Forties, and in the growing number of critical articles written by him at this time. McLaverty had been in the habit, since the early Thirties, of writing down his thoughts and observations, though the character of these was to change over the years. When he was writing his early stories of children on islands, and the loneliness of the human spirit, he was influenced by the writing of James Joyce, Liam O'Flaherty and Daniel Corkery. It was the prose style of such writers as these, and the Russians, Chekhov and Tolstoy, which inspired the young McLaverty in his first rush of enthusiastic writing. From them, and from his wide and careful reading, he learned his craft, and it was not till the early Forties that he stopped seeing himself as an apprentice at the feet of his literary masters, and began to consider instead what sort of writer he was to be. At this point begins the probing of conscience which leads to the apparently strange denial in 1949 of the short story form.

As early as 1941, he set out in the journal his idea of the novel:

For me a novel:

(i)   must be in serious relation to actual living.

(ii) The characters must be normal, credible.

(iii) Each sentence should have significance.

(iv) Technical ability and poetic sensibility.

(v) The style depending on the compulsive quality of the matter in hand.

(vi) The events to be inevitable (no forcing)

A novelist should recreate reality and illumine it.[18]

Elsewhere he declares his dedication to truth, and his abhorrence of writing which might "lead others into sin."[19] This seems to be the beginning of the scrupulous examination of the writer's moral as well as aesthetic responsibility, which was eventually to lead McLaverty to his renunciation of the short story, and to draw him away from his place in the public eye.

One intriguing line in a fragment of an unpublished essay of 1941 states that "Man is good and evil—and it is the integration of these that..."[20] Tantalisingly, the entry ends there but the theme of the duality of man's nature and the necessity of overcoming the intrinsic tendency to evil recurs. He does not mention Blake, but with this entry there becomes apparent a striking similarity to the thought of "Auguries of Innocence." However, although Blake is not acknowledged, one name recurs very often at this time— that of Gerard Manley Hopkins. A journal entry of 1941 makes the first reference to a most significant influence on the author at this time, as he reminds himself to "Write article on Hopkins from notes already made."[21] Observation of his surroundings and notes on the moral responsibilities of the individual alternate and merge, so that a page of delicate observation of the workings of nature may be followed by an intense examination of man's moral responsibility, for the journal is above all a record of the author's spontaneous thoughts and reactions. A typical page reads thus:

> Anger is a horrible sin. Man loses his reason and descends to brute level; there enters into the unguarded mind all the vices that flesh and spirit are heir to.

> Downpatrick—the roads—people—Nature—books—feeling. Language—edge of dark—cutting away—heel of evening— moon in full bloom—blossom on the sun today.
> Avoid stale phrases—read poetry.[22]

One of the most interesting of the journal entries of this time refers to the German air raids on Belfast in 1941, remarkable for its capturing of the spirit of comradeship and resilience that seems to have characterised the townspeople at that difficult time:

> Suddenly the siren went and a nervous hush spread across the people, and those who were lying got up and stood about. The silver barrage balloons were put up; an old man looked at them contemplatively: "You might as well put me up!"
> The crowd laughed. Presently there was a noise like machine-gun fire and the crowd raised their eyes to the blue sky. But the sound faded; it was only an old motor car running over broken slates on the road. Silence again. Then there came a faint drone like an aeroplane and once again all raised their eyes. Then from a wooden box spread

out at the feet of two women an alarm-clock suddenly
went off and the people jumped away from it in fright.
Then they laughed at their folly and the man said again
with contempt: "We can take it!"[23]

It would seem to have been the case that the writing of
short stories was no longer of primary importance in Mc
Laverty's mind, for while his concern for the quietly
desperate was manifesting itself in the fine stories, "The
Poteen Maker," "The Road To The Shore," and "The
Mother," the main energies of the author were at this time
going into the development of his moral as well as his
aesthetic sense and, especially, into the writing of his third
novel, published eventually in 1945 as *In This Thy Day*.[24]

Increasingly, criticism and the education of the minds
of younger artists was assuming greater importance to
McLaverty. As early as 1942, he addressed a meeting of the
Belfast branch of PEN, the authors' society. His title was
"The Young Poets." In the last paragraph of this short
piece, he touches again on the morality of the author:

Out of the emotional and intellectual interpretation of
life these poets are conveying feeling and thought in
concentration, and as their poetry in general manifests
that man has more than natural needs to satisfy they will
probably escape from that materialistic conception of life
that impoverished much of the poetry of the 1930s. So far
they have evaded the schools of poetry that are already
cropping up with ready-made tabulated ingredients and
prepared plans. A poet should write as he himself feels; it
is his task to elucidate and integrate his experiences and

> if he possesses a Christian philosophy of life his work will,
> I think, be more universal and greater as literature.[25]

This was not the first time he had lectured on a literary topic; he had spoken before to the members of Irish PEN in 1940, on "The Irish Short Story,"[26] and in the same year had addressed the members of the Young Ulster Society on the topic of "Irish Fiction."[27] Yet, he had not, in these previous lectures, addressed the question of the author's moral responsibility to his readers. From this time onwards his private writings and critical articles delve further and further into the nature of artistic accountability. So, while his journal entries for the early years of the decade continue for a time to reflect his love of minute detail and his accurate ear for the rhythm of colloquial speech, his next critical piece, delivered as another lecture to Irish PEN in May 1944, makes clear the change that has come upon him.

The subject of this talk was the Jesuit poet, Gerard Manley Hopkins, and the text was, perhaps, the article which he had earlier been exhorting himself to produce. In it McLaverty examines with admiration and a developing critical sense his view of, not only Hopkins's literary value, but also his renunciation of poetry, because of the poet's fear of his own sensuous responses to the natural world. He notes particularly the importance to Hopkins of renunciation, and marks, in the margin of his paper, a comment on Hopkins's self-imposed penance: "cf Habit of Perfection. Self-sacrifice." It is this quality which McLaverty most admired in Hopkins, and, in this article, he commends Hopkins' embracing of the philosophy of Duns Scotus as an indication of the poet's reconciliation of his aesthetic with his moral responsibility. Hopkins' concern for the perfection of detail, for the working and reworking of verse or prose, provided the vital link for McLaverty, especially when considered in the context of the poet's Catholicism:

> With Hopkins embracing and absorbing the philosophy of the Church of which he was a member, his work gained as he grew older a fine positive and intellectual control. It is true that one who shares his beliefs may get more spiritual value from his work than one who doesn't but one does not fail to notice that there is behind them a unification of experience—not to grow is to live in a world "that's all in pieces, all coherence gone," or as Yeats remarks,
>
> > Things fall apart; the centre cannot hold.
> > Mere anarchy is loosed upon the world.[28]

McLaverty's significant conclusion on Hopkins' work is that "Hopkins is always serious, never cheap and never flashy," and that "the Catholic outlook on the world gives his poems unification."[29]

In this way, McLaverty developed and refined his moral standpoint. In his fiction, though clearly reducing his output in the short-story form, he produced short-story length extracts from his forthcoming novel, set in County Down. This seems to indicate a pragmatic approach to the problem of keeping his work in the public eye, with a kind of disregard for the short stories these self-contained extracts might have been, for it is a fact that in the third novel, *In This Thy Day*, the characters of the grandfather and his granddaughter, so vivid in the extract, rarely have the chance to impress the reader as fully rounded characters. There is no doubt, however, that McLaverty was now determined to spend more time on what he hoped would be his definitive novel. Years later, he would write on the flyleaf of one copy of the novel the explanatory subtitle, "An Exploration of Charity." This, the examination of charity and its opposites, spite and rejection, rather than the memories of childhood and the celebration of his people, was to be McLaverty's new theme. To underline it, he left the spiteful Mrs Mason grieving for her lost son and repenting too late for her limited vision. That this also left the young heroine without any hope for the future seemed to the author an inevitable corollary of Mrs Mason's lack of charity, and he believed strongly that his novel required this bleak and uncompromising ending.

His publishers, however, did not agree, and it was at this time that McLaverty left Longmans rather than change his ending.

He decided, too, from that time onward to make clear the aesthetic and moral principles by which he worked. In this, he was determined to be guided, not by his critics or publishers, but solely by his own conscience. Some echo of his feeling of betrayal and disappointment is evident in the last line of his final letter to Longmans: "Though the reading public may despise my book my faith in it will not alter."[30] It was at this point that Roy McFadden mounted his defence of McLaverty's method, but, though this showed that some of his fellow authors applauded his attention to detail, perceiving beneath it what Padraic Fiacc called "the vein of his terrible pity,"[31] great damage had been done to the author by the critical reception of his novel. In his own mind, he was essentially alone, and this sense of isolation would not leave him.

His feeling of alienation from the general reader is expressed once more, in a letter written by him in 1945, the year of publication of *In This Thy Day*. This letter was to John O'Connor, author of *Come Day, Go Day*, and reflects the forbearance coupled with determination of a man deeply disappointed at the reception of his work:

> A letter like yours, unexpected and unsolicited, brought me keen satisfaction and made me feel that the writing of novels is worthwhile. The fact that you quoted a few passages increased my satisfaction and scattered, somewhat, an idea that I was forming about novel-readers, namely that they do not read but skim, following the physical aspects of the story, that only and no more. My idea may be true of the mass of readers but, on them, literature does not rest for sustenance, nor to them does a creative writer primarily address himself.[32]

From this time onwards, McLaverty wrote to satisfy his moral as well as his aesthetic impulse. Increasingly, the two were becoming one.

The Three Brothers[33] was his first completely moral, Catholic novel. It was published in 1948, and is largely the reason for his declarations at this time of lack of interest in the short story. Since the trying time of *In This Thy Day*, McLaverty had been determined to prove to himself and the reading public that he was a moral novelist, and that his being so would not take away from the aesthetic appeal of his books. With this book, he set out to show that the different characteristics and moral attitudes of the eponymous three brothers brought them either peace and reward or torment of spirit. Much emphasis was laid here, as in the previous novel, on the necessity of accepting the consequences of actions performed with free will.

The epigraph to the novel, ascribed to an anonymous source but actually written by himself, reflects not only a Blake-like concern with the inevitable tension of opposites within man's flawed nature, but also the crystallisation of the author's view of the necessity of suffering and repentance:

> Sorrow and suffering and joy are three strands in the tether of God; sorrow and suffering strengthen fervour, and joy strengthens hope. Without fervour and without hope the spirit breaks loose, and when the spirit breaks loose from the tethering, Man roams like an animal without a home.

A note made in the journal in the same year underlines further the shift away from compassion for man's frailty, towards the acceptance of suffering and struggle as the only means towards redemption:

> 23 February 1948
>
> When you feel at peace with the world and at rest, if you feel no more within you a struggle against this world and your soul's salvation, then is the time to re-examine your conscience ruthlessly. To be lukewarm and indifferent is to be in danger. A soul is alive when there is an unceasing daily struggle.[34]

This emphasis on suffering and struggle sets the tone for a critical article published in London in 1948, entitled "Letter To A Young Novelist," which contains much of the spirit of McLaverty's 1945 letter to John O'Connor. He warns the fictional apprentice against the darkness of the vision of such writers as Mauriac, and emphasises that the sincere novelist must, "from the shuffled material of experience... integrate and clarify the night and day of life, its sorrow and joy." He concludes, as he had more tentatively in 1942 while writing of the young poets, that "A Christian philosophy comprehends the whole of life and gives meaning to all human experience."[35]

One of the most interesting features of this article is McLaverty's ambivalent attitude to a writer whom he could not help but admire and with whom he had more than a little in common. This was François Mauriac, who had, himself, felt the danger of corrupting his readers, and had dedicated himself, with *Le Noeud de Vipères*,[36] to the Catholic novel. Mauriac explained his moral position thus:

> I am a metaphysician working on the concrete. I try to make the Catholic universe of evil perceptible, tangible, odorous. The theologians give us an abstract idea of the sinner. I give him flesh and blood.[37]

McLaverty, in an interview given in 1978, uses remarkably similar terms:

> I have always tried to explain evil and the effects of spite and hate in my work, and their opposites.[38]

Similarity exists, too, to the dilemma posed by Conor Cruise O'Brien, writing as Donat O'Donnell, in *Maria Cross*, where woman, however loved or hated, is at once the temptress and the source of salvation.[39] The subtitle of the study: "Imaginative Patterns in a Group of Modern Catholic Writers," could apply as well to McLaverty's as to Mauriac's work. Journal entries refer at this time again and again to Mauriac, and McLaverty's own interest in O'Brien's thesis is reflected in those pages.[40]

As if concerned that the epigraph to *The Three Brothers* had not made plain his moral and artistic beliefs, McLaverty went on to set out clearly his formulated opinion of the role of the novelist This article, entitled "Michael McLaverty Explains His Methods," appeared in August 1948 in *Forecast*, the official publication of the American Literary Foundation.[41] No one could now doubt his dedication as a moral and, like Mauriac, Chesterton and Hopkins himself, a specifically Catholic writer. All his journal entries of this time reflect his deeply self-critical moral sense.[42] The importance of struggle towards redemption, very much in the spirit of *Maria Cross*, is reflected time and time again, and with it there is outright condemnation of any writing which might corrupt the mind of a single reader. Into the dangerous category of writers who might undermine the moral integrity of their readers comes, increasingly, Mauriac, of whose *Thérèse Desquéroux* McLaverty wrote in 1948: "One wonders was the book worth writing."[43]

For readers in the Forties, who may have wondered whether "Six Weeks On and Two Ashore" would represent a significant change in theme in McLaverty's work, the following entry, dated 30 January 1949, seems to indicate that a sense of disgust at the usual portrayals in fiction of sex and related matters, combined with his unshakable belief in the responsibility of the author for his readers' moral health, would preclude any more such writing from McLaverty:

> 30 January 1949
>
> Many critics quarrel with writers who are too con- templative—it is a niggling sort of criticism to condemn a man for the nature which God has endowed him with. If all through his life he has met "chaste, quiet and virginal women," why should a critic condemn him for writing about the life he knows. To write otherwise would be to write what is untrue to himself—to what he knows and feels and thinks.[44]

"Six Weeks On and Two Ashore," the last short story written before the renunciation of the form, represents an end to a period of the author's life, though, happily, not to his career as a short-story writer. No-one could have predicted the subtle and unobtrusive way in which the body of McLaverty's short fiction would grow, gradually regaining a life of its own, until, thirty years after his renunciation, his short stories would provide for him, when he most needed it, an affirmation and celebration of his life's work.

McLaverty the man, and McLaverty the writer, coalesce to make what McFadden calls "the whole man." This study is not concerned with biographical information, beyond that which affects author's work, but attempts instead to trace the development of a complex mind. McLaverty withdrew from his prominent position in Irish letters because of an inner moral imperative. This work sets out to show the gradual movement in his writing towards this point of renunciation and dedication in 1948, and to examine the consequences throughout his career of his decision to become a moral novelist.

His decision was made in a spirit of dedication to the dilemma described in *Maria Cross*, the necessity of redemption by suffering and renunciation. It shows itself most clearly in his deep affinity with the work of Gerard Manley Hopkins, confirmed in a talk given to the English Society of Queen's University, Belfast, at the beginning of December 1949. Its title, "Night and Day: A Note on Literature," reflects the author's over-riding concern with the duality of man's fallen nature:

> In his [Hopkins's] mature work there is underlined this continual attempt to come to grips with the Night and Day of human experience, and it is this truth to life, to the acceptance of the Cross—blended with the original form and verbal freshness of his poetry, that give it its meaningful significance.[45]

In such a spirit of renunciation McLaverty wrote on the last day of 1949 to John Pudney those oddly final-sounding words: "I have turned my back on the short story." He then settled to his self-appointed task of wrestling with the demands of the contemporary moral novel. When McLaverty became, with the publication of *The Three Brothers*, a Catholic novelist, he may have echoed Mauriac's move towards orthodoxy on the writing of *Le Noeud de Vipères*, but he did so in the spirit, not of the French writer, but of the scrupulous Jesuit, Gerard Manley Hopkins:

> The only just judge, the only literary critic, is Christ, who prizes, is proud of, and admires, more than any man, more than the receiver himself can, the gifts of his own making. And the only real good which fame and another's praise does is to convey to us...some token of the judgement which a perfectly just, heedful and wise mind, namely Christ's, passes upon our doings.[46]

REFERENCES

1 Roy McFadden, "A Note on Contemporary Ulster Writing," *Northman* XIV, 2 (Winter 1946), 21.

2 McLaverty to McFadden, 23 October 1942. Letter in possession of Roy McFadden.

3 McFadden, op. cit., 20.

4 Robert Greacen, "Writing in Wartime Belfast," *The Irish Times*, 16 March 1976.

5 St John Ervine, "Mr McLaverty's Clocking Hen," *Belfast Telegraph*, 10 August 1945.

6 See bibliography.

7 June Shepperd, "Looking Back: June Shepperd Talks to Michael McLaverty," *Ulster Tatler* (June 1983), 74-76.

8 ibid., 75.

9 ibid.

10 ibid.

11 Sheila, Colm, Kevin and Maura McLaverty.

12 Raymond de Micheaux, "An Ulster Novelist: Michael McLaverty," unpublished thesis presented to Université de Lyon for Diplôme d'Études Supérieures, 1960, 134.

13 Seamus Heaney, Introduction to *Collected Short Stories of Michael McLaverty*, Dublin, 1978.

14 See bibliography.

15 McLaverty to John Pudney, 31 December 1949. See *In Quiet Places*, Dublin, 1989, 141.

16 "Six Weeks On and Two Ashore," *Irish Writing*, 4 (April 1948), 36-45. See also *Collected Stories*, 182-93.

17 "After Forty Years," "New Irish Writing," *Irish Press*, 13 March 1976.

18 Journal, 1941; *In Quiet Places*, 75.

19 ibid.; *In Quiet Places*, 75-6.

20 ibid.; *In Quiet Places*, 77-8.

21 ibid.; *In Quiet Places*, 79.

22 ibid.; *In Quiet Places*, 81.

23 ibid.; *In Quiet Places*, 84-5

24 See *In Quiet Places*, 91-2; 100-103.

25 "The Young Poets," *The PEN in Ulster*, Belfast, 1942, 3.

26 Unpublished lecture delivered to Belfast branch of Irish PEN, March 1940.

27 Lecture to Young Ulster Society, 27 February 1940. See *In Quiet Places*, 67-9.

28 "Gerard Manley Hopkins," lecture to Belfast branch of Irish PEN, May 1944. See *In Quiet Places*, 97-8.

29 ibid.; *In Quiet Places*, 98.

30 McLaverty to Julie Kernan, 15 December 1944. See *In Quiet Places*, 103.

31 Padraic Fiacc, "Good and Evil: Prolegomenon to Study of McLaverty's Work," *Irish Bookman* I, 5 (December 1946), 37-41.

32 McLaverty to John O'Connor, 23 September 1945. See *In Quiet Places*, 104-6.

33 *The Three Brothers*, New York and London, 1948. Poolbeg (pbk) edition. Dublin, 1982.

34 Journal, 1948. *In Quiet Places*, 117.

35 "Letter to a Young Novelist," *The Key*, London, 1948; *In Quiet Places*, 114-16

36 François Mauriac, *Le Noeud de Vipères*, Paris, 1932.

37 François Mauriac, quoted in *Writers at Work: The Paris Review Interviews*., ed. Malcolm Cowley, Harmondsworth, 1981, 37 (Penguin edition).

38 Elgy Gillespie,"The Saturday Profile: Michael McLaverty," *The Irish Times*, 28 September 1978.

39 Donat O'Donnell, *Maria Cross: Imaginative Patterns in a Group of Catholic Novelists*, London, 1954.

40 Journal, 1949; *In Quiet Places*, 132-5.

41 "Michael McLaverty Explains His Methods," *Forecast*, Milwaukee, Wisconsin (August 1948), 6-7.

42 Journal, 1949; *In Quiet Places*, 131-5; 154-8.

43 Journal, 1948; *In Quiet Places*, 118-19.

44 Journal, 1949; *In Quiet Places*, 131.

45 "Night and Day: A Note on Literature," talk delivered to Queen's University English Society, 2 December 1949. See *In Quiet Places*, 142-8.

46 WH Gardner, ed., *Poems and Prose of Gerard Manley Hopkins*, Harmondsworth, 1978, 185.

SECTION I

VALEDICTION AND LOSS

1932-41

CHAPTER ONE

THE ISLAND

1932-4

Apart from Hopkins the only SJ I ever liked was Father John Joy—he came from a family of fourteen, a Kerryman; he had another brother also an SJ, and he opened his *Irish Monthly* to my first efforts at the short story. I think my first story to appear was "The Green Field"; then came "The Turf Stack," "The Wild Duck's Nest"(it has gone round the world and was translated into Russian along with "Pigeons" a few months ago). There are other things in the *Irish Monthly*.[1]

Michael McLaverty's memory of his earliest fictional writings is largely accurate. When he wrote his first short story, it was to the Jesuit periodical, the *Irish Monthly*, that he sent it. Fr Joy accepted it, and "The Green Field"[2] was published in August 1932. In this first story, his desire to follow Corkery's injunction to "sink himself in the heart of his own people"[3] finds its first expression. In taking as his subject two young island people, he establishes a pattern not often repeated in his later short stories but one which is at the very heart of the novels *In This Thy Day* and *The Three Brothers*.[4] In the short stories which follow "The Green Field," McLaverty examines in detail various aspects of life on islands, concentrating less on young adults than on the young of the human and often the animal species. In this he seems to follow the example of Liam O'Flaherty, whose *Spring Sowing* [5] is a text admired by him. In tone, he follows the pattern set down by Chekhov in his letters, when Chekhov exhorts the writer to distance himself from his subjects in order to give "their grief as it were a background, against which it stands out in greater relief." He follows Chekhov, too, in his descriptions of natural objects, endeavouring to "seize upon the little particulars, grouping them in such a way that, on reading, when you shut your eyes, you get a picture."[6] Above all, he tries to suggest rather than state, in emulation of the spirit of Kuno Meyer's phrase "the half-said thing."[7]

It is interesting to note that in the novels, *In This Thy Day* and *The Three Brothers*, he returns to the themes of the first short story, "The Green Field," which tells of a young woman who endures her life as a teacher on an island while waiting to be married to the man she loves. It is the story, too, of a young and eligible farmer who loves her and hopes she will be his wife. McLaverty handles with great delicacy the unspoken hopes of the young man, as he meets the girl by accident and tries to help her remove an insect from his eye:

> Frank stooped and the girl leaned forward. She pulled down the lid gently. The young man thrilled as he felt her soft, gentle hand cool against his cheek.

"It's out now; it was only a midge," she said, with-drawing to her former position.[8]

The reader is allowed to suppose that this will be a match, especially since the young man owns a green field which "always brought thoughts of the home she would share with him she loved." Even when the hero's sister—"an elderly woman of forty"—gives it as her opinion that Maura is too flighty to make a good wife to him, the reader shares Frank King's quiet confidence that she will one day be his. At the Regatta dance, he is filled with happiness to be chosen by her for one dance, especially as she has spent most of the evening with a smartly-dressed fellow teacher, a stranger, like her, to the island:

> From the corner of his eye Frank furtively glanced at Maura. She was on her feet and approaching him. He assumed an air of indifference by talking to the man beside him. The next instant he was on the floor oblivious of everything but her presence and the thought that she had chosen him from amongst all the dancers. He never felt so happy, yet when he had resumed his seat he knew he had blundered. It was the last dance and he hadn't offered to leave her home. A twinge came to his heart when he saw her leave the dance with the grey-suited teacher.[9]

Frank King avoids the implications of what he has seen, even though he follows the pair out into the moonlit night, and hears with "inexpressible loneliness" Maura's laughter, "clear and silvered in the deathly stillness of the night." He visits her house the next day, and McLaverty, with a control which displays the author's sense of the comic as well as of the unhappy aspects of this situation, allows King to find out in the cruellest way imaginable that he is not Maura's choice:

> That night Frank King found himself entering Maura's house. They were alone. They sat on opposite sides of a clean-swept hearth, gazing into a furnace of turfen fire. The girl broke the stillness.
>
> "Frank, I have something important to tell you...You're one of the best friends I have in Innisdall...I want to remain here all my life, but this—depends on you."
>
> Frank couldn't understand this riddling talk. "Is it proposing to me she is?" he thought.[10]

Her only proposal is that he sell her his green field so that she may build a house there, in which she will live with her teacher from the mainland. Frank leaves the house, too stunned to think or speak. The first example of McLaverty's transference of mood to the physical manifestations of weather or landscape is given as he moves from the misery of King's realisation to the desolation of his final noble gesture:

> Rising up, he crossed to the dresser, pulled out a drawer and rummaged for paper amongst the contents of fishing tackle. He found an envelope, and, tearing a piece of a white paper-bag, he wrote: "Dear Maura, the green field is yours, and may you be happy always. —Frank." He folded it, placed it in the envelope, and went out softly by the back door. His feet made squelching sounds as he walked

over the sodden grass of the green field. Jumping over its
stone fence, he came to the school—grey as a ghost,
deserted and abandoned, with the rain dripping heavily
from a broken gutter. He stood very still, listening to the
rain, and then, slipping the envelope under the porch
door, he walked across the green field towards his home.[11]

"The Green Field" is closer in theme to the third and fourth
novels than to the short stories to follow, and perhaps it
touches on too wide a subject for the compact shorter
form. The author himself has expressed this view, but regrets
that for years he undervalued the story, dismissing it as an
unimportant first attempt.[12] It is much more than that: the
beginnings of control of imagery, the detachment from
the subject which contributes to its pathos without drowning it in sentimentality, and above all the understanding
of and compassion for a situation which is so common as
to be almost a comic stereotype, make this a worthy first
work. It is not without faults, one of the most distracting
being the constantly shifting point of view between the
two main characters. In later stories McLaverty learns to
control this, and on several occasions to use the shift
between characters as an advantage. An urge to tell too
much at the beginning is also evident as in the heavily
adjectival opening sentence:

Maura Murphy, a slim, fair-haired, girlish figure, stood in
the porch of her small one-roomed island school overlooking the sea and the mainland.[13]

This, too, is a tendency which is modified as time passes, but McLaverty's power over adjective and verb becomes increasingly obvious as the story continues and he develops his theme. Houses on the mountain become "scraps of white paper blown against a black hoarding"; curraghs "wriggled like upturned beetles." Above all, the symbolic importance of the green field itself, an "oasis" in an unyielding land, is made clear early in the story and is emphasised by the heroine's innocent pleasure in the living things of the island.

Frank King is the prototype of the recognisable hero of McLaverty novels, quiet, good-living, and hopeful of finding a good woman to make a home for him. The young woman, Maura, whose heart is not in her work, reappears throughout the novels in several guises. Sometimes she is trying to live out her family's wishes for her, like Mary in *In This Thy Day* or Anne in *The Three Brothers*. The spinster sister, Brigid, reappears under different names in all but the first two of McLaverty's novels. She is always alone, slightly envious of the young, warped by her unfulfilled existence, and although not deliberately unkind, at some stage in the novels she provides a stumbling block to the course of true love.

It is clear that this first short story is McLaverty's earliest exploration of types which were of importance to him, although he was not to develop these themes until considerably later. The concern for "the half-said thing," for the Chekhovian detachment which leaves the reader free to consider the implications of the insights afforded by the short story, leads McLaverty in his second published story to one of his favourite themes. This is the awareness in children of the darkness and harshness of the world into which they have been born. If the concerns of the young people of "The Green Field" emerge under different forms in the novels, the plight of the child in the midst of incomprehensible adult requirements finds its fullest expression in the novel *Call My Brother Back*.[14] The hero of McLaverty's second short story, "The Turf Stack", is a twelve-year-old boy, Kevin Black, who tries to please his father by building a turf-stack for him before he returns from his long day's fishing:

> The boy was alone and lonely. He had neither brothers nor sisters. His mother being dead and his father out at the fishing, he had no one to help him to draw the turf. Since early morning he had been working feverishly to build a big a stack as the Cloughmore boys. As he sat tapping the rock with a peeled stick, he recalled with a feeling of sadness the rhyme they shouted at him yesterday, and he coming from the school—"Kevin, Kevin, Kevin Black! Has only got a wee turf stack!"
>
> Their laughs rang in his ears, and he found himself clutching the stick tightly. Then he thought of all the turf he had heaped at the gable-end of his thatched home, and a sweet unrest embraced him as he pictured the big stack he would build this evening.[15]

Kevin is the first of the boy heroes whose most famous example is Colm McNeill of *Call My Brother Back*, and, like Colm, he is an island boy. A suggestion that he is a native Irish speaker is contained in the phrase "and he coming from the school." Its very theme, the effort of the boy to show his solidarity with his father in a lonely and desolate period of their lives, is balanced by the fact that his father does care for him, and allows him at the end to regress to the state of dependent child. Nonetheless, the great difficulty of the task of building the turf-stack, the poverty which necessitates such an effort from a child, and the inescapable loneliness of the motherless boy left by himself all day are suggested most skilfully in a series of images. The first occurs at the opening of the story, where the idyllic, if over-adjectival, picture of the child on the hillside is thrown into relief by the darkness of the shadows:

> It was a Saturday evening in late August. Kevin Black, a small, bare-foot, fair-haired boy of twelve years, sat on limestone rock, that made a grey patch in the black-cloaked bogland of Illaunmore. His blue jersey showed holes at the elbows, and his grey homespun trousers with their frayed edges flapped gently in the cold breeze that blew up from the cliffs. The sun sent large, black, cooling shadows and cooling shafts of mellow light across the hummocky bogland. The boy, sitting high above the sea, looked a glorious figure of freedom in the golden atmosphere of the setting sun.[16]

McLaverty's awareness of the darker side of island life receives its finest expression in this story through the central image of a hawk, who tears a wounded gull to pieces before the boy's eyes. Kevin seems to see his own vulnerability reflected in the plight of the wounded bird. The power and ruthlessness of the hawk are the symbols of the odds piled against the boy. His determination to make an effort— however futile—is encapsulated in his instinctive David-like hurling of a stone at the predator and, in a masterly transfer of feeling, the pain of the victim becomes the boy's sudden memory of a gash on the desk at school. Thus, in this story, McLaverty approaches his greatest strength as a short-story writer—the movement to symbol through precise observation, following Willa Cather's dictum that "Description is revelation."[17]

This is the first of the darker McLaverty stories and is important for its introduction of his recurring character— the island boy. Once established, this boy does not change greatly, although his name is not always the same. He is always an earnest, affectionate, mildly mischievous but fundamentally nervous and ambitious boy who lives much in his imagination and is most anxious to please. He becomes Colm McNeill in "Leavetaking," and later in *Call My Brother Back*, thereafter disappearing, his role completed.

Island boys are at the centre of the three stories published by McLaverty in 1933. Each story, in its own way, breaks new ground. The first, "The Boots," was published in the *Irish Monthly* in May of that year; "The Grey Goat" and "The Letter" appeared in the same publication in August and December respectively. "The Boots" is the first story of leavetaking; "The Grey Goat" is the first animal story; and "The Letter" is the first of the tragic studies. Some elements of all these are to be found in the later stories; in some, such as "The Wild Duck's Nest," "Pigeons," "The Game Cock" and "The White Mare," all are present.

The theme of leavetaking is one which recurs throughout McLaverty's work. The valedictory note changes as time goes on, becoming increasingly sombre, until it finds its fullest expression in the short stories of 1939 and 1940,

"Stone," "The White Mare," "The Sea," and "Becalmed." In the novels, the saddest parting is that of the old grandmother from her home in *Lost Fields*,[18] but the feeling of final parting is present in *In This Thy Day*—notably at the ending—and contributes to the autumnal atmosphere of *The Three Brothers*.

In the first story of leavetaking, there is little sadness and much gentle humour. An island boy, Padraig, is leaving his grandmother's home for the first time to find work on the mainland. He is happy and excited at the prospect, and his proud grandmother has purchased for him his first pair of boots in honour of the occasion. It becomes clear as the story continues that they have been chosen solely for their handsome and sturdy appearance but with no consideration for size. As the boy walks proudly down to the boat wearing the boots, he is as much disturbed by an unaccustomed discomfort as delighted by his proud possessions:

> He walked awkwardly, and as he stumbled now and then on the rough road his face became wry with discomfiture...
> He stopped and pressed the toe of his right boot towards the ground, but his efforts at relief were futile...at the pier some boys were in their bare feet and they eyed him with childish envy.[19]

The finest image in the story, showing clearly the boy's complete unfamiliarity with the ways of the mainland, is that of a steam train. It is an image to which McLaverty returns, in the later story "Aunt Suzanne," when he wishes once more to show the strangeness felt by a child in the face of an unknown situation. In "The Boots," the train, "a

big black monster hissing and grunting with impatience"
allows the author to show the boy's wonder and touching
innocence:

> At each issue of steam Padraig retreated, for he feared that
> at any moment it would blow up or leap upon him. He
> surveyed open-mouthed the wheels, the funnel, the man
> with the glossy peaked cap—never had he seen such a
> black-looking man. Still watching fixedly the engine, and
> trembling with each hiss and snort, he sidled over to join
> the three Boyles from his own side of the island.[20]

His innocence is further indicated by the fact that, despite
excruciating pain, he never considers removing the boots—
until, that is, he is rejected by prospective employers
because, "It's a kind of stiff he is about the feet." In the
face of such shame, the magical world of the town becomes
in an instant "a picture without a breath of life." He removes
the boots, his relief from crippling pain indicated by a
clever transfer of the adjective "swollen":

> He sat down, saying "A-a-a-h!" as he removed each boot.
> Unrolling his stockings and tying his boots together, he
> placed them around his neck, as he had seen island visitors
> do when crossing swollen streams. Rejoicing with his
> newly-won freedom, he stood erect with his feet, feeling
> deliciously cool as the sun streamed down on him. A little
> bronze-faced farmer, driving a cart and horse, was watching
> him. Padraig smiled and stood with his chest puffed out
> as the man halted and spoke.[21]

He is hired, of course, and in his new-found status is referred to by the author not as Padraig but Sweeney. As for the boots, the farmer takes them to give to "a wee handful of a boy," and Padraig is able to send the money he receives to his grandmother.

It is such a cheerful story that it is hard to realise that it is one of valediction, and that the innocent boy disappears at the instant of his hiring. The loss of innocence, and of childish association, is explored less in this story than in those later written on this theme, but it is present, for the boy is clearly leaving behind his childhood. Nonetheless, this is a story which indicates a movement towards the more important valedictory stories, and displays a light-hearted approach not frequently evident in the author's early work. To an extent, this lighthearted approach is maintained in the second story published in 1933, "The Grey Goat." The first of the animal stories, it seems to show something of the influence of Liam O'Flaherty, echoing the unsentimental tenderness of "The Wild Goat's Kid," just as the incident of the hawk in "The Turf Stack" recalls O'Flaherty's "The Wounded Cormorant."[22] "The Grey Goat" has its own character, however, and is clearly the forerunner of "The Game Cock" and "The White Mare" in its exploration of the relationship between animal and man, a theme to which McLaverty constantly returns in story and novel. It is the story of a pet goat who is to be sold to alleviate the hardship of lean times. No one in the family, parents or children, wants to see her go, but the acceptance of harsh necessity which makes the boy, Kevin Black, attempt to do a man's work in "The Turf Stack" enables the heart-broken children of this family to prepare in silence for their pet's departure:

> "Poor Bess, you'll never see Rathlin again!" he said as he
> cut off from her long grey coat three pieces of hair. The
> goat never flinched, for many a time she had provided
> Brendan's father with fishing flies of a silky greyness. But
> now she was leaving for ever. The sight of a plait of Bess's
> hair somewhat mollified Ethna, who immediately ran into
> the house and placed it in her prayer book. Young Bob
> disappeared for a time, and on a little hill behind the
> house he dug a grave with a spoon. Into the grave he
> reverently placed the hair, covered it with clay, and at the
> head he placed a flat stone with crude nail-carved letterings:
> "Our Bess—R.I.P."[23]

There is no doubt of the grief felt by the main character,
Brendan, for the loss of the animal, but McLaverty takes
pains to establish that this is a happy home despite the
temporary failure of income, and that these are careful and
well-intentioned parents who do not wish to inflict suffering
on their children. In a sense this is a story of leavetaking,
as is the later animal story, "The White Mare," but the
emphasis in both stories is on the effect of the parting on
the person left behind, so that when McLaverty describes
the discomfort of the goat in the cramped boat, he is in
fact revealing the misery of the boy who is powerless to
alleviate her distress. Later, in "The White Mare," his sense
of the owner's desolation darkens the story into tragedy:
here he is concerned primarily with the knowledge of the
many sides of island life revealed by the necessity of the
parting. Despite the near-disaster of a threatened purchase

by an unattractive red-faced woman, the goat is reprieved when the woman rejects her as "a poor thin island crayture," and the story ends joyfully as the family, no better off but determined to manage rather than part with their pet, return to the island with Bess.

The third story published in 1933, "The Letter," could not be said to be slight, although it is one of McLaverty's shortest. It is a very sad story. In the terrible disillusionment of the little boy who has to read to his mother the letter containing the news that the mainstay of the family, his sister, has died in America, there is something of the quality of Corkery's "Vision."[24] Its uncompromising starkness, in the unsentimental treatment of the boy's humiliating visit to the shop to ask for credit from an unsympathetic grocer, is reminiscent of stories by Chekhov, of whom McLaverty was to write twenty years later:

> His best stories are conflicts of the spirit, his drama taking
> place within the life of the mind. He avoids the exceptional
> in life and eschews all flashiness and falsifications, the
> precious bane of many Irish writers.[25]

The story is set in the heart of winter, and the opening paragraph, one of McLaverty's best at this early stage of his career, emphasises the bleakness of the landscape in order to convey the dreary hopelessness of the situation endured by Tameen and his mother. McLaverty is always responsive to the effects of the sun, and in this story it can do no more than cast a few spent chilly rays on a dead land. Part of the sadness implicit in this story, however, is the powerlessness of the widow and her son to do anything to improve their position, and it is this inability to contend with the destructive forces of change which gives power to this, as to his later studies of loneliness and bereavement:

> Winter had come to Roecarra. A December wind blew over the naked-grey land, whistling sharply through the unmortared stone hedges and making the donkeys shiver in their beds of sapless bracken. The morning sky was ice-blue streaked with white skeletons of clouds.[26]

At the end of this first period of his writing career, McLaverty synthesises these themes—of the island boys, of the relationships between man and animal, and of the overwhelming effects of loss and parting on the human spirit—in one story, rightly acknowledged as one of his finest: "The Wild Duck's Nest" which appeared in the *Irish Monthly* in April 1934. The 1934 version is not the same as that made famous in anthologies since its appearance in the *Game Cock* collection of 1947. In the later version, a boy, Colm, finds a wild duck's nest on Rathlin Island; he touches the egg, replaces it, and then spends a night of agony wondering if the bird will forsake it. It is only when he returns and finds that she has not only not forsaken the egg but has laid another beside it, that he is relieved of the heavy burden of guilt which has weighed upon him. It is the slow mounting of tension that gives this story its character. The original version is as dark a story as its predecessor, "The Letter." In it, the boy goes back and sees the bird on the nest. The bird is disturbed by his presence; it flaps and flies away in panic. In the later version her leaving reveals two eggs in the nest, and the boy goes away, happily relieved of the consequences of his thoughtless action:

> He turned to go away, hesitated and glanced back at the
> dark nest; it'd be no harm to have a look. Timidly he
> approached it, standing straight, and gazing over the edge.
> There in the nest lay two eggs. He drew in his breath with
> delight, splashed quickly from the island and ran off
> whistling in the rain.[27]

It is this ending which most people associate with the
story. The original could not be more different, even though
it begins in very similar style:

> She was on, her shoulders hunched up, and her bill lying
> on her breast as if she were asleep. Colm's heart thumped
> wildly in his ears. She hadn't forsaken. He was about to
> turn stealthily away. Something happened. The bird
> moved, her neck straightened, twitching nervously from
> side to side. The boy's head swam with lightness. He stood
> transfixed. The wild duck, with a panicky flapping, rose
> heavily, squawking as she did so, a piece of straw and a
> white object momentarily entwined in her legs. The egg
> fell on the flat wet rock beside the nest, besmearing it
> with yellow slime. A sense of tremendous guilt seized Colm,
> a throbbing silence enveloped him as if everything had
> gone from the earth leaving him alone. Stupefied, numbed
> to every physical sense, he floundered across the black
> water, running wildly from the scene of the disaster.[28]

The control of short and long sentences, the precise but
emotive imagery and the inescapable finality of the word

"slime", prepare the reader for the despair of the boy, "floundering" away from "disaster." Yet, when McLaverty submitted it to John Middleton Murry for inclusion in *Adelphi*, the periodical of which Murry was editor, he objected to the ending. Murry believed, McLaverty recalls, that the duck would not be so insensitive as to let her egg drop. McLaverty was reluctant to change his ending, having gone to pains to emphasise the heaviness of the rain in order to give verisimilitude to the idea of the bird's heavy, wet feathers and consequent impaired control of her muscles. Once he conceded that his work might lack general, as opposed to particular, truth, McLaverty accepted the advice of the experienced Murry and changed the ending.[29] In so doing, he seems to have changed the character of the story. Certainly, the later version provides relief for the reader as much as for the boy, but the earlier story seems much more in keeping with McLaverty's style as it was emerging in 1934.

After "The Letter," he seems to have been in a mood to probe the darkness attendant upon loss. The first version of the story also contains a new and important pre-occupation: the necessity of accepting the consequences of wrongdoing. This theme was to be explored in depth in his novels, and in the original version of this story it finds its first expression. In the amended version, the boy is absolved from the sin of interfering with nature: in the earlier, he is doomed from the instant of his transgression. Seen in this light, the change is a major one. It is undeniable, however, that the process of changing the story also affects other parts of it, in some cases for the better.

The finest descriptive writing, however, remains. As in

the earlier stories, McLaverty's descriptions are best when, according to the principles laid down by Chekhov and admired by McLaverty, they reveal the attitude or state of mind of the character whom he wants us to understand. Here, the boy Colm's familiarity with and obvious joy in his surroundings lend an extra dimension to the quality of the fine imagery, and a poignancy to the shattering of innocence for which this idyllic scene-setting was originally intended as preparation. This following extract describes the moment when he touches the egg, and, ironically, discovers the nature of sin:

> The nest was his. He lifted the egg, smooth and green as the sky, with a faint tinge of yellow like the reflected light from a buttercup; and then he felt he had done wrong. He left it back quickly. He knew he shouldn't have touched it and he wondered would the bird forsake it. A vague sadness stole over him and he felt in his heart that he had sinned. Carefully smoothing out his footprints he hurriedly left the islet and ran after his cow. The sun had now set and the cold shiver of evening enveloped him, chilling his body and saddening his mind.[30]

Such a loss of innocence seems deliberately reminiscent of the account in Genesis of the Fall and, indeed, in the earlier version of the story, the boy's childhood is as firmly behind him after this action as was Adam's vision of Paradise after his sin. The writing in both versions of the story is powerful, the Chekhovian "conflict of the spirit" so well-evoked that the actual ending does not affect the reader's involvement with the main character and his moral dilemma. Whether or not he is reprieved, the boy has dared to interfere with the rhythm of nature and must bear the knowledge of that sin for the rest of his life. In either version, it is an exceptionally well-written story, and marks a watershed in McLaverty's career. Although this is not the last of the island stories, it is the one where he achieves his clearest vision of the many sides of island life. He depicts in it the peace and innocence of the life but does not avoid the loneliness and attendant harshness of experience which is inextricably linked with the superficially idyllic setting. In Colm, McLaverty finds the name and the character of the definitive island boy and, while he writes other stories which touch on the themes of lost innocence and sadness in the lives of island children, as in "The Trout" and "The Prophet," he never surpasses the distinctive achievement of "The Wild Duck's Nest." It represents the completion of a phase in his development, and from this time onward he looks not to the island for his chief inspiration but to the city of his childhood, Belfast. The island stays in his mind, however, and comes to life in the nostalgic and lyrical first novel, *Call My Brother Back*, which marks the end of McLaverty's apprenticeship as a writer.

REFERENCES

1 McLaverty to Sophia King, 1982. Letter in possession of S King.
2 "The Green Field," *Irish Monthly*, 60 (August 1932), 497-504. See *In Quiet Places*, Dublin, 1989, 5-12.
3 Daniel Corkery, *Synge and Anglo-Irish Literature: A Study*, Cork, Dublin, London, 1931, 243.
4 *In This Thy Day*, New York and London, 1945; *The Three Brothers*. New York and London, 1948.
5 Liam O'Flaherty, *Spring Sowing*, London, 1924.
6 Louis S Friedland, ed., *Letters on the Short Story, the Drama and Other Literary Topics*, by Anton Chekhov, with a preface by Ernest J Simmons. London, 1965, 97.

7 Kuno Meyer, *Selections from Ancient Irish Poetry*, London, 1928.

8 "The Green Field," *Irish Monthly*, 60 (August 1932), 498; *In Quiet Places*, 6.

9 ibid., 502; *In Quiet Places*, 9-10.

10 ibid., 503; *In Quiet Places*, 11.

11 ibid., 504; *In Quiet Places*, 12.

12 In conversation with S King.

13 "The Green Field," op. cit., 497; *In Quiet Places*, 5.

14 *Call My Brother Back*, New York and London, 1939.

15 "The Turf Stack," *Irish Monthly*, 60 (December 1932), 751; *In Quiet Places*, 13.

16 ibid.

17 Phrase attributed by McLaverty to Willa Cather in conversation with S King and quoted by Seamus Heaney in "Fosterage: For Michael McLaverty," *North*, London,1975, 71.

18 *Lost Fields*, New York, 1941; London, 1942.

19 "The Boots" *Irish Monthly*, 61 (May 1933), 303; *In Quiet Places*, 20.

20 ibid., 311; *In Quiet Places*, 20-21.

21 ibid., 312; *In Quiet Places*, 22.

22 *The Short Stories of Liam O'Flaherty*, London, 1937; "The Wounded Cormorant," 226-230; "The Wild Goat's Kid," 185-94.

23 "The Grey Goat," *Irish Monthly*, 61 (August 1933), 518; *In Quiet Places*, 26.

24 Daniel Corkery, "Vision," *Earth Out of Earth*, Dublin and Cork, 1939.

25 "Anton Chekhov—a man of sympathy and a gentle, ironic humour," *Belfast Telegraph*, 5 November 1955.

26 "The Letter," *Irish Monthly*, 61 (December 1933), 750; *In Quiet Places*, 29.

27 "The Wild Duck's Nest," (later version), *The Game Cock and Other Stories*, London, 1949, 27-8.

28 "The Wild Duck's Nest," (early version), *Irish Monthly*, 62 (April 1934), 240; *In Quiet Places*, 36.

29 Recounted in conversation with S King.

30 "The Wild Duck's Nest," (1934), 238; *In Quiet Places*, 35; 1949 version, 26; *Collected Stories*, 196.

CHAPTER TWO

THE CITY

1935-7

Although the city was to be the main source of inspiration for McLaverty in this period, he did not devote himself exclusively to writing about it. After "The Wild Duck's Nest" there seemed still to be some residual concern for the theme of lost innocence, as can be seen in the 1935 story "The Trout."[1] The beginnings of the preoccupation with the problems of the old can be seen in "The Return"[2] and "The Race,"[3] although this theme was not to be fully explored until the stories of 1939, "Stone," "The White Mare" and "The Sea." The main stories of this period are those dealing with the city, beginning with the gentle "Evening in Winter"[4] and culminating in the well-known stories published in 1936 and 1937, "Pigeons,"[5] "Aunt Suzanne"[6] and "The Game Cock."[7] Oddly, the last story of this period, "Leavetaking,"[8] is an island story, but, as it becomes with very few changes in style or content the third chapter of McLaverty's first novel, *Call My Brother Back*, it has its place here as the link between the two major themes which are combined in the first full-length work. 1937 is the year, too, when McLaverty began to receive both encouragement and pressure from publishers to produce not a collection of his short stories, which he would have liked to do, but a novel.[9] By the end of this period, therefore, McLaverty was no longer a dedicated writer of short stories, but an aspiring novelist. To write his novels he called upon the two themes most thoroughly explored by him until that point: the island and the city.

The stories published in 1935 reflect, to a minor degree, the major themes of the island, the city and the loneliness of the uprooted old. "The Trout," published in January 1935 in *The Irish Monthly*, tells of a young boy who plays truant to go fishing but is found out when a poacher, from whom, he tells his mother, he received the fish, calls unexpectedly at the house and exposes the child's lie.

Of all McLaverty's stories, "The Trout" is closest in mood to "The Wild Duck's Nest,"[10] especially in the ending, where the child realises that his true transgression has been not his truancy but his deceit:

> The poacher, perplexed, looked up at the woman. There was silence, broken only by the rattling loom within. Without speaking they turned to the boy seated at the table, his face ablaze, his head hanging in shame.[11]

It is not a major story, but a variant in a minor key on the recurrent theme of the island boys. The next story to appear in *The Irish Monthly*, "Evening In Winter," published in May 1935, is the first of the stories to deal with the city theme. However it is, unlike later stories such as "Pigeons" and "The Game Cock," much more a nostalgic evocation of the Belfast of McLaverty's childhood than a realistic portrayal. The houses, streets and church, ironically the same noticed in passing by Colm as he runs for the priest when his brother is shot in *Call My Brother Back*, are seen here through the wondering eyes of a small, protected child, safe with his father in a world which offers no threat:

> A tram passed, groaning up the hill where they were walking. Sparks, green ones and red ones and blue ones, crackled from the trolley, but the tram went on and slithered out of sight. And now there was nothing on the road only the snow and the black lines where the trams ran. Up above were the telephone wires covered with crumbs of snow, but the trolley wires were all dark. Presently they lit up with gold light and soon a black motor-car came slushing down the hill, covered with snow. Then it was very quiet...[12]

Another ironic difference between this child and those of the later stories is seen in his attitude to official authority. To Charley, policemen are to be avoided because they chase boys "playing football in the streets," but he is not afraid on this occasion, "walking with his hand clutched tightly in his Daddy's—inside the big warm pocket." To Frankie in "Pigeons," as to Colm in *Call My Brother Back*, policemen are fearsome because of their guns and because of the child's awareness, in both cases, that he is in some inexplicable way endangered by them. None of this is to be found in "Evening in Winter." It is a story of celebration of past happiness and of a time when keen observation revealed nothing but gratifying confirmation of security:

The organ began to growl and people to sing. Charley put his fingers to the flaps of his ears. You could hear the noise very small, then it would get big like thunder, and if you moved your fingers in and out the noise would go ziz-zaz and a ah-aha-aaah! But it soon stopped. People bowed their heads and Daddy bowed his head too. Charley covered his face with his hands, but looked through his fingers to see what was going on. Someone coughed far, far away. Someone else coughed. Then it became so still you could hear your heart thumping.[13]

Apart from its preliminary exploration of the world of the city, "Evening in Winter" is important for its examination of the self-absorbed world of the younger child, for it is the shattering of security which concerns McLaverty in the later stories, "Pigeons" and "The Game Cock."

The third of McLaverty's major themes to be touched upon in his writings of 1935 was that of the grief of the old, forced to part with their homes. This was the theme of "The Return," published in the spring of 1935 in the American periodical, *Catholic World*. In this story, an old man, Martin Conneely, leaves his island home, going instead to the new home being built by his son and daughter-in-law on the mainland. He is not unwanted and there is no question of his staying on the island. The first line of the story indicates that his going is part of a general evacuation: "The people were leaving Innishleen." The old man's grief is personal and he does not manifest any outward reluctance to leave, beyond a helpless inability to take an active part in the removal. He knows that the island is a dead place, but it, and the dead who already rest in its graveyard, are more alive and real to him than the incomprehensible young. The story's importance lies in its preliminary exploration of the theme of uprooting, of loneliness among friends and of the need to return home.

The year 1936 saw the publication of one of McLaverty's most famous stories, "Pigeons," which is to Belfast as "The Wild Duck's Nest" is to the island. It was published in the April/May edition of *New Stories* in 1936 and was the first and only short story to deal directly with the political theme of the "Troubles" in Ireland. It was personally important for McLaverty that this story should be accepted, for the volume's editor, Edward J O'Brien, was an important anthologist. Apart from his position as one of the founder editors of *New Stories*, with which he was associated from 1933 until 1935, he was also the editor from 1915 until 1940 of a well-known annual collection called *The Best Short Stories*, in which he was to include McLaverty's "Wild Duck's Nest" in 1937. Until his death in 1941, he continued to give McLaverty much encouragement and introduced him to the publishing house of Longmans Green, who subsequently published his first novel. His death in 1941, at the age of fifty-one, was a sad loss for McLaverty.[14]

The story is written in the first person, another departure for the author. From the first paragraph he effectively catches the innocent but unsentimental tone of the little boy who has lost his elder brother:

> Our Johnny kept pigeons, three white ones and a brown one that could tumble in the air like a leaf. They were nice pigeons, but they dirtied the slates and cooed so early in the morning that my daddy said that someday he

would wring their bloody necks. That is a long while ago now, for we still have the pigeons, but Johnny is dead; he died for Ireland.[15]

Because he captures accurately the child's tone of voice, and because by 1936 he was practised in avoiding sentimentality, this opening paragraph allows the author to move unhindered in a place, time and state of mind very familiar to him. He effectively moves away from the eldest or only child of the islands, to examine the world of a younger child in a large family, to whom the harsh lessons of experience come as a greater shock, but who is cushioned from their full effects by a large and supportive family. The fusion of these two styles, of the islands and of the city, results in 1939 in *Call My Brother Back*. In "Pigeons," the last phrase of the opening paragraph, "he died for Ireland," is repeated throughout, as a barely-understood incantation with which the child may ward off his grief. There is no wavering in the point of view in "Pigeons"; McLaverty keeps strictly to the experience and understanding of a small boy. His plain, unaffected style establishes early the little boy's hero-worship of his brother, which, in turn, prepares the reader for Frankie's uncomprehending grief at the end of the story. To be with his brother, he shares in his enthusiasm for keeping and flying pigeons, but the narrator's admiration is more for the magnificence of his brother than for the feats of his birds:

All day we would sit, if the weather was good, watching our pigeons flying, and Brownie doing somersaults. When they were tired they would light on the blue slates, and

Johnny would throw corn up to them. Saturday was a
great day for us and for our pigeons, but it was on Saturday
that Johnny died for Ireland.[16]

When the man comes for Johnny, "a strange man in a
black hat and burberry coat," all that the boy notices is
that "Johnny looked very sad and he didn't laugh at Brownie
any more." He gives his young brother his penknife, a key
and a blue notebook, in which he has written down on
page after page his expenditure for the pigeons' corn, which
comes to an expensive half-crown; his sixpence for an
unnamed club; another sixpence for three packets of cheap
cigarettes; and twopence for Frankie. The little boy Frankie
cannot understand the pointless repetition of these columns,
and remarks only that "if he had been at school he would
have got slapped for wasting the good paper." Thus at one
stroke, McLaverty preserves the innocent viewpoint of his
narrator, while informing the reader of the poignant
significance of Johnny's notebook. He further underlines
the impending tragedy, without attributing to the child-
narrator information he cannot know, by providing a
stormy, windy night as the background for the family's
long vigil. This is similar to the device used to prepare the
reader for disaster in the first version of "The Wild Duck's
Nest," and it is particularly effective here because of the
contrast of the anxious but powerless family trapped in a
house whose comfort is as meaningless to them as to
Johnny, lying dead in the wet street:

The clock on the mantelpiece chimed eleven and my sisters
blessed themselves—it got a soul out of Purgatory when

you did that. They forgot all about my bedtime and I was
let stay up though my eyes felt full of sand. The rain was
falling. We could hear it slapping in the yard and trindling
down the grate. It was a blowy night for someone's back
door was banging, making the dogs bark. The newspapers
that lay on the scullery floor to keep it clean began to
crackle up and down with the wind till you'd have thought
there was a mouse under them.[17]

After a "dim knock," and a "cry of disbelief" from his
mother, Frankie is sent to bed. He wakes in the morning
to an unaccustomed stillness, and, nervous "because the
house was strange," he goes to the room he has shared
with Johnny. There he finds his mother, in a black dress
with "the smell that kills the moths." He is puzzled even
by her endearments and her curious greeting, "You're the
only boy I have now." Then he sees his brother. McLaverty's
single-minded protection of the boy's ignorance allows him
to reveal the grisly details of Johnny's death through the
child's uncomprehending and puzzled observation:

"What's wrong, Mammie?" I asked, looking up at her wet
eyes. "Nothing darling: nothing, pet. He died for Ireland."
I turned my head and looked at the bed. Johnny was
lying on the white bed in a brown dress. His hands were
pale and they were joined around his rosary beads, and a
big crucifix between them. There was a big lump of wadding
at the side of his head and wee pieces up his nose.[18]

By using the narrator's voice McLaverty is able to comment
on the father's reaction to patriotic cliché at the wake,

where he writes: "One man told my daddy he should be a proud man, because Johnny had died for the Republic. My Daddy blinked his eyes when he heard this, and got up and went into the yard for a long time." The device of the candid narrator permits him also to show the sinister connotation of the police presence at the funeral, recalling in grimmer fashion the childish fear of the boy in "Evening in Winter." The control of emotion attendant upon lack of comprehension allows McLaverty also to present the only moment of unrestrained grief, when the child begins to realise at the graveside that he will never see his brother again. Lest the story degenerate into sentimentality, however, he quickly reminds the reader that the child's distress is as much for himself—lest he should have to part with his pigeons—as for his brother's death:

> Daddy had his head bowed and there were tears in his eyes, but they didn't run down his cheeks like mine did. The priest began to pray, and I knew I'd never see Johnny again, never, never, until I'd die and go to Heaven if I kept good and didn't say bad words and obeyed my Mammie and my Daddy. But I wouldn't like Daddy to tell me to give away the pigeons.[19]

Even in the midst of grief, the child can contemplate, as perhaps his parents cannot at that moment, the possibility of resumption of normal life. Frankie knows he will turn again to his former interests; in the last paragraph of the story, McLaverty shows that this must be so. The poignancy of Frankie's assumption of his brother's role is balanced by the pragmatic awareness of self which saves the boy from the full effects of his loss. It is this instinct for self-preservation which distinguishes the young city boys from the less worldly island children, and it is this kind of incipient street-wisdom that gives the city stories their distinctive quality. By the end of this story McLaverty has not only the theme of his first novel, and its original title, *Waste Ground*, but also the authentic voice of the people he remembered from his childhood in Belfast. The elegiac tone which is a feature of the stories between 1936 and 1940 is noticeable here for the first time. The celebration of childhood and innocence which preoccupied his mind for the first few years of his writing becomes a nostalgic recreation of a lost time. Yet, even in nostalgia, he makes it clear that the darkness of reality is never far from the brightness of a child's vision:

> Yesterday I was lying on the waste ground watching the pigeons and Daddy came walking towards me smoking his pipe with the tin lid. I tried to show him the pigeons flying through the clouds. He only looked at them for a minute and turned away without speaking, and now I'm hoping he won't wring their necks.[20]

McLaverty's next Irish publication was in *Ireland Today* in March 1937, entitled "Aunt Suzanne." In it the note of sadness struck in "The Letter," "The Trout," "The Wild Duck's Nest," "Pigeons," and to a lesser extent in "The Turf Stack," is evident once more, but its undoubted pathos is lightened by the author's sense of humour, apparent here as in "Pigeons." While his affection for the city of his childhood is clear, it is tempered here by his acute awareness of Belfast's hostility towards those who do not conform to its standards. The safe world of "Evening in Winter" exists only for those who do not deviate from the norm. "Aunt Suzanne" is an exploration of the plight of one such outcast, and prepares the way for the often grim face of the city glimpsed in the novels *Call My Brother Back* and *Lost Fields*. In this story his sympathy is not for the plight of a young child or for an old person. "Aunt Suzanne" is the story of a woman in the prime of her life, who is, without wishing to be so, a tragic and lonely figure, one almost anticipatory of Brian Moore's Judith Hearne.[21] The story concerns a family of young children whose widowed, stern father asks his late wife's sister to come to Belfast to care for his children. Aunt Suzanne comes gladly, and the growing affection between the children and their aunt is explored in some depth. In particular, McLaverty dwells on the special affection which the aunt displays for the youngest child, and only boy, Arthur. His undisguised curiosity at her iron leg is revealed with McLaverty's customary unsentimental delicacy, as is the natural but pathetic restiveness of the motherless children, in a passage whose central image of the steam train is as effective a way of showing the children's anxiety and vulnerability as in the earlier story, "The Boots:"

> At the station they had to wait, Mary telling and retelling Arthur not to be forgetting his manners, occasionally taking his hands out of his pockets, and pulling down his brown jersey...
>
> Presently there came a vibrating tumble like thunder and the train came panting in, smoke hitting the glass roof with all its might.

Mary fidgeted. "Now you two hold on to me tight. Don't get lost; look out for Aunt Suzanne. She's small; she'll be in black; she has a—She has a—She has a—Oh! I see her! There she is!" People hurried past, brushing roughly against wee Arthur till he was ready to cry from fright, but Mary's gleeful shouts sent a breathless, weak excitement over him. And then, as if she had jumped out of the ground, he was looking up at Aunt Suzanne.[22]

The building up of tension is skilful; the author places the three children in a place, the railway station in Great Victoria Street, which would have been familiar to generations of Belfast people, and then renders it strange and unfamiliar through their nervous reaction to this forthcoming meeting. All their apprehension is conveyed in these reactions, and the reader learns of Aunt Suzanne's handicap not through outward description, but through Arthur's merciless candour. Surveying the "wee woman, not as tall as Mary," he is surprised and intrigued by "something funny:...one boot, and where the other should be was a ring of iron." Aunt Suzanne is seen through Arthur's eyes until the turning point of the story, when he discovers that she drinks. Gradually it becomes apparent that this was also a failing of their late mother's; their father has an understandable antipathy to the repetition of familiar but unacceptable behaviour and eventually asks Suzanne to leave. As she goes, Arthur, the little boy in whom she has taken a particular interest from the first, but whom, since the discovery of her secret, she has come to fear, is already oblivious of her presence as he buys chocolate with the money she has given him as a parting present:

> At the station before getting into the carriage Aunt Suzanne gave Arthur a penny. Her eyes were wet as she held Annie's and Mary's hands and stroked them lovingly. They couldn't look up at her, but stood awkwardly swaying to and fro. The train slid out and they lifted their arms and waved them wearily, tears filling their eyes. Arthur stood watching the smoke and the back of the receding train. Then he plucked at Mary's coat. "Come on quick," he said, but they didn't seem to hear him, and he ran on in front to the chocolate machine with the penny Auntie Sue had given him.[23]

Despite her affection for him and for the little girls, to whom she turns for company after Arthur's defection, she has no choice but to go and leave them alone again. She does not challenge the sentence of perpetual banishment; indeed she seems to accept that she has broken an unspoken law. There is no doubt that the reader is meant to feel sympathetic towards the lonely, maternal woman and to the equally lost and lonely children. Yet, within the story, McLaverty seems to change his mind about one of the children, Arthur, the little boy to whom Aunt Suzanne pays particular attention. He seems unable to decide whether Arthur is a frail but lively child, full of mischief but incapable of anything worse than tactlessness, or the unattractive little bully who tries to blackmail his aunt in a very unpleasant fashion. In the following extract, he has discovered Aunt Suzanne drinking directly from a "bottle of gurgling yellow liquid":

She gave him a half-penny. "Don't tell your da that poor Auntie has to take medicine, he'd be vexed to hear it. Now go and gather your cinders."

Later he returned with an almost empty bucket and found Aunt Suzanne snoring on the sofa. He started to sing loudly so as to waken her, and she got up and poked the fire vigorously. "Give's a penny for the pictures?"

"If I'd a penny I'd frame it, and you with no cinders!"

"G'on," he whimpered, "or I'll tell me da about your medicine."

"Get out of my sight! Do you think I'm made of money!" she said crossly.

"G'on!"

She lifted the poker in anger, and Arthur raced into the yard. He barricaded himself in an old disused goat-shed and started to sing:

"Boiled beef and carrots,

Boiled beef and carrots

And porter for Suzanne."[24]

With this incident, the story changes direction, reverting to the gentle, nostalgic tone of the opening only at the very end. The little boy, until now a central character, becomes a shadowy threat; his watchfulness is distasteful, and it becomes difficult for the reader to bear in mind that he is a small child. Aunt Suzanne herself loses credibility to an extent in the poker incident; and it is interesting, if disconcerting, to note that her thoughts and feelings are very rarely explored after this point. She is seen, like the others, from the outside, as if the dramatic reversal of her fortune becomes more important in the author's mind than her reaction to it. She is not truly reinstated in the eyes of the reader. Established as a volatile, unreliable character, her games and songs with the "sensible children" and her fervent prayers for abstinence serve only as reminders of the excess to which she might have been driven in the incident involving the poker. Her fall is complete when, driven by cold-induced pain in her leg, she slips out on a bitter winter's night to a local public house and drinks herself into a stupor.

Very little happens after that; it is over. Daniel puts her belongings together as she lies oblivious on the sofa, and only a detached concern reminds him to toss an overcoat across her before he goes to bed. In McLaverty's world, island or city, there are no second chances. The finality of Suzanne's transgression is indicated as Daniel silently gazes at the winter night. Nothing is said, but through the imagery of cold and desolation, it becomes clear that she will not be forgiven:

> He went into her room and bundled all the things he could find into her band-box...The snow was falling, falling with a sparkle against the lamp lights, and falling quietly on the window-sills and the hut doors. Over the white-silent roofs the cold sky was sprayed with stars. A man with bowed head passed and said: "That's a hardy night." Daniel heard him kicking the snow off his boots against a doorstep, and a door closing. He came inside.[25]

There is little more to be said; two terse paragraphs cover Aunt Suzanne's departure and Arthur's final betrayal. "Aunt Suzanne" is a flawed story, but one which it is difficult either to overlook or forget. It looks forward in its vitality and humour to the tragi-comic "Game Cock" and to the second novel, *Lost Fields*.

From 1936 onwards, McLaverty began to receive letters from publishers, enquiring about the possibility of his producing a novel. There is evidence in his correspondence to suggest that the author was beginning at this time to consider such an undertaking. In particular, a letter from the firm of Chapman and Hall, dated April 1936, refers to a letter by McLaverty which seems to have indicated that he could not complete a novel for another year, and subsequent correspondence reinforces the impression that he was indeed working on what was to become *Call My Brother Back*.[26] In this context, his next story, "Leavetaking," published in July 1937 in *Ireland Today*, presents a problem. With few alterations, this becomes Chapter Three of Part One of *Call My Brother Back*, and the difficulty for the reader is to know whether it was written as part of the longer work, and converted to a short story for publication, as later extracts from novels were to be, or intended as a short story but later absorbed into the novel.[27] The strong tradition of island stories would suggest the latter. However, since the author had been moving since 1936 towards the themes of city life and the problems of the old in his short stories, it seems equally possible that the early part of the novel, including Chapter Three, was substantially written as early as 1937.

"Leavetaking" is the story of a boy's last day on Rathlin before he goes away to school in Belfast, and centres on his visit to his elderly aunt and uncle. It unites, therefore, the familiar themes of the island and of leaving, and incorporates in the characters of the old aunt and uncle the newer theme of the old who see their way of life disappearing. Its tone is elegiac, celebrating a way of life already over for Colm. The possibilities of his new life are as exciting to him as the memories of his old one are dear, and his nostalgia is not tinged with despondency:

> The road climbed gradually out of the village, up into the hills, where the air was clear and cool. Here he could see Fair Head and dark Knocklayde bulging strangely near. Away beyond that lovely mountain he would soon be going to Belfast, and as he looked at its cold, sodden folds, he wondered if he would be able to see it from the town.[28]

His visit to his uncle and aunt's house is more than a duty call, for he is attached to them and finds their home a place full of fascinating objects—such as the ship in a bottle, a relic of his uncle's seafaring days, which lies amid the accumulated clutter of the old people's lives. Colm's inability to understand how the ship got into the bottle, and his uncle's stubborn refusal to part with his secret, contribute to the humour and innocence of the story.

The old uncle delivers the eulogy for this and all McLaverty's islands, in a passage not included in *Call My Brother Back*, as he says: "It's sad to see so many young people leavin' the island and none comin' back. There'll soon be nothin' on the island only rabbits—with nobody marryin', the ould dyin', and the young goin' away."[29] Colm's emotional reaction to this is transferred, in McLaverty's familiar device, to the natural world. The author's old failing, of intensifying the image to the extreme, is saved by the homely and humorous picture of the dog, who jumps at that emotional moment on to the bed and is roughly removed:

> They fell silent. A wet sun shone into the room, splintered in a thousand pieces upon the lake, and withdrawing its light, lost itself in a bundle of clouds. Colm lowered his head and stretched out a hand to the dog who licked it and jumped joyously on to the bed.
>
> "Get down o' that or you'll have the place full of fleas," shouted Robert.[30]

This lapse into the earlier style of "The Boots," a story not dissimilar in theme, is not repeated. Instead, McLaverty introduces the central image of the story, that of the swans on the lake about to fly away as a storm gathers.

> One of the swans rose heavily, and with loud flaps from their wings and white splashes from the water the others followed. Necks a-strain they circled the lake and as they flew low over the cottage old Robert heard with delight the bing-bing of their powerful wings. Sadly Colm watched them flying northwards, while the dog jumped around him barking with joy.
>
> "He done that well; he's a good dog," said the Uncle, when they came in again. "But keep him outside or he'll dreep the place."[31]

As the storm breaks, all Colm's impressions, not only of his day, but, by implication, of his life on the island, are gathered into it, as the storm takes on a life of its own.

When it is over, the land is quiet and clean, and it is time for Colm to leave, with fresh butter, "snail-cold in the cabbage leaf," and a pair of socks hand-knitted for him by his aunt. The story ends on a gentle, reflective note, as he thinks of the swans, settled, as he will be, in an unfamiliar place, "pushing into the shelter of rushes in the night-grey waters of a lonely lough." Like Padraig in "The Boots," Colm can never return to his childhood, and the farewell is a final one, just as this is the very last of the stories of island boys.

"Leavetaking" is not, however, the last story of the island. The others to be written, including "Stone," "The White Mare" and "Becalmed," deal with the old. This is the aspect of island life touched on in "Leavetaking," and it is to the vigour and endurance of the old that he addresses himself in a story published in *The Capuchin Annual* in 1937. Entitled "The Race," it seems to owe something to the spirit of Liam O'Flaherty's "The Reaping Race," having as its theme the preparation for and performance of an old man in an island race. The old man, Shamus "The Mackerel" lives with his sister, a patient and lively-spirited character similar to Maggie in "Leavetaking," who, when she hears of his determination to take part in the forthcoming Veterans' race, comments: "I suppose it's off to Nell's pub you are, where they'll egg you on and make you the laughin' stock of the whole island." Naturally, he goes straight to the pub, and, encouraged by his cronies, begins at once to plan his training:

Shamus slipped across the road away to the rock heads and in a little secluded hollow, unseen and unseeing, he began to do physical exercises—bending and stretching his short legs with many a grimace. Then he would run fifteen yards or so and pull up awkwardly, blowing funnels of breath into the cold morning air. For two weeks before the race Shamus performed this ritual of surreptitious training, and at home he ate his food with slow deliberation and made endless excuses to Ellen for not going to fish.[32]

It becomes clear from the tone and atmosphere that Shamus and his friends have changed little in their attitudes to one another over the years, and indeed the importance to Shamus of saving face at all costs in front of his friends puts him closer to the level of the boys of the early stories than that of the dignified old men of the later works. In the outside world he would be, despite his endurance and will to win, a laughing stock. This is the fundamental truth of this slight story, which serves to emphasise the harsh facts of island life in a humorous and affectionate way. Therefore, though there is gently comedy in his laboured preparations, and broad humour as one of the elderly competitors jumps the gun so that all are "called back puffing and blowing while young spectators laughed at their discomfiture," the reality of the decline of island life as they have known it is never far away. From this time onward, the idea of loss, even in the midst of seeming happiness, is never far distant in McLaverty's short stories.

The third of the stories published in 1937 is arguably one of McLaverty's most famous. "The Game Cock," published in *Ireland Today* in October 1937, stands with "Pigeons" as one of his most highly-regarded stories. As in the earlier Belfast stories, the city and its people are represented with affection and respect but without romantic or nostalgic idealisation. McLaverty knows the city intimately, and within the narrow circle in which his characters move, he lingers with sympathetic understanding and with respect over every detail. Like "Pigeons," a story with which it has much in common, it is written in the first person, and the narrator is a young boy who feels the implications of a tragic event without fully understanding the human error or effort involved therein. Although there cannot be any true comparison between the death of a bird and the death of a human, the cruel end of the game cock of the title impinges as much on the consciousness of the young boy in this story as does the death of his brother on Frankie in "Pigeons." Like Frankie, this boy moves in a restricted circle, circumscribed by the movements of his family; like him, he accepts with confidence the judgement of his elders and the relative unimportance of the happenings of the world outside his home and family; like him he reveals, through a voice deliberately innocent of emotion, a tragedy of human neglect. The opening sentence, although not used by McLaverty as a refrain, lingers in the mind: "When I was young we came to Belfast and my father kept The Game Cock and a few hens." The memory grows in definition as the narrator recalls the great pride the family had in the game cock.

> We called him Dick. He was none of your ordinary cocks. He had a pedigree as long as your arm, and his grandfather and grandmother were of Indian breed. He was lovely to look at, with his long, yellow legs, black glossy feathers in

the chest and tail, and reddish streaky neck. My father would watch him for hours in the long summer evenings, smiling at the way he tore the clayey ground with his claws, coming on a large earwig, and calling the hens to share it. But one day when somebody lamed him with a stone, my father grew so sad that he couldn't take his supper.[33]

McLaverty's ironic observation of the father's concern at the laming of Dick reminds the reader that this sensitive man is all the while training the bird to kill or be torn to pieces in a barbaric ritual. This is the central irony of the story, as the cock is at once a pampered pet and a victim fattening for the slaughter. The father's friends gather like Shamus the Mackerel's companions to discuss the cock's chances in the same tone that they use to discuss the price of coal, but it is the narrator's detached relation of the unbelievably cruel cutting of Dick's comb and wattles which shows to greatest effect the author's mastery of ironic understatement. The boy's sisters' protests are dismissed; like small children, which they may be, they are fobbed off with a lie. It is possible that the father believes the cock does not feel the pain; it is certainly more convenient for him to say so:

"Now," said he, "try and cut it with one stroke."

When my sisters saw the chips of comb snipped off with the scissors and the blood falling on the tiles they began to cry. "That's a sin, father! That's a sin!"

"Tush, tush," said my father, and the blood on his sleeves. "He doesn't feel it. It's just like getting your hair cut—Isn't that right, Jimmy?"

"That's right; just like getting your toenails cut."

But when Dick clucked and shook his head with pain, my sisters cried louder and were sent out to play themselves, and I went into the scullery to gather cobwebs to stop the bleeding.[34]

To keep him peevish and aggressive for the fight, which is to be held in the town of Toome on Easter Monday, the cock is first starved for two days, then given hard-boiled eggs, "but they didn't agree with him and made him scour." The blind man prescribes a diet guaranteed to keep him scour-free, "a strict diet of barley and barley water." Kept in a dark box, his feathers and tail clipped, the cock is trained to fight with a straw-stuffed flannel bag. His easy, friendly nature changes radically, and one day he pecks at the boy, who gives him "a clout that brought my father running to the yard." Once again, the thoughtful father, who has taken pains to "sponge the feet and head" after the day's terrible training, runs to protect the bird from injury, but his proudest moment is, ironically, when he sees the cock ready for combat, with his steel spurs on, and pronounced by the men "the picture of health." On the day of the fight, as in the earlier Belfast stories, the Falls Road of McLaverty's childhood comes alive in vivid imagery, and there follows a highly comic episode, reminiscent of Chaucer, where the cock, pursued by the two heroes, escapes across the tramlines and makes his way to North Howard Street where he pauses, "contemplating a dark green public lavatory." He has no intention of being caught, and defies them, causing the father, torn between exasperation and admiration, to lose the last shreds of his dignity.

When he is finally caught, his heart is "going like a traction engine," and the boy's father fears he will be "bate." He himself is exhausted, "punctured," in the local phrase, and perspires and puffs freely during the train journey. The boy's main worry is that he will be blamed. Neither considers for an instant the ordeal in store for their lively and playful pet. The curious lack of concern continues when they reach the house of the boy's maternal grandmother, who welcomes them to her home in the quiet country town and helps to conceal the illegality of their enterprise—for it is made clear that cock-fighting is against the law.[35] Her heart and sympathy are with the cock-fighters and with the poteen-distillers, who, "Poor fellas...run great risk to make that." Similarly, the rebellious determination to partake and rejoice in any activity specifically forbidden by the authorities causes the boy's uncle, who lives with the grandmother, to lecture him on the iniquities of the landed gentry, cursed for taking the land from its rightful owners:

> We walked to the Big House and saw the lake covered with rushes and weeds. The Big House was in ruins and crows were nesting in the chimneys. When I asked my uncle where were all the ladies and gentlemen and the gamekeeper, he looked through the naked windows and replied: "They took the land from the people and God cursed them."[36]

It is in this way that the boy is occupied while the cock is engaged in combat, and no more is heard of him till the return of the father. Once again McLaverty shows his command of irony when he follows the catalogue of wrongs done to the Irish people by the gentry with an understated account of the father's triumphant return, side by side with the torn and bleeding cock:

> The cock's comb was scratched with blood, his feathers streaky, and his eyes half shut. He was left in the byre until the tea was over. While my father was taking the tea he got up from the table and stood in the middle of the floor telling how Dick had won his fights: "Five battles he won and gave away weight twice."
>
> "Take your tea, Mick, and you can tell us after," my granny said, her hands in her sleeves, and her feet tapping the hearth.[37]

No comment is made on this callous failure to tend the wounded bird; even when the father boasts of his great success, it occurs to no-one, not even to the grandmother, to look after the cock. They board the train for home, and the boy hears in the rumble of the wheels his uncle's strange spell-like words, "They took the land from the people...God cursed them..." hypnotising him as do similar incantations the child in "Pigeons."

Neither of them thinks to look at Dick during the journey, each lost in his own reflections of the day. When they do remember about him he is long since dead of his injuries, and there is nothing for the father to do but consider a way to preserve the time of his glory as the owner of so fine a cock. The ending is grimly reminiscent of the ending of "The Grey Goat," but the ironic implications make it memorable in a way that the milder story could not be:

He took him out gently and raised his head, but it fell forward limply, and from the open mouth blood dripped to the floor.

"God-a-God, he's dead!" said my father, stretching out one of the wings. Then he put him on the table without a word and sat on a chair. For a while I said nothing, and then I asked quietly: "What'll you do with him, Da?"

He didn't answer, but turned and looked at the cock, stretched on the table, "Poor Dick!" he said; and I felt a lump rise in my throat.

Then he got up from the chair. "What'll I do with him! What'll I do with him? I'll get him stuffed! That's what I'll do!"[38]

When this story was republished in an anthology entitled *Stories of the Forties*, a reviewer in *The New Statesman*, noting its similarity to the style of the short stories of James Joyce, wrote of its "minute and brilliant observation...in the great tradition of *Dubliners.*"[39] There is no doubt that it is one of McLaverty's most carefully crafted stories. It is a fitting end to his most productive period as a writer of short stories, demonstrating his assimilation of the lessons learned from the masters whose style he had studied, and the discovery of a personal, unmistakable voice. In the novels *Call My Brother Back* and *Lost Fields,* he would once more use the themes and character of "The Wild Duck's Nest," "Pigeons" and "The Game Cock" to excellent effect, but with the publication of "The Game Cock," his explorations of childhood had found almost their last expression in the short story form.

REFERENCES

1   "The Trout," *Irish Monthly* 63 (January 1935), 47-53.
2   "The Return,"*Catholic World* (Spring 1935), 657-63.
3   "The Race,"*Capuchin Annual* (1937), 223-4.
4   "Evening in Winter," *Irish Monthly* 63 (May 1935), 314-8.
5   "Pigeons," *New Stories* (April/May 1936)
6   "Aunt Suzanne," *Ireland Today*, II, 3 (March 1937), 48-57.
7   "The Game Cock," *Ireland Today*, II, 10 (October 1937), 51-58.
8   "Leavetaking," *Ireland Today*, II, 7 (July 1937), 45-51; *In Quiet Places*, 55-62.
9   Correspondence in possession of McLaverty family.
10 "The Trout," *Irish Monthly*, 63 (January 1935), 50-1; *In Quiet Places*, 40. "The Wild Duck's Nest," *Irish Monthly*, 62 (April 1934), 236-240; *In Quiet Places*, 33-36.
11 "The Trout," op. cit., 52-3; *In Quiet Places*, 42.
12 "Evening in Winter," op.cit., 315; *Collected Stories*, 128-9.
13 ibid., 317-8; *Collected Stories*, 130.
14 Edward J O'Brien (1890-1941), editor of *New Stories* (1933-5) and *The Best Short Stories* (1915-40).
15 "Pigeons," *New Stories*, II, 8 (April-May 1936), 561; *Collected Stories*, 17.
16 ibid., 563; *Collected Stories*, 19.
17 ibid., 564; *Collected Stories*, 20.
18 ibid., 566; *Collected Stories*, 22.
19 ibid., 568; *Collected Stories*, 24-5.
20 ibid., 569; *Collected Stories*, 25-6.
21 Brian Moore, *The Lonely Passion of Judith Hearne*, London, 1955.
22 "Aunt Suzanne," op. cit., 48-9; *Collected Stories*, 27-8; *In Quiet Places*, 44.
23 ibid., 57; *Collected Stories*, 38-9; *In Quiet Places*, 54.
24 ibid., 53; *Collected Stories*, 33; *In Quiet Places*, 49.
25 ibid., 57; *Collected Stories*, 38; *In Quiet Places*, 53-4.
26 AW Garfield (Chapman and Hall) to McLaverty, 20 April 1936. Letter in possession of McLaverty family.
27 Other novel extracts (from *In This Thy Day*) are "Sea Road," *Capuchin Annual*, 1943, 486-90; "The Passing Generation," *Lagan* 2 (1944), 13-7.
28 "Leavetaking," op. cit., 45; *In Quiet Places*, 56-6.
29 ibid., 47-48; *In Quiet Places*, 58.
30 ibid., 48; *In Quiet Places*, 59.
31 ibid., 49; *In Quiet Places*, 59-60.
32 "The Race," op. cit., 223. See also *Ulster Tatler* XVI, 6 (June 1982), 41-2.
33 "The Game Cock," op. cit., 51; *Collected Stories*, 82.
34 ibid., 53; *Collected Stories*, 84.
35 ibid., 55, 56; *Collected Stories*, 89.
36 ibid., 57; *Collected Stories*, 90.
37 ibid., 57; *Collected Stories*, 90.
38 ibid., 58; *Collected Stories*, 54.
39 *New Statesman* review in possession of McLaverty family.

CHAPTER THREE

UPROOTED

1939-41

In February 1939, Michael McLaverty's first novel, *Call My Brother Back*, was published in New York by Longmans Green, and the course of his career was changed. He did not stop writing short stories, as can be seen by the appearance in the *Capuchin Annual* for that year of no fewer than three stories, and of another in its next issue,[1] but the short story form was never again to command his whole attention. Something of the exhilaration felt by him at this period is conveyed by an autobiographical fragment, written when he was over eighty, in which he recalls the formation in his mind of the first novel, under the helpful influence of the American anthologist, EJ O'Brien:

In my spare time I did a Master of Science degree. Tried my hand at short stories. 1929 did a Master of Science degree and from that time rediscovered my library. At that time an anthologist EJ O'Brien—he gave me great encouragement. He told me I should try to write. I thought of my pigeon house and the places around. I was really

willing and felt power stirring in me. I thought not only
of my pigeon shed but also of Rathlin island where we
went for our holidays for years. The two combined to
make a first novel: the first section depicts Rathlin island
with its swans. The second section: the strife-torn city.[2]

The themes explored in the short stories of the Thirties
provided an ideal springboard for a work which would
unite both island and city, and in which the theme of
uprooting, centred in the character of the island boy, could
at last be fully explored. McLaverty recalls that the book
came easily to him, commenting that "that book wrote
itself," and he has never had quite the regard for it that
critics and readers have shown. This is evident in a letter
written many years after its publication in which the author
remarks: "*Call My Brother Back* is my most popular book
but not in the same street as the later novels which were
misread and misunderstood in the land and by the people
that inspired them."[3] Perhaps in his distrust of the easily
achieved, he is inclined to overlook the many years of
thought and preparation which made the novel compar-
atively easy to write. He does not, however, underestimate
its effect on his career or the debt of gratitude owed by him
to the anthologist Edward O'Brien, who took pains to put
McLaverty's work before the American publishing company,
Longmans Green, and introduced him to one of its editors,
Julie Kernan, who was a significant influence on his career
until his change of publisher. The American publishers'
enthusiasm prompted the London firm of Longmans to
publish the novel in September 1939. This enthusiasm did
not extend to McLaverty's original title, *Waste Ground*; they

suggested, as a substitute, *Call My Brother Back*. The original title, although unacceptable to his publishers, was not chosen at random. The idea of the waste ground as a symbol for the strife in the city of Belfast is first found in the short story, "Pigeons," and McLaverty was to use it again in his second novel, *Lost Fields*. An account of the inspiration for his first novel, given to the compiler of a volume entitled *Catholic Authors*, underlines the importance to him of the contrast between the island and the city:

His first novel which contrasts the lyrical life of Rathlin with that of the anti-Catholic, anti-Nationalist life prevailing in Belfast came to him on a visit to Rathlin, and in an old house overlooking a lake he discovered a faded newspaper containing an account of the 1935 Belfast pogrom. As he read it, all the twisted life of that city, which he had experienced as a boy, suddenly surged with compulsive force into his mind, and seeing a few swans in the lake below him he thought of Yeats's beautiful poem, "The Wild Swans at Coole." The recollection of this poem re-illuminated for him the tranquillity of the island life compared with the pitiable waste of blood that was spilt in the poorer quarters of Belfast. He appended Yeats's line, "They paddle in the cold companionable streams," to convey the atmosphere of the Island section in his book, and for the city section lines by Louis MacNeice, the Belfast poet:

Frost will not touch the hedge of fuchsia

The land will remain as it was.

But no abiding content can grow out of these minds.

Fuddled with blood, always caught by blinds.[4]

In *Call My Brother Back*, the limitations imposed by the straitness of the waste ground behind their back-street house are in complete contrast to the freedom experienced before the move to the city of the Rathlin-born McNeills. The character of Alec grows from that of Johnny, the hero brother of "Pigeons," and the memories of Rathlin mirror the musings of Colm as, in "Leavetaking," he is about to leave the island. In the novel the process is reversed: looking at the Black Mountain behind the narrow town house, he thinks of Rathlin, and recalls all the island boys. At the same time, standing in the pigeon shed abandoned by his brother who has now committed himself to the IRA, he recalls to the reader's mind Frankie, the boy bewildered by violent events outside his control in "Pigeons." Colm McNeill represents all the boy-heroes of McLaverty's early stories:

> For the first week after he went back to school he climbed every evening up the ladder to the shed. His mother had given him a stool; Jamesy had made a table for him out of old butter boxes; and so he was able to do his exercises and learn his lessons. Finished, he would stand for a while at the window which overlooked the yard-walls...He would stand and think of Knocklayde and compare it with the mountain before him: the one barren and desolate, the other green and near. Then he would turn away, do some dumbbell exercises, pencil his height on the boards of the shed, and then out to the waste ground to play football until dark.[5]

In Book One, McLaverty recalls in lyrical prose the island of childhood celebrated in the early stories. In Book Two he is less successful in conveying the character of the city and its effect on the island family. The first section is written with the same assurance as the earliest stories, but the second seems episodic, almost picaresque in its earnest attempt to incorporate all the author's impressions of the city into the daily life of one boy.

The McNeills could be any of the island families of the early stories. Colm, the second of three sons, is about to go to a well-known boys' school in Belfast and will be leaving the island for the first time. His older sister and brother, Theresa and Alec, already live and work in the city. Still on the island are his parents and his younger brother and sister, Jamesy and Clare. His kind, dependable father dies suddenly, when a chill caught on the boat from Ballycastle develops into pneumonia, and the headship of the house falls suddenly on the eldest brother, Alec. Alec, newly returned from Belfast, seems even early in the novel curiously remote from the others. His detachment is one of the main characteristics attributed to him. He sees no point in Colm's going to school now that circumstances have changed and, but for the intervention of the island priest who pays his fees, Colm's future would surely be sacrificed to Alec's ambitions. The priest prevails and Colm is sent as a boarder to the school in Belfast. At first his life is peaceful, and McLaverty clearly enjoys evoking the sights, smells and sounds of his own old school, St Malachy's College, on which he has said St Kevin's is based:

Outside in the grey evening lay two playing fields, black with mud, the goal-posts white and dirtied by smacks from the ball. On one side was the dark jail wall, and on the opposite side the top windows of terrace houses overlooked the grounds. The fields were desolate, and already the gulls were swarming and calling as they lit on the ground.

Inside, the Study Hall glowed with dry warmth from the hot pipes. All the boys stood at their yellow desks waiting for the priest to enter. Some were combing their wet-streaked hair and others exchanging twopenny detective stories...[6]

Without warning, Alec moves the entire family to Belfast and Colm becomes a day-boy, travelling across from his new home in the heart of the nationalist community in the west of the city. McLaverty takes pains here, as in "Pigeons" and "Aunt Suzanne," to depict the humour and vitality that are as much a part of the city as its darker, puritanical side. One memorable chapter describes Theresa's wedding. In it McLaverty indulges his love of the colloquial, showing a genuine affection for the characters and their concerns:

She [Theresa] had her mouth full of hair-pins and her small pink hat lay on the table. She wore a pair of brown suede shoes and a pink dress down to her heels.

"I'm a holy show," she whimpered into the square looking-glass on the wall. "My hair's cut too short. Them hair-dressers'll do nothing you tell them!"

"I never seen you looking better in my life; you're

gorgeous, child," placated the mother. "I hope you're warm
enough; it wouldn't suit you to get a cold on your wedding-
day. Have you yer heavy chemise on?"[7]

Despite the author's efforts to make him human and
comprehensible, Alec never truly comes alive in the novel.
Nonetheless, there is a feeling of real desolation when he
is shot, but the focus of attention is less on the martyred
brother than on the grief and desolation of the survivors.
A measure of the artistic distance travelled by the author,
from the time of his first exploration of the city in "Evening
in Winter," is seen in Colm's nightmare journey along the
Falls Road to fetch a priest for Alec. Colm covers the same
ground as the little boy Charley in "Evening in Winter"
but the world is changed and there is now no guarantee of
safety for the innocent:

His bare feet thudded on the pavement and made a pinging
sound as he passed corrugated railings. Up the hill he ran
and then at the corner of a street two black figures jumped
out to meet him, but he swerved and ran past them,
harder and harder. Behind him he heard them shout:
"Halt! Halt!" and it echoed and reechoed in the night air.
They shouted again, but he didn't stop. There were shots
and their noise filled up the whole world and re-sounded
from the empty road. But Colm found himself going on.
Then he turned the corner of the convent grounds with
its black granite walls and came in sight of the church. A
lamp with a broken mantle blinked and snored, and a
bullet whined.[8]

After Alec's death, Jamesy leaves for England with his married sister, and Colm's promising career at the college comes to an abrupt close. He is left supporting his mother and sister in the waste ground that Belfast has become and, in the last lines of the novel, he recalls the images of his life, carefree on Rathlin, dispossessed in Belfast:

> ...rabbits wild and free on the hills around Belfast...swans moving across black water...oil-lamps warming the windows in Rathlin...a rusty tin in the fork of a thorn bush...a rickle of bones falling dead in York Street.[9]

Call My Brother Back is to a large extent an autobiographical novel, in that McLaverty calls on his own memories of life on the Falls Road, mass in St Paul's Church, school at St Malachy's College, shopping in Smithfield market. He remembers the Raglan Street siege in which he has Alec take part.[10] It may be the solid factual base for the fiction which gives to the novel its impressive vivacity and colour, qualities immediately noticed by the critics, who were for the most part favourably disposed. *The Southport Guardian* compared the novel to Robert Flaherty's film, *Man of Aran*; the *Johannesburg Star* noted the author's "reticence and impartiality"; *America* spoke of "realism of the right kind that avoids the sordid while giving a clear picture of real conditions"; and *The West Australian* of Perth described it as "a novel of great distinction," commenting on McLaverty's "prose style of a singular purity."[11] His prose style caught the eye of most of the critics. Horace Reynolds of the *New York Times* felt that establishment of character was sacrificed to style but was nonetheless full of praise for the quality of the writing.[12] Others did not warm to the style to the same extent. An unnamed reviewer in the *Oxford Times* believed that "the reticence is overdone," and that "a little more imagination would have improved greatly a book that, as it is, emerges too rarely from the prevailing monotone."[13] Another anonymous reviewer, in the *Saturday Review of Literature*, objected to "the unswerving lyricism" of McLaverty's writing, believing that the second half should have been marked by a change of style.[14] This objection recurred in reviews on both sides of the Atlantic and several of the reviewers gave as their opinion that the second half of the novel did not live up to the promise of the first. One of the least favourable of the reviews is among the most interesting for its analysis of McLaverty's talents. Harry Sylvester, writing in *Commonweal*, felt the main failing of the book was that it was written by an author whose gift was for the short story:

> Mr McLaverty's book may be called a novel only by courtesy and by virtue of his use of the third person. It is a rather pedestrian picture of already-known aspects of Irish life, spotted with purple here and there and only once or twice lifting to interest...What is surprising is that Mr McLaverty has written distinguished short stories...He is not, of course, the first good short story writer to meet defeat in the novel, although it is a problem how a man who can get fine implications and meaning into a short story can keep them out of a longer work.[15]

The decline in power of the second half of the novel requires some examination. The lack of the constraint necessarily imposed by the short story form seems at once to release and hinder the author. Accomplished as a painter of miniatures, he finds the sudden change to a broad canvas exhilarating; yet he continues to paint tiny masterpieces on a space too large. It is the lack of motivation, the absence of form in the novel, that leaves it so curiously unsatisfying in the end. This may be a common fault in a first novel. McLaverty's burden was heavier because he was an established writer, in a different form. Yet, his years of work in the short story did not help him, beyond allowing him his favourite imagery and ironic observation of character. In his abundance of material, he seems not to know which of his rich memories to use next. Consequently, in a very short book, the reader witnesses a wedding, two deaths, a birth, a spell in school, a stay in hospital and a move from innocent childhood to disillusioned adolescence. The involvement of Alec in the IRA seems extraneous, imposed on the story almost as Alec himself is, for the real theme of the novel is the effect on the family, and especially on Colm, of the move to the city. Not till the end of the novel, with the events leading up to Alec's cruel death described and done with, does the reader experience again the calm harmony between author and character so remarkable in the early stories and, indeed, in the first part of *Call My Brother Back*:

A chill mist rose from the ground. Two men passed with greyhounds on leads. Swans with wings akimbo were moving up to the quieter reaches for the night, a fan of wavelets widening behind them. No birds were singing. The waterfall lumbered into a pool and wrinkles of froth with groups of bubbles came and broke in the eddies. The grass on the banks was combed by the water. The fields were deserted and their grass limp and grey.

And all this beauty, all these quiet places flowed into his heart and filled him with a tired-torn joy. And turning out of it he came to the city and the lights of the tram at the end of the road.[16]

The mood of "Leavetaking" is recovered in that passage, its Hopkins-like sadness a development from the nostalgic tone of the short story and of its revised version in the novel. As an elegy for the city of his youth, it is powerful and moving, the undoubted vitality of McLaverty's writing staying in the memory. If the novel is flawed, it is still remarkable in its parts if not as a whole.

The last short story to be published before this novel was "Leavetaking," and there seems to have been a continuity of thought in McLaverty's mind as he returned to his theme of uprooting, a variation on the theme of valediction, for three other works published in that year. These three stories, entitled "Stone," "The White Mare" and "The Sea" appeared together in *The Capuchin Annual* in its edition of 1939. They explore the world of older people who see the ends of their lives approaching. The first, "Stone," is as stark as its name suggests. Deliberately chilly and sepulchral, it tells the story of an old Rathlin man, Jamesy Heaney, whose life has narrowed to the single desire for a monument that will cause envy among his neighbours and be a more lasting memorial than children might have been. The imagery, reminiscent of that in the earlier story, "The Letter," suggests the coldness of the grave.

Not even his meagre fire can warm this "small grasshopper of a man, withered and worn, and cold to look at."

The last of his family on the island, he is alone and unloved, except for the one warm and friendly creature in the story, his black and white collie. Although he considers his grave his real home and looks forward to the envious discontent which, he hopes, his splendid monument will occasion in the other old men, he still derives some satisfaction from the possession of his cottage, even if he has no comfort in living there. As he walks up the hill to the graveyard, it becomes clear that he is not going to pray for his dead like the old man in "The Return." He goes to feed his envy on the one thing which fills him with something like warmth or passion, the monument of a neighbour who died a lonely bachelor. To Jamesy, this stone, "a large Celtic cross of blue granite, its panelled arms and shaft decorated with an interlacing design," is more beautiful than anything in the world. Determined to confound the other old men, he goes down that evening to inform them that the only permanent thing in the world is stone. Unfortunately, he chooses as an example of the endurance of stone a hill which is the site of an infamous massacre, where the men of the island were hurled from the cliffs before the eyes of their families. His argument is quickly demolished by the cronies:

"A hill is only a hill if it has no memories; it has no life!" And then in excitement he raised his voice: "I declare to God when I look at Croc-na-Screilan 'tisn't a hill I see at all, but our people—the McDonnells, the McCurdys, the McQuilkins, and the rest—fighting the invaders in the hollow, and our women and children screamin' and shoutin' at them from the hill. 'Tis that what the hill means to me."

"Aren't all them people dead and gone and the hill's the same," Jamesy answered.

"They're not dead!" they shouted at him in chorus.

"Aren't their children's children here still? Aren't we the same stock?" added Johnny John Beg.[17]

A fearsome storm, reminiscent of that in "Leavetaking," begins to blow up and, amid its rage, Jamesy begins to be afraid that he will lose his chance of immortality by dying "before he had the arrangements made for his Stone!" Jamesy fails to understand the warning of the storm, even though his tree, like a banshee, is "bent to the wind like an old woman with flying hair," and eventually crashes down by the house. He takes it only as proof that the life of stone is superior even to that of a strong tree, and superior certainly to the tenuous connection with immortality provided by children or grandchildren:

From the crest on the road his house, bare of the out-spreading arms of the tree, looked desolate. Looking at it Jamesy became sad and regretful; awakened memories of the tree's companionship arose within him and made him linger on the hill. But the shouts of playing children came to him faintly on the calm, chill air and he grinned to himself cunningly and strode off towards the village.[18]

As he creeps "slyly" to the graveyard for reassurance of the permanence of stone, he sees to his amazement that the

McBride monument is gone; "a great vacancy held the sky." Desolate, he escapes blindly from the scene of the wreckage, forgetting all his old rituals in the collapse of his last and only dream. Meanwhile, the children, living proof that the other men are right, laugh at their play in seeming mockery of his plans. It is a grim, bleak story, the other side of the gently humorous story of old men on the island, "The Race." It prepares the way for a new perspective in McLaverty's stories. He has not finished his explorations of loss and farewell but he considers them from this time onward from the point of view of the old, lonely and dispossessed, rather than the young and innocent.

Loss of a similar kind is at the heart of the second story in the group. Here, it is an old man living with his two unmarried sisters who loses the thing dearest to him—his white mare. Paddy is ailing but takes pride in doing the work he has always done. With his white mare, he has worked in his fields for many years. She too is old, but together they make the daily effort because the work must be done. One day, having exhausted himself the previous evening in finishing the ploughing of a field, Paddy lies in bed to recover. His one day becomes three. Unknown to him, his sisters, acting as they think in his best interests, sell the mare. Paddy's desolation, as he tries frantically to call back the boat that is carrying her away from him to the mainland, is complete, far greater than that of the children in "The Grey Goat" as their animal is taken away, and equalled only by the sense of loss at the end of "The Letter," "The Wild Duck's Nest" or "Pigeons." Rushing wildly down to the quay, ignoring the warning pains in his heart in a desperate effort to save "the beast, the poor beast that hated noise and fuss, standing nervous on the pier with a rope tied round her four legs," he is in time only to see the boat pass him by. In a chilling reminder of the early stories of island boys, and in token of his future helpless status in the family, he receives in response to his frantic signals the cheerful, dismissive wave reserved for children. Helpless and bereft, he turns his way homeward without comfort or hope for the future:

> For a long time he looked at the receding boat, his spirit draining from him. A wave washed up the rock, frothing at his feet, and he turned wearily away, going slowly back the road that led home.[19]

Stronger than "The Grey Goat," more poignant than "The Return," "The White Mare" deserves its place as the title story of McLaverty's first collection, four years later.[20]

The third story in the trilogy is again a story of loss sustained by the old. Unlike Jamesy Heaney in "Stone," Robert Neeson, hero of "The Sea," puts his trust for the future in a young boy, Peter McCloskey, an orphan whom he treats as his own child. Like Uncle Robert in "Leave-taking," Neeson tells Peter story after story of his seafaring life, unwittingly stimulating in the boy the desire to go to sea himself. When Robert's wife, Alice, dies, he is left desolate. His only comforting thought after a day spent from home on business is that the boy will take her place in preparing a welcoming fire and meal for him. When he arrives, the boy is gone. The betrayal in this story is felt not only by the deceived; Peter, on the Liverpool boat, craning his neck to see St John's Lighthouse near Robert's home, feels the pain of remorse:

> A piercing sense of utter worthlessness crept into his soul,
> the tears flowed thickly down his cheeks, and he could no
> longer see the lighthouse beams that marked the land.[21]

In this way, McLaverty succeeds in dividing the narrative
point of view, providing a broad sweep from one character
to another without disturbing the involvement with one
figure, Robert. The reader is not meant to sympathise with
Peter, who has done a worthless thing in abandoning
Robert. The theme of the all-seeing beam of the lighthouse,
introduced in "The White Mare," is reintroduced, and recurs
at the crucial point of the story, when Robert fires Peter's
imagination with his tall tales, ironically precipitating his
departure. It does not matter that Robert's wife Alice, like
the aunt in "Leavetaking," tells Peter later that "it'd have
taken him forty years to ramble the countries that he says
he was in," for the damage is done:

> Peter listened to him in silence.
>
> "What d'ye think of that for a life?" Robert finished.
>
> Peter startled, his eyes were shining, and he gave a
> nervous little laugh.
>
> Behind them the beam from St John's Lighthouse was
> lengthening in the falling dark. They rowed with long
> slow sweeps and soon they rounded the point and came
> into their own quiet bay. Alice had the light in the window
> and its beam made a shivering path upon the sea.[22]

It is a long story, designed for careful reading, as layer upon layer of clues to the eventual outcome is planted in the mind of the reader. It is filled too with memorable images. The opening sentence, "Oh, Sister, look at the boats!" was to inspire the title of the story when it appeared in the collection, *The White Mare and Other Stories*. The central image of the story, a gentler reflection of the power of the lighthouse beam, is that of the welcoming light in the window. Alice provides this on the first night Peter comes to the house, and it remains a symbol throughout the story for home and security. Through Robert, this message is conveyed, as they sit in the house on Peter's first evening. He asks, rhetorically, what they consider "the nearest thing to death about a house." His answer, "a hearth without a fire and a house without a woman," prepares the reader for Robert's great loneliness at the end of the story, when darkness and cold finally replace light and warmth.

Loneliness is the fate, too, of the woman at the end of the fourth and last story written by McLaverty between *Call My Brother Back* and *Lost Fields*. Appearing in *The Capuchin Annual*, at Christmas 1940, this was entitled "Becalmed." (It appeared in the 1943 collection, *The White Mare*, as "The Schooner.") The heart of the story lies in the silent grief of an islandwoman whose generosity prompts her to lend a precious possession, a model schooner made by her late husband, to a little boy, who loses it. His main regret, even when he has taken in what he can of her story, is that there will be nothing to play with when he comes next year. This child is not of the island, but a visitor, a stranger unfamiliar with the rhythm of life there. One of the important images in the story, here as in "The

Sea," is of the reassuring light at the window. Paddy, the islandman in whose house the little boy is staying, recalls the day his sister's husband, married but three months, set out on a small boat to reach the great ship becalmed off the island. He was to sail as a member of its crew to Canada. All during the still time of the ship's enforced stay, Annie kept up what contact she could, providing light in the darkness, waves of encouragement from the shore. After the ship was lost, Paddy tells Terence, "She always felt that he was alive and that he'd come back...She's got very old waiting...For a while she used to walk about the house at night, opening and shutting doors, but she got over that."

The boy Terence unheedingly launches the model boat on a stormy day and causes it to be lost in an unconsciously cruel mimicry of Annie's original loss. Ironically, she waits in the lighted doorway, confident this time, at last, of the boat's return. There is sadness, too, in the revelation that her brother cares little for the boat or its importance to her, and is unlikely to make any effort to find it. When Terence asks him if he will look for the little schooner, he replies that he will, "But the abstracted way he answered made Terence feel that the schooner meant nothing to Paddy; he knew he would never see it again and that he'd have no schooner to play with when he'd come back next year." Like "The Sea," it is a long and intense story, filled with descriptive imagery and layers of suggestion.

In these four stories of people dispossessed, McLaverty seems both to recall his earlier preoccupation with the lives of island children and to look forward to his new concern for the losses of the old. All four lead to the work which represents the culmination of McLaverty's concern with uprooting and loss—his second novel, *Lost Fields*.

In his book, *Catholic Authors*, Father Hoehn records McLaverty's inspiration for this second novel:

> The idea for his second novel, *Lost Fields*, was derived from a boy's essay in the Belfast school where he was teaching. The boy wrote a short description of a cantankerous old grandmother who had come from the country to live with her poor relations in the city, and ended her days threatening to go back to her home in the country where she had her fields, her hens, and the Angelus Bell. From the few words the lad wrote Michael McLaverty created his *Lost Fields* which reveals the socially maladjusted life of country people in an industrial city and how their minds are preserved from sourness and deformity by the spiritual attitude they adopt to their scanty livelihood.[23]

Part of a draft was sent to Longmans Green in the summer of 1940, and Julie Kernan, who first dealt with McLaverty as the result of an introduction by Edward O'Brien, wrote to express her opinion that Longmans Green would want to publish it. Such enthusiasm and encouragement must have been gratifying to McLaverty, who seems to have submitted the manuscript, with a tentative title, *They Lived in the City*, before the end of October 1940. Miss Kernan wrote on 31 October 1940, no less enthusiastic about the content, but once again with alternative suggestions as to its title, thinking McLaverty's working title "a little pedestrian." McLaverty replied on 6 December that he favoured the title *Lost Fields*, for the appeal of its "poetic loneliness." On 19 December 1940 he sent his manuscript to Longmans Green in London, who replied after many letters from him on 17 February, saying that they were unable to publish the book because of wartime difficulties. It was at this point that McLaverty approached Cape, and Jonathan Cape replied on 25 March 1941 that he would "be willing to make an agreement...to publish it—sometime." Shortage of paper was his main constraint and the London edition of the novel was not published until the end of January 1942.[24] In the meantime, Cape had asked McLaverty for a paragraph on the novel itself, and McLaverty submitted the following on 5 April 1941:

Enclosed is the requested paragraph on my book, *Lost Fields*.

God forgive me if I have made claims for it which it does not possess.

In this novel the Irish author of Call My Brother Back *reveals—within a short compass of time and with consummate technical skill—the attitude to life of three generations of people.*

The story concerns the Griffin family, their neighbours, and their continual makeshift employment. An old woman is wheedled from her home and fields in the Antrim countryside to live with her son's family in the noise-swarming streets of Belfast. Against her uprooted life in the city she is in revolt; and it is only her spiritualized struggles against selfishness that persuade her to remain with a family for whom her old age pension brings comparative wealth. Her cantankerous moods, her recurring threats to leave for the country, and her daughter-in-law's counter-manoeuvres to get her to remain, and the death of the old woman provide scenes of tenderness, humour and deep tragedy. Then there are her grandson Hugh and his girl

Eileen against whose marriage the old woman bars the way.

Amongst the neighbours there are many unforgettable characters—Stick McCormick for ever whistling and chopping sticks in his back yard; the cup-reading Liza McCloskey and her good natured husband with the foolish habits; brilliant studies of children, a boys' reformatory, and a girl's vocation for the convent.

It is all told in a prose pared to the bone and taut with emotional intensity; and throughout the book the lyrical urgency of the style evokes for us the rainy streets of Belfast and the quiet fields around the lonely reaches of the river Bann.[25]

The newly-found confidence of the author is unmistakable. He seems quite sure of what he wants to say, and has a careful structure to impose on his story. He was moving away, too, from some of his earlier literary influences, reading less by Corkery and turning to a wider range of authors than before. He recalls, in particular, that *Lost Fields* was influenced by the novel he was reading at the time, *Le Notaire du Havre* by Georges Duhamel.[26] Certainly in its evocation of a crowded, poverty-stricken family life, the sacrifice of the desires of one character to the selfish dreams of another, and in the final truth that happiness is not dependent on the hope of returning to the joys of the past, Duhamel's novel prefigures McLaverty's. In Duhamel's world, life passes by as the family wait to hear of their inheritance from Le Havre. In McLaverty's, the lost fields of the title are idealised to the point where happiness in the present, in the city, seems impossible.

Even if the germ of the idea came from Duhamel's work, *Lost Fields* remains McLaverty's own story. For the central figure, that of the grandmother, he recalls that he drew upon his memories of his own grandmother, already vividly depicted in "The Game Cock," the story closest in mood to this novel. The grandmother is prevailed upon by the wife of her poverty-stricken son to leave her comfortable home in Toome and move to a cold, antiseptic-smelling "wee room" in her son's Belfast house, so that she may eke out their meagre income with her old-age pension. Once she makes the move, the quality of her life deteriorates at an alarming rate, as does the bright, expansive tolerance of her character. The children lean on her, sapping her energy and ultimately her goodwill in a relentless siege of demands that recalls the story "Aunt Suzanne."

Eventually, slowly and painfully, the grandmother dies; and, in a twist of irony, her son and some of his family go to live in her house in Toome. One member remains in Belfast. The aggressive, self-absorbed brother Hugh, resembling in his dedicated self-seeking Duhamel's "papa," stays in the Belfast house with his new wife, unconscious or careless of the havoc wrought in the old woman's life. In a letter to Julie Kernan dated 4 November 1940, McLaverty had given his view of this difficult character Hugh and of some of the others, as he typed the last pages of the novel:

At last I am able to send you the remaining chapters of my book. My delight last night in typing out the words: The End: was inexpressible. And yet the relief in finishing the book was tinged with a little sadness, and for this reason—the characters so preoccupied my mind that I now feel lonely at despatching them into the world.

I am pleased with the book though I agree with you that it may not make a great appeal. I feel that within the short compass of time in which the action takes place I have successfully depicted three generations of people and their different attitude to life: the old woman with her thoughts on death and her spiritual struggle against selfishness; Johnny and Kate preoccupied with the struggles of their family; Hugh and Eileen—Youth—with their doubts, hopes and ambitions: Hugh's selfishness (not having reached the stage when he'll be a family man like his father and can forget the "self" in the rearing of children) and then the incipient stages of Eileen's pregnancy manifesting itself in her anxiety for the children. For Eileen and Hugh the wheel will go full circle and they'll pass in time through the whole gamut of existence as that of the two previous generations.[27]

The dominant figure in the novel is undoubtedly the grandmother. She is at first a dependable, comfortable personality, full of quirks and wise ways. On the day the postman tells her that her son's family has survived an attempted eviction in Belfast, her pleasant life comes to an end. Her peace of mind shattered by the news, she decides, against her better judgement, that she must accede to her family's request that she go and live with them. Her resolution is made, not in words, but in a transfer of mood, characteristic of McLaverty's established style:

She stood at the door as the postman mounted his bicycle and rode off along the wet-black road. She gazed forlornly at the bare hedges and the cold-looking sky.

"God forgive me," she breathed aloud, "for not believing Johnny—he was always a great one for the truth."

Above the hill in the demesne a rip came in the clouds and she saw the silver spokes of the sun stretch towards the earth, flicker for a moment and disappear. The air became colder, and she turned to go into the house, stopped, put her hand to her ear and heard over the bare country the rumble of the morning train as it sped over the bridge at Toome.[28]

The contrast between the lively, authoritative woman of the opening of the novel and the pathetic, tetchy pensioner of the later pages is very marked, but the decline is made quite credible, mainly through the constant reference to the cold, bare, distempered room in which she ends her days. This unattractive apartment is coveted by Hugh, her grandson, so that he can marry Eileen without having to find a house of his own. Earlier, the room belonged to the quiet, withdrawn daughter, Mary, whose one desire in life is to enter a convent. Nothing can cheer this room, in which even Mary's attempts to brighten it, with her crucifix and some drapery for the rails of the bed, serve only to increase its resemblance to "a wake-house." Soon afterwards, as the children in the street outside celebrate the coming of May, the grandmother falls from a chair while attempting to reach a secretly-stored bottle; she lies unnoticed for a long time, while the children shout at their play and a lark escaped from its cage flutters, panic-stricken, about the room. The cause of her fall brings to mind the incident in "Aunt Suzanne" where Arthur catches his aunt taking her "medicine," and its consequences are no less disastrous.

The family finds her burdensome and, Hugh, the eldest son, begins to voice his opinion that she should be put in the workhouse. In an icy winter she fails, not only physically but in charity and trust, becoming cantankerous and short with adults and children alike. Eventually, in pain and misery, she dies in the spare room, and is taken home to Toome to be buried.

The unity of the novel depends on the strong figure of the grandmother. McLaverty is at his best in the passages where he writes of her, at home with the details of description, and fired by enthusiasm for what is to be his major theme in the next two novels—the effect on human relations of lack of charity. Other characters are less successful. One of these, Peter, seems at the beginning of the novel to be of importance, despite his inauspicious introduction as a petty thief, raiding his mother's purse, and later stealing a bicycle. It is through him that the grandmother is introduced in the novel, as Peter flies to her after the impulsive thievery. Here she is a rock of strength.

Quietly he got off the bicycle...At the bare window he saw her sitting in the fire-glow, her silver spectacles glinting, and her finger following the words in the prayer-book. Her lips moved and now and again she turned her right hand as if rolling a ball of wool. She licked her thumb to turn a page in her prayer-book and then she saw him at the window. She opened the door and he stood in front of her, outlined against the light from the sky. She took off her spectacles and slewed him round so that the light from the sky shone in his face: "Sweet God in Heaven, is it Peter?"[29]

Eventually Peter is sent to a reformatory and becomes unimportant, except as a worry to his sister, Mary. It seems as though McLaverty finds it difficult to keep in mind the many minor characters he introduces into this novel, dwarfed as they are by the figure of the grandmother. Mary is characterised by her desire to be a nun. This desire seems neither burning nor vital, for vitality is a quality quite absent from her make-up. If anything, her ambition seems to be rather weary and sad, lacking in anything approaching joy or zeal. A final encounter between Mary and Peter, depending as it does on such phrases as "a subdued inertness" and "a pained smile," does not succeed in eliciting sympathy for her sorrow—as she is always sorrowful—or in awakening compassion for the imprisoned Peter, who has long since been at a distance from the reader's consciousness.

Curiously, Mary reappears later in the novel, no longer a major figure, but a failure, having been sent home from the convent. In the disintegration of the family peace that precedes in the novel the solution of a divided house, she declines even more rapidly than before, becoming careless of her appearance and bringing upon her head the wrath of the overbearing Hugh. In the end she is one of those who move to the country, and in the letter which ends the novel, Kate tells how Mary has found a position in service in Ballymena with a kindly Protestant lady who "plays the harmonium all day." Mary is a half-realised, unsatisfactory figure, and the novel undoubtedly suffers from the introduction of such underdeveloped characters, as does *Call My Brother Back*. Nevertheless, though the reader might be confused between the characters of the brothers Frankie and Peter, or between Peter and Hugh, or wonder which of the three little sisters is which, the essential figure of the grandmother unifies theme and plot.

There is much in the novel of humour and pathos, and McLaverty displays a sense of control not evident in the enthusiastic flow of *Call My Brother Back*. *Lost Fields* has a strong opening, in which the scene is set with clarity and care, and an equally well-handled ending, despite the impression that the author is trying very hard to tie up many loose ends. In the final paragraph, he suggests the possibility of lives made better by the harrowing experience endured by the grandmother. Reparation for his action in bringing his mother from her home is symbolised in Johnny's removal to her old house in the country, bringing with him the children most at risk from the harsh city influences. Hugh, remote as Alec in *Call My Brother Back*, but better able to make his way in the town, inherits without a qualm the house whose maintenance cost his grandmother her life. Eileen, Hugh's wife, is to be the mother of the tribe of survivors, those who can and do adapt to city ways, and make a success of their lives there. As in the earlier novel, the last image is of the waste ground; but here it is a place where children play and are happy. The woman who watches them has hope for the future and does not grieve for a life in the country of which she has no experience and which would not suit her city children:

She waited until she saw Hugh wheeling his barrow towards the drying shed. She waved to him, and pushing his barrow with one hand he waved back. She smiled and looked up the waste ground to where little girls were gathering in a ring to play some kind of a game.[30]

Reviewers were generally well disposed to the novel, commenting approvingly on its style and precision of detail. John C Moynihan in the *Boston Post* considered that McLaverty had "managed to inject dramatic coloring, sympathetic character portrayal, and skilful plot handling into a study of fundamental human values," and went on to say that, to him, it "seems to come pretty close to fulfilment of the highest creative ideals."[31] Others noted its episodic tendency. A reviewer identified only by the initials ED described it as "a novel of episode rather than of plot," and an anonymous reviewer in *Books of the Month* commented on both on the author's "exceptional skill" and the novel's lack of "form." McLaverty's favourite review, of which he is justly proud, came from Edwin Muir, writing in *The Listener*. Muir noted McLaverty's "curious quietude" and referred to him as "a born artist."[32] Muir here seizes upon the very qualities McLaverty hoped to convey; his "precision," his "fine lack of emphasis" and the indefinable "curious quietude" are the very best features of his work. It was right and just that Muir should notice and praise them as highly as possible. Nonetheless, the other features, the lack of tight control in plot and characterisation, need to be mentioned, if only for their detrimental effect on the overall impression.

The poet John Hewitt, reviewing the book for *The Bell*, took note of the unsatisfactory as well as the undoubtedly inspired in this book. To him, McLaverty's "ponderous care for minute detail tends to clutter up the earlier sections of the book, so that the human figures scarcely emerge from the matrix of material objects," and the book comes to life only in the second half. Hewitt concludes:

> This is an advance on *Call My Brother Back*, but Mr McLaverty will do better yet when he allows his richly demonstrated sympathy for cockfighters, tippling teachers and miching schoolboys to cram the pages of the fat, raucous, turbulent novel that Ulster life offers and no writer yet has encompassed.[33]

It is clear from the reception of *Lost Fields*, and, in particular, from the views expressed by the two distinguished reviewers quoted last, that Michael McLaverty had made his mark with his novels of the waste ground, and that great things were expected of him. It is equally clear that a different style of writing was required from the novelist than from the short story writer. Reviewers and, by implication, the reading public, were not prepared to take the time over careful, minute detail in the novel that they would afford it in a short story. In the strength of this message and the puzzled reception of it by McLaverty, lies the beginning of a growing distance between the writer and his public. After the publication of *Lost Fields*, McLaverty seems to have felt he had explored as fully as he could the earliest themes of valediction and loss. By 1942, he was already planning a novel on the theme of charity, which would, ironically, bring into the open the difference between his own concept of his role as a writer and that of his publishers and critics.

REFERENCES

1 "Stone," "The White Mare" and "The Sea," *Capuchin Annual* (1939), 150-75; "Becalmed," *Capuchin Annual* (1940), 209-18.

2 Unpublished autobiographical fragment. MS in possession of McLaverty family.

3 McLaverty to Liam Miller, (Dolmen Press), 18 April 1970.

4 The Rev Matthew Hoehn OSB, *Catholic Authors; Contemporary Biographical Sketches (First Series), 1930-47*, Newark NJ, 1947, 473.

5 *Call My Brother Back*, New York, 1939, 182-3; Poolbeg (pbk) Dublin 1979, 132-3.

6 ibid., 75-6; Poolbeg ed., 59-60.

7 ibid., 125-6; Poolbeg ed., 93-4.

8 ibid., 234; Poolbeg ed.,166.

9 ibid., 261; Poolbeg ed.,184.

10 Recounted in conversation between McLaverty and Sophia King, 1982.

11 Reviews in possession of McLaverty family.

12 *New York Times*, 26 February 1939.

13 Review in possession of McLaverty family.

14 *Saturday Review of Literature*, 2 February 1939.

15 *Call My Brother Back*, op. cit., 259-60; Poolbeg ed.,182-3.

16 "Stone," op. cit, 150-151; *Collected Stories*, 41-42.

17 ibid., 155; *Collected Stories*, 49.

18 "The White Mare," op. cit., 163; *Collected Stories*, 116.

19 *The White Mare and Other Stories*, Newcastle, Co Down, 1943.

20 "The Sea," op. cit., 175; as "Look at the Boats," *Collected Stories*, 220.

21 ibid., 171; *Collected Stories*, 211.

22 Hoehn, op. cit., 474.

23 See *In Quiet Places*, 70-4 for correspondence with Longmans and Cape about the publication of *Lost Fields*.

24 Publicity enclosure, 5 April 1941. In possession of McLaverty family.

25 Georges Duhamel, *Le Notaire du Havre*, Paris, 1933. Author's own copy with inscripton on flyleaf: "cf *Lost Fields* may have influenced. Feb. 1982." In possession of Sophia King.

26 McLaverty to Julie Kernan, 4 November 1940. See *In Quiet Places*, 70-1.

27 *Lost Fields*, London, 1942, 31; Poolbeg (pbk) edition, Dublin 1980, 23.

28 op. cit., 252; Poolbeg ed., 207-8.

29 John C Moynihan, *Boston Post*, 14 September 1941.

30 Edwin Muir, *The Listener*, 23 April 1942.

31 John Hewitt, *The Bell*, IV, 4 (July 1942), 303-4.

SECTION II

QUIET DESPERATION

1941-8

CHAPTER FOUR

"AN EXPLORATION OF CHARITY"

(FROM "MOONSHINE" TO *IN THIS THY DAY*)

The period between 1941 and 1945 was a happy and productive one for Michael McLaverty. He had the satisfaction of seeing two of his novels and a first collection of his short stories, *The White Mare*, in print and he was busily working on another novel.[1] Yet, in all this time, he published only four new short stories, for, with the exception of "A Schoolmaster," all the stories in *The White Mare* had been published elsewhere. Of these four stories, two, "Moonshine"[2] (later renamed "The Poteen Maker") and "The Road To The Shore"[3] are acknowledged as good examples of his mature style but the other two, "Vigil"[4] and "A Schoolmaster"[5] are disappointing.

"Vigil" is a very short story, the only one McLaverty ever wrote about the Blitz in Belfast. The jottings in his journal for that time show his characteristic eye for detail and ear for accurate colloquial speech and catch the camaraderie among those who experienced the Blitz. However these are not communicated to the same extent in the story, where a mother presides over the wake of her son, dead of an unnamed but painful and lingering illness. "A Vigil" is unsatisfactory because it lacks a central image, an insight into the ways of humanity from which the author can rise into imagery or allusion.

"A Schoolmaster," originally entitled "My Queerest Relation," is written in the first person and with a retrospective air. The tone of this story, which reads more as an anecdote, is one of exasperated disbelief at the outrageous behaviour of the schoolmaster. Incident follows incident, but there is no heart to the story, no carefully prepared centre to be though over, and, as such, it fails to engage the reader's deeper attention.

The small output of short stories and the unsatisfactory quality of two of these suggest that the writing of novels was taking up not only a great deal of the author's time but also much of his creative energy. The first concerns for the morality of the novelist manifest themselves in the journals and letters at this time, and there seems no doubt that McLaverty no longer saw as his first responsibility the nostalgic celebration of his own life or the lives of his people. In the few short stories published in these years, as in those of the later part of the Forties, his concern is with those who, in Thoreau's phrase, "lead lives of quiet desperation."[6] One of the best examples of his concern for the struggles of people in their middle years is "Moonshine," the last story to be published by McLaverty before the appearance of his first collection, *The White Mare*. Written in the first person, it tells of a man's memories of his master in the school at the edge of his home-town. He recalls the respect his parents had for the teacher despite his apparent poverty, and in spite, too, of the drinking which causes others in the town to mock him. The master's clothes may be threadbare and his school draughty but he instils into the children a love of learning, using where necessary the very drawbacks of his building to make his point:

During his last December he was ill for two weeks and when he came back amongst us he was greatly failed. To keep out the draughts he nailed perforated plywood over the ventilators and stuffed blotting paper between the wide crevices at the jambs of the door. There were muddy marks of a ball on one of the windows and on one pane a long crack with fangs at the end of it; "So someone has drawn the River Ganges while I was away," he said; and whenever he came to the geography of India he would refer to the Ganges delta by pointing to the cracks on the pane.[7]

His gentle ways are contrasted with the officious style of the teacher next door, who, when Master Craig slips out "for five or ten minutes," comes in to deal with the noise, "her lips compressed, her fingers in her book." Her stale colloquial phrases, "An altar boy on Sunday and a corner boy the rest of the week!" are caught by McLaverty's unerring memory for the spoken word, and he has his narrator recall that the class "let her barge away, the buckets plink-plonking as they filled up with rain, and her own class beginning to hum, now that she was away from them." The authentic voices of both mischievous schoolboy and harassed teacher are heard there, providing a usefully unsentimental background for the sad story of the schoolmaster. It is in such humour and through innocent, unconscious irony on the part of the narrator that the heart of the story is revealed. The boy describes a frequently repeated experiment named "Evaporation and Condensation," which is actually the master's device for distilling illegal liquor, the "poteen" of the later title. One bitterly cold day, as he repeats his experiment yet again, the school inspector enters, unannounced. The misery of the cold day and the total surprise of the inspector's visit are well suggested by the stares of the scholars at the intruder. Unshaken, but "in a strange voice," Mister Craig takes the boys through the experiment "as if we were seeing it for the first time." There is no doubt that there is risk involved, and McLaverty, in describing the gamble, admires the courage and even the bravado of the downtrodden schoolmaster:

Mr Craig would fill up his tumbler and say: "As pure as crystal." And then one day, the door opened and in walked the Inspector. He was muffled to the ears and snow covered his hat and his attaché case. We all stared at him—he was the old kind man whom we had seen before. He glanced at the bare firegrate and at the closed windows with their sashes edged with snow. The water continued to bubble in the retort, giving out its pleasant smell...Then the inspector took the warm tumbler and questioned us on our lesson. "It should be perfectly pure water," he said, and he sipped at it. He tasted its flavour. He sipped at it again. He turned to Mr Craig. They whispered together, the Inspector looking towards the retort which was still bubbling and sending out its twirls of steam to be condensed to water of purest crystal. We smiled when he

again put the tumbler to his lips and this time drank it
all.[8]

Such is the mutual good humour of the teacher and the
inspector, as a result of this experiment, that the boys are
allowed to go home early, and the narrator, who carries
the inspector's case to the railway station, is praised by Mr
Craig and given a penny for himself. There the recollection
ends but the conclusion of the story is memorable, as the
narrator describes the school as he finds it on his return to
the master's funeral, with "an ugly iron barrier near the
door to keep the homegoing children from rushing
headlong on to the road." He does not go in, having heard
that there is "a young teacher in the school now, with an
array of coloured pencils in his breast pocket." The detail
of the pencils, out of place in the grey, tumbledown school,
effectively distances the modern and efficient teacher from
the old-fashioned but gentle master of the narrator's
childhood. His nostalgia is for a lost time as much as for
the loss of a friend whose problems he had but half
understood. Yet the unspoken loneliness of the "decent,
good-living man" is poignantly suggested in every line.
Like Annie in "Becalmed,"[9] Master Craig is a valiant survivor,
hiding the marks of deep trouble. In both cases, the nature
of the problems and the courage which surmounts them
are suggested less by what is said than by what is omitted.
Thus, McLaverty demonstrates again the effectiveness of
the "half-said thing."[10]

In 1943 a first selection of Michael McLaverty's stories
was published by Richard Rowley's Mourne Press. It took
as its title story "The White Mare," and was illustrated by

the distinguished artist, Mercy Hunter. In recognition of McLaverty's courtesy and willingness to accommodate his publisher, Rowley wrote to him on 1 September 1943 about the forthcoming publication:

> If you knew the ways of some of my young contributors you would not miscall your own courtesy and promptitude by apologising for delay. You are a very model of the author whom a publisher likes and respects...
>
> The five stories, The Prophet, The Game Cock, The White Mare, Look at the Boats and Moonshine, will make a delightful volume. Plenty of variety, both of incident and character, and a lot of delicious writing.[11]

The order was not as Rowley outlined it. The first story was "The Game Cock," followed by "The White Mare"; "Moonshine"; "The Prophet"; "Look At the Boats" (formerly "The Sea"); and "A Schoolmaster." It was generally well-received by the critics, who had by 1943 noted the publication of *Call My Brother Back*, and *Lost Fields*, but may not have been familiar with McLaverty's considerable work in the area of the short story. One reviewer, writing on 11 December 1943 in an unidentified newspaper, comments on the stories' "simple, natural beauty," and the "humour and exquisite quality of tenderness running though every page." Another, identified only by the initials BK, and in another unidentifiable newspaper cutting, notes that McLaverty's "eye for significant detail and significant form...so notable in the novels *Call My Brother Back* and *Lost Fields*, is alert and watchful here." His particular favourite is the "Game Cock," "whose poor, mutilated, vicious existence might be a pathetic and dreadful allegory of all exploitation." It is interesting to note that this reviewer objects to the wet weather of McLaverty's stories, missing the significance of the rain as a vehicle of suggestion.[12] One other review is notable here. Written by the novelist Kate O'Brien, it appeared in *The Spectator* on 7 January, 1944. Oddly, Miss O'Brien does not seem to be aware of McLaverty's work before the novels. She assumes that he has lately taken to the short story. Her review is generally favourable, finding his style both "lyrical" and "tender" but pointing out that "the writing of fiction is not another form of painting, for its main concern is not with the appearance of things." This objection to McLaverty's minute attention to detail was to be echoed by St John Ervine in a scathing review of the author's third novel, *In This Thy Day*, published in 1945.[13] Yet, Kate O'Brien does not have in that selection the whole range of McLaverty's short stories. Of the group in the *White Mare* volume, only three, "The Game Cock" "The White Mare" itself and "Look at the Boats" are examples of McLaverty's most incisive writing. The others, "The Prophet," "Moonshine" and the inferior "A Schoolmaster" are typical of the more lightweight, even whimsical writing which is not representative of his narrative and descriptive powers at their best. While this is undoubtedly an important volume, therefore, it does not fulfil the task of displaying the full extent of McLaverty's gift as a writer of short stories.

The impression that the author was, in a sense, marking time while he prepared *In This Thy Day* is further reinforced by the appearance in 1943 and 1944 of two short-story length extracts from this forthcoming work. Each stands well enough on its own, much as the short story "Leavetaking" has a life separate from *Call My Brother Back* but the fact that these are clearly published as extracts shows the relative importance of the novel to the author.

No attempt is made to turn them into short stories, although it could have been done. The first, "Sea Road," which appeared in *The Capuchin Annual* in 1943, deals with the incident of a fire begun by the careless daughter, Barbara, at the beginning of the novel, and could stand on its own. The other, "The Passing Generation," which appeared in *Lagan* in August 1944, is concerned with the relationship between a grandfather, Dan Scullion, and another of the daughters of the Devlin house, Tessie. Since all these characters tend to become dwarfed by the dominant personality of Mrs Mason in the novel itself, it is at once gratifying and frustrating to note the possibility of their meriting stories of their own. Yet these are not stories, but vignettes, and the stories they might have been are absorbed into the novel.

One last story was published before McLaverty's third novel. This was "The Road to the Shore,"[14] which appeared in *Selected Writing,* edited by Reginald Moore, in 1944. This story is in the tradition begun by "Moonshine," in which McLaverty investigates the quiet endurance of people oppressed by circumstance. This is the theme which runs through his best work of the Forties, and which is most in keeping with the preoccupation with personal morality revealed in the letters and journals. On the surface, "The Road to the Shore" is the story of an outing made to the sea by a small group of nuns, under the guidance of their Reverend Mother. McLaverty wrote some years later, in a letter to Daniel Corkery, that "I got the idea for the 'Road to the Shore' when cycling south from Cork out by Inishannon, and happened to see a load of nuns who had unfortunately knocked a cyclist into the ditch."[15] The outing is abandoned for that day, and the reactions of the nuns to the crisis reinforce the impressions of their characters, created by slight and seemingly unimportant incidents and allusions earlier in the story. One such episode shows the reactions of each character when a bee flies into the car:

> The breeze whorled in, and as it lifted their veils they all smiled, invigorated by the fresh loveliness of the air. A bumble bee flew in and crawled up the pane at Reverend Mother's side of the car. She opened the window and assisted the bee towards the opening with the tip of her fountain-pen, but the bee clung to the pen and as she tried to shake it free the wind carried it in again. "Like everything else it hates to leave you," said Sister Benignus. Reverend Mother smiled and the bee flew up to the roof of the car and then alighted on the window beside Sister Paul. Sister Paul swept the bee to safety with the back of her hand.
>
> "You weren't one bit afraid of it," said Sister Clare. "And if it had stung you, you would in a way have been responsible for its death. If it had been a Queen bee—though Queens wouldn't be flying at this time of year—you would have been responsible for the deaths of potential thousands. A Queen bumble bee lays over two thousand eggs in one season!"
>
> "'Tis a great pity we haven't a hen like that," put in Sister Francis, and they all laughed except Sister Clare.[16]

Here, as apparently elsewhere, Reverend Mother takes the necessary decisions, assisted by Sister Paul, whose secret sadness is at the centre of the story. Sister Clare is inquisitive and intrusive, reducing everything to soulless fact; Sister Benignus is dutifully supportive of her leader; Sister Francis is straightforward in her response and apparently unaware of any subtlety. It is Sister Paul who is the second in command, the equivalent of the innocent but thoughtful and sensitive children of the earlier stories, who willingly shoulder the half-comprehended burdens of their parents' lives. Once the differences of character are established, through layer upon layer of apparently trivial happenings as the party tries to begin its outing, McLaverty displays in the central incident of the story the deep sorrow which has maimed Sister Paul, and which has led her to seek the guidance of another strong personality in the absence of her much-loved father. It happens when Sister Paul suddenly calls the attention of the others to a line of young poplars: "'Look, look!' she was saying. 'Look at the way their leaves are dancing and not a flicker out of the other trees. And to think I never noticed them before!'" Soon she is "lost in her own memory," oblivious of Sister Clare's persistent questioning about their precise nomenclature, and recalling only that her father called each of the poplars in their garden by the names of his daughters, tending them with equal care. Clare's insensitivity provides an appropriately clamorous background, as she compels the quiet, gentle Sister Paul to speak of her life-long sorrow:

"Can you not think of what special name those trees had?" pressed Clare. "Did their leaves tremble furiously—

tremula, tremuloides?"

"They didn't quiver very much," said Sister Paul, her head bowed. "My father didn't plant aspens, I remember. He told us it was from an aspen that Our Saviour's rood was made, and because their leaves remember the Crucifixion they are always trembling...And I remember," said Paul, folding and unfolding her handkerchief on her lap, "how my poor father had no gum once to wrap up a newspaper that he was posting. It was in winter and he went out to the poplars and dabbed his finger here and there on the sticky buds and smeared it on the edge of the wrapping paper."

"That was enough to kill the buds," said Clare. "The gum, as you call it, is their only protective against frost."

"It was himself he killed," said Paul. "He had gone out from a warm fire in his slippers, out into the bleak air and got his death."

"And what happened to the poplars?" said Clare. But Sister Paul had turned her head to the window again, trying to stifle the tears that were rising to her eyes.[17]

At this point, their car accidentally knocks down the cyclist, and the rest of the story is a demonstration of Reverend Mother's ability to turn an unfortunate incident to the convent's advantage. The worthy, abstemious young man so unfortunately knocked from his bicycle is offered the job of dealing with the convent grounds, abused at the beginning of the story by a lazy handyman, and Sister Paul is deputed to tell the rest of the sisters that the outing will be attempted again on the following day. Reverend Mother's authority is once more established and Sister Paul, her past reburied, is relieved to have the decision made for her, and to rejoice, both in her superior's wisdom, and in the prospect of the next day's pleasure:

> "Isn't Reverend Mother great the way she can handle things?" she said to herself. "And to think that on tomorrow I'll be able to see the poplars again."[18]

The fact that "The Road To The Shore," "Moonshine" and *The White Mare* all appeared between the publication of *Lost Fields* and *In This Thy Day* does not alter the fact that the writing of short stories was no longer McLaverty's primary concern. His correspondence and journal entries make it clear that his mind was increasingly occupied with the form of the novel and the role of the novelist. As early as February 1941, he was planning another full-length work, which he intended as a "long historical novel." War and its confusions intervened; McLaverty was involved in the teaching of evacuated children in County Down and later in Belfast, and found he had little time to devote to his writing.[19] Gradually he abandoned the idea of the historical novel, and began to plan one set in Strangford, where he was living during the war. Encouraged by the reception of *Lost Fields*, he began to find the energy to tackle this next novel. He wrote to Julie Kernan on 5 June 1942:

> I think I told you that I had put aside my historical novel as I am far too distant from the libraries where I intended to do a bit of research for it. However when the war is over I shall be able to go to it with vigour and greater maturity. Meanwhile I am at work on another novel and

I shall do my best to let you have it before the end of the
year. All I can say about it at this stage is that the sea air
is blowing through its pages from first to last.[20]

The novel did not progress as quickly as he hoped, and his
letters to Julie Kernan at the end of 1942 and the early
months of 1943 show how difficult he found it to discipline
himself to write. There is no record of any new short stories
in 1942 or 1943, so it seems reasonable to assume that the
unsettling influence of wartime disruptions affected his
creative ability. Something of this feeling finds its way into
the correspondence, as he writes to Miss Kernan:

I find it difficult to write, to contemplate, in times like
these when the whole blood-boltered world is growing
dehumanised. I trust in God it will all end soon and a
blessed peace follow after it.[21]

Gradually, however, the work took shape, and he was able
to report to Longmans in June 1943 that he had his "teeth
in it" and felt he could "forge ahead." At this point, all
seemed well between McLaverty and his publishers. The
tone of their letters is friendly and professional. Miss Kernan
had written on 11 January 1943 that she liked "very much"
the first chapter of his new book, and expressed the hope
that she would see all of it "before too long." Her
encouragement continued throughout the summer but in
November 1943 McLaverty was in the position of apologising for delay, and of sending Julie Kernan a copy of his
White Mare volume, which neither he nor she seems to
have considered, at that time, of any lasting importance.

Miss Kernan thanked him for "the lovely little volume"; McLaverty sent more chapters, and matters progressed satisfactorily. Miss Kernan gave as her opinion on January 1944 that "so far (we) think the story is excellent" and wrote on 13 March "So far I like the book very much." McLaverty did not manage to finish the book by May, as he had hoped but felt confident by that month that he was nearing its conclusion and confident, too, of the quality of its writing:

> Here are two long chapters which contain, I think, some of my best writing. I have about three more chapters to send you and then the book is complete. These will follow within the next six weeks but I don't suppose that will give you sufficient time for your autumn list. However do what is convenient. I am terribly sorry to have disappointed you so often but many things upset me. I trust the book will do better for you than my last.
>
> About a title: what would you think of any of the following:
>
> *Bread of Sorrow* (it's taken from a psalm)
>
> *A Fire in Spring*
>
> *Stony Limits*
>
> You may of course have some interesting suggestions.
>
> I am now living in a new house well out from the smoke and smudge of the city.[22]

The difficulties of commuting and the pressures of wartime restriction were eased by his removal to the new house. There is a note of regret, heard from this time onwards, that the novels do not sell as well as he might hope, but

McLaverty was sure of what he wanted to write, and was not disturbed that the reading public had not yet realised the value of it. Jonathan Cape was expressing interest in the new novel, even though he had had to let *Lost Fields* go out of stock through shortage of paper. McLaverty's main difficulty at this time, with both Longmans and Cape, seemed to be in the choice of a title. Jonathan Cape wrote to McLaverty on 12 September 1944 that he was unhappy with the author's suggestion of *Bread of Sorrow*, and accepted reluctantly the alternative title, *In This Thy Day*. On 14 September McLaverty wrote to Julie Kernan, enclosing the final chapters of the novel, and making clear that his only concern over the novel was the correct choice of title.[23] On 23 October, however, a letter came from Julie Kernan indicating the embarrassing presence of a much larger problem. The readers in Longmans Green could not come to a final decision about the novel, and unless the author could "submit an additional chapter giving a ray of hope— so far as Mary is concerned at least," she feared the firm would not publish it.[24] It was a long time before McLaverty received this bombshell. Evidence exists in his correspondence, and, obliquely, in the tone of his journals, to show his reaction to it; he was not prepared to change his story in any way, and he regarded as "preposterous" the suggestion that he should do so.[25]

Briefly, the story of *In This Thy Day* concerns two families. Ned Mason, the son of a prosperous family whose head has recently died, leaving the land to his wife "for her day," wishes to marry Mary Devlin, the worthy daughter of a rather shiftless family. Ned's mother opposes the match and effectively prevents their marriage. In the end, almost in the instant that Mrs Mason perceives her folly in blocking the happiness of the young pair, she realises that it is too late. Ned has run away to sea, and Mary, like her namesake in *Lost Fields*, goes resignedly into service. McLaverty saw nothing wrong with this ending, believing it to be in accordance with the principles of general truth. When he did not hear from Longmans, therefore, it did not occur to him that the ending might be causing a problem. On 27 November 1944, he was still discussing the question of title with Cape, and expressing, without knowledge of the storm that was brewing, some disquiet with his American publishers.[26] The following day, on 28 November 1944, McLaverty was again writing to Cape. His position was that he did not "intend to alter the inevitable sequence of the story," and intended "to make a friendly departure from Longmans." McLaverty had included, in his letter to Cape of 27 November, a description of the novel for publicity purposes. In the light of the disturbing events related above, it is interesting to note the author's unswerving faith in the "general truth" of his novel, as he writes: "It is all blended with a fine coherence and written with that quietness of tone and fresh lyricism of phrase that characterised his previous novel, *Lost Fields*."[27]

Most important of all, in McLaverty's eyes, was a proper understanding of his title. The phrase "In This Thy Day" comes from Luke 19: 42: "When he was come near he beheld the city, and wept over it, saying, If thou hadst known, even thou, at least in this thy day, the things which belong unto thy peace, but now are hid from thine eyes!" This, in McLaverty's opinion, explained and justified his bleak ending, where the mean and stony-hearted Mrs

Mason realises too late that her priorities have been mistaken. These are the last sentences of the novel:

> "All of you go to bed...And say nothing about it to the neighbours...Lower the lamp a little, Sarah, it's too bright...and hand me my beads like a good girl."
>
> Ann and Delia went upstairs. From under her mother's hands Sarah lifted the tablecloth, the knife and fork and cup and saucer. She brought her her prayer beads and patted her mother's shoulder: "Don't be fretting, Mother," she said, "he'll come back. We must have faith in God's goodness."
>
> "O God," she moaned, "what did I do that You're so hard on me!"
>
> She lifted her beads but her mind sped from the prayers she was saying, her heart hardened to John Devlin, and bowing her head on her crooked arm she wept bitterly.[28]

To its author, the novel was, as he wrote on the fly-leaf of one copy, "an exploration of charity."[29] Consequently, he was not prepared to move on this. Despite the advice of Jonathan Cape to stay with Longmans if he could, McLaverty preferred to respond to Cape's suggestion that he try the Devin-Adair company in New York.[30] Finally, still in spite of misgivings voiced by Cape, McLaverty parted with Longmans on 15 December, when he wrote to Julie Kernan:

> The hint given in that final chapter fits in with the title: In this thy day if thou hadst known the things that are to thy peace. Neighbourliness, love—old Dan has it and

> Luke—that is the positive life-giving force of the book and
> not Mrs Mason's which concerns itself with negations, a
> soul-destroying attitude. However, the book may have
> failed to reveal these implications and the fault therein
> lies with me. Though the reading public may despise the
> book my faith in it will not alter.[31]

To this dignified defence of his novel, Miss Kernan replied,
on 11 January 1945, with similar courtesy and equal
firmness, that she accepted McLaverty's decision "with
genuine regret," and that while she acknowledged that it
was the work of "a true artist," she and her employers were
compelled "to think of sales and appeal to the public, which,
especially in these dark days, is not greatly attracted by the
sombre and dark side of life."[32] It was a sad but inevitable
parting, for the differences between the author and his
publishers were irreconcilable. It left McLaverty in a strange
position. The link forged by Edward O'Brien now broken,
McLaverty was for the first time independent of his first
mentors. For the first time, too, he was losing confidence
in his readership; but he was confident to the point of
stubbornness of the importance of leaving his novel
unchanged. To this end, he was determined to find an
American publisher who would accept his work as he had
written it. His correspondence with Devin-Adair has not
survived but a letter written on 23 February 1945 from
Alfred A Knopf to Little Brown and Company reveals that
McLaverty had not confined himself to one publisher in
his search for a new firm, and that Longmans Green was
by no means the only company to find the ending unacceptable.[33] On 5 March, having cabled Devin-Adair and

found out that the book was with Knopf, McLaverty wrote to offer it to Houghton Mifflin.[34] A certain anxiety is evident in this letter; despite his indifference to public acclaim, it appears that he very much wanted the novel to be accepted. Devin-Adair did not choose to publish it, but expressed interest in the short stories. Ironically, from that interest there came the collection of stories entitled *The Game Cock and Other Stories*, regarded by many as representative of his finest work. McLaverty wrote to Cape on 6 March 1945:

Devin-Adair want to publish a collection of my short stories which they have seen in American magazines, and I am now going to make an agreement with them to do so. But I can't understand them with regard to the novel: I feel it is the best I have written so far and though it wouldn't bring them in a fortune in America yet it would pay its way respectably. I don't hold much hope now with Knopf as I feel the script is pretty well-mauled and dejected looking by this time. I am going to send my corrected copy of the proofs to Macmillan as soon as I hear definitely from Knopf.[35]

On 18 April Houghton Mifflin declined the novel.[36] Nothing more of the correspondence has survived, but the novel was accepted and published by the American Macmillan Company; and there began a most happy collaboration, matched only by that with Jonathan Cape, between McLaverty and his Macmillan editor, Cecil Scott.

This long, painful experience marks a watershed in McLaverty's career. Surviving a series of rejections that might have caused a lesser man to lose confidence in his ability to write anything at all, he became quietly confident that he could and would continue on his chosen path. He would write novels about conscience, about charity and its opposites, spite and calumny, exploring what he would later term "the sins of the mind."[37] There would be no more autobiographical novels; in the longer, as in the shorter form, he was now determined to write of the struggles of ordinary people to rise above their own natures.

In the meantime, his trial by ordeal was not yet over, for reviews of the novel were much more mixed than previously. Many, like the *Times Literary Supplement*, praised his skill, although the reviewer thought the book "hardly large enough to call a novel." Concern about the novel's length had already been voiced by the reviewer of the *Brooklyn Eagle*, who wrote: "In a longer book, he could have resolved things better...Also in a longer book the author might have been able to decide whose was the story."[38] The question of technique had concerned the *Sun*, New York, which made the distinction between McLaverty the novelist and McLaverty the short-story-writer:

The quality of the writing is that of McLaverty's short stories, many of which have appeared in magazines and collections here and abroad. His descriptions of the countryside and of the animals and birds are poetic, full of colorful imagery and sometimes of lyrical emotion. His conception of people, however, is cool and objective. Their tragic loves and hates are told quietly, without humor and without warm, pulsing life. We look on with the author, but he does not arouse our pity for them.[39]

Once again, as after *Lost Fields*, the charge of failure to transpose his art from one form to the other was levelled at McLaverty. One reviewer seemed to be saying that he did not tell enough, another that his attitude was too detached. Yet these were features which, in such short stories as "The Game Cock" or "Pigeons," had given his writing its strength and restrained compassion. To be accused of lack of understanding, of poor planning, must have been a blow. This is not to say that the reviewers doubted his ability. Richard Church, in *John O'London's Weekly*, perceived McLaverty's interest in the theory as well as the practice of writing, noting his affinity with O'Faoláin and O'Connor, and noting with approval his skill in avoiding "over-picturesque phrases and lush Irishisms."[40] The reservations expressed by so many of the reviewers seem to depend upon a definition of appropriate technique: none doubt his superior abilities but several wonder about the wisdom of applying his carefully restricted methods to the less stringent, broader form of the novel. The observation of his greater sympathy with animals and nature than with people concerned Oliver St John Gogarty, in a review for the *Inquirer* of Philadelphia. He perceived the author's compassion but believed he had consciously withdrawn it in the name of art. Gogarty gave qualified approval of the novel, but not without minor reservations about the intensity of the imagery and major ones on authorial detachment.[41] Roy McFadden, reviewing the novel for the *Dublin Magazine*,[42] saw the density of the imagery as essential to McLaverty's unique talent; unlike Gogarty he found much of humour and sympathy within the pages of the novel. To him, McLaverty was to be compared with Wordsworth, animating his excellent descriptive prose with a faithful representation of colourful local speech. The last and, possibly, most significant review came from the Ulster writer St John Ervine, who reviewed the novel in some detail for the *Belfast Telegraph*. He praised the authenticity of McLaverty's vision, as had Roy McFadden, but took him to task over painstaking detail and accused him of sacrificing plot to style. The title of this review was "Mr McLaverty's Clocking Hen," and Ervine took as the focus of his objection McLaverty's attention to small details, including even the precise cataloguing of the movements required in trying a string to the hen's leg:

What is the significance of all that particularity? Do we care what Mary did to the clocking hen? Is our knowledge of Mary increased in the slightest degree by Mr McLaverty's information? If this were an exceptional statement of insignificant detail complaint could not justifiably be made of it; but it is not exceptional: it is typical and altogether too frequent. I beg Mr McLaverty to believe that all this cataloguing and listing of events is a danger to his work and must be avoided. It will become a trick, if he is not careful, which he will perform automatically...When I criticise Mr McLaverty's work, I am criticising him on the level of great writers, not because I think he is one already but because I think he has the potentialities of one. He makes me aware of his people. They stay in my mind as living creatures. It is for this reason that I beg him to beware of tricks...[43]

McLaverty's response to this detailed criticism has not

survived but two letters on the subject, written to him by Jonathan Cape, indicate something of his reaction. Cape wrote to ask McLaverty's opinion of Ervine's review at the end of August and, having received a reply which has not survived, wrote again on 7 September 1945, thanking the author for a "thorough and complete exposition of your own reactions to St John Ervine's review." He also expressed the view that it was important for McLaverty "to think out your own attitude in this reply to an unperceptive criticism by a reviewer."[44]

Clearly, *In This Thy Day* was a work which caused McLaverty much trouble, both in its composition and in its reception, but he did not lose faith in it. Rather, he drew from its long difficulties increased faith in his ability to perceive the true task of the novelist, and seems to have begun at about this point to see himself not solely as a writer but also as a critic and student of critical theory, particularly with regard to his own work. Although always modest and unassuming about his own abilities, he seems to have felt from this time onwards that he was no longer a novice and could safely venture opinions on literature.

As a novel, *In This Thy Day* demonstrates more clearly than the first two, dependent as they were on some of his early experiences and memories, the nature of the stylistic and thematic problems with which the author was faced. An experienced writer of short stories for thirteen years, schooled in detachment coupled with close observation, determined to leave open to the reader all the possibilities inherent in a short story, McLaverty found himself labouring under the very different constraints of the novel. Here development was more important than careful sketching;

background was needed in more than shadowy form; words had to be spoken, emotions made explicit. The obvious had never been part of McLaverty's concern; he had striven always, even in the first two novels, for the "half-said thing." At this point, he was something between a short-story writer and a dramatist, practising in the novel form. It is possible that his refusal to change his surprising ending, which seems abrupt even today, may have arisen not so much from an unwillingness to be advised (for he had demonstrated in his readiness to change "The Wild Duck's Nest" that this was not a mark of his character) but from a curious lack of confidence in the autonomous life developed in the course of the novel by the characters themselves. Perhaps it was the very control which he had worked so long to develop in the shorter form which prevented a move in a different direction when the novel itself seemed to demand it. This is speculation: McLaverty has stated his reasons in his letters and in his writings, and the fact remains that he believed in the novel.[45] Some of his friends and reviewers agreed with him; some did not. What is certain is that this novel represented a change in direction for McLaverty, and it was to be the route chosen here which would lead him in 1949 to his renunciation of the short story as his primary form, to his dedicated adoption of the novel and to his establishment as a critic of more than ordinary perception.

Beyond this pivotal significance, there remains the question of the novel's value in itself. It begins with the lyricism typical of McLaverty's finest writing:

Winter was at an end and the first spring winds blew fresh and cold from the sea, coaxing the hedges to bud and stirring the lark to rise from the withered grass and burst in song. Horses were led along the sea-road to the forge, ploughs gritty with rust were carried in creaking carts, and in the dark barns the doors were flung wide and men were busy riddling the potatoes for seed. On the shore the black and white shelduck were moving in pairs, and further inland crows were breaking off the young shoots from the trees and flying with them to build their nests.[46]

Much of the novel recalls the style of the earlier stories, and two chapters were used, as has been noted, as short-story-like extracts in periodicals before the publication of the novel. In a discussion which anticipates the later story, "Six Weeks On and Two Ashore," and has its origin in a journal entry, two minor characters, "The Curate," an odd-job man, and the grandfather, Dan Scullion, discuss the north-west wind.[47] Scullion, a vivid if peripheral character in the novel, features in the extract "The Passing Generation," published in *Lagan* in 1944:

Outside the wind dunted against the house and died away again, and he recalled, when he was a young lad, crouched around the fire, how his father used to question him about the different natures of the winds. He licked the back of his spoon and looked at The Curate: "Do you hear that wind, Jimmy? How'd you know it was a nor'west wind supposin' you didn't know the lie of the land?"

Tessie took the empty bowl from him.

"It's a cold-rifed wind," said Jimmy, taking a pin from the lapel of his coat and dislodging a piece of meat from between his teeth.

"Sure every wind is cold—that's no answer," and his rough hands rasped as he rubbed them together. "Listen to it—do you remark anything peculiar?"

They all listened and heard it lurch and bump against the back of the house.

"They've all the same sound, Granda," Tessie said.

"They have not! Listen again with the ears the good God gave you!"[48]

Other characters suggest themselves as the subjects of short stories: Jimmy Neil, the aforementioned "Curate," who loses his health and confidence in his neighbours through malicious gossip and comes in the end to the workhouse; the priest's housekeeper who fears that she, too, will end her days in the workhouse and spills out her story one lonely day to Mary Devlin:

"...And that group," she said, showing her a group of children in an orphanage flanked by two nuns with joined hands: "I'm in that but you couldn't pick me out. That's me with the thick head of curls. You wouldn't believe it, but it is. I was a fine wee girl, and when I was leaving the nuns, Sister Laurentia cut off one of my curls as a keepsake—she did indeed. I could have been married twice. The first time I was asked I was too young and I refused because he had bad teeth and the next time I was too cautious and I held on too long, and he went and married a postmistress that was old enough to be his mother..."[49]

McLaverty's skill in transferring emotion to the observation of nature is used to good effect in the nearest he is prepared to come to a love-scene between the two young people, Ned and Mary, whose hope of happiness is blocked by the unbending attitude of Ned's mother, Mrs Mason, to Mary and her shiftless family:

> They remained so still then that a sparrow with a worm in its mouth fluttered into the nest above their heads and out again. A young foal gazed unflinchingly at them over the hedge, its ears pricked, a startled expression in its wide eyes. Its mother stood nearby, its eyes half-shut, and no movement from her except a slight shivering of her flanks when the flies tormented her. Sparrows hopped about, scolding harshly because they were deprived of their nests.[50]

It is for writing such as this that the reader returns to *In This Thy Day*. Because of the freshness of its imagery, the hints of passion and grief beyond expression which are not developed, the reader is left waiting for more of such writing. The expectation of a resolution of the young people's problem is not unreasonable but no solution is offered by the author except the very bleak one, rejected by Longmans Green, where Ned is driven away and Mary is left to deal as best she can with a broken heart. The abrupt ending, however justified by the author's aesthetic intention, leaves the reader who has been involved with the story curiously dissatisfied, as at the end of an unfinished novel. A strict and unbending sense of moral justice, the keynote of McLaverty's work from this time onwards, decides the time and nature of the conclusion. Yet, in opting for the triumph of retribution, McLaverty seems to lose sight of the impulse towards life and renewal, the celebration of which had so illuminated his earlier short stories and novels. His severity with his characters seems, in conjunction with his letters and journals of the time, to grow out of an equally stern attitude to himself and his talent.[51] He would not allow himself to write less than the truth, and his attempts to define as precisely as possible his responsibility to artistic and moral veracity were leading him onwards to the point of renunciation of the role of lyrical writer and adoption of that of moral novelist. In this light, the controversy over *In This Thy Day* represents the turning point of McLaverty's career.

REFERENCES

1   *In This Thy Day*, New York and London, 1945.
2   *The Bell*, II, 4 (July 1941), 34-9.
3   *Selected Writing*, 5, London, 1944, 19-26.
4   *Northern Harvest: An Anthology of Irish Writing*, Belfast, 1944, 34-9.
5   "A Schoolmaster," *The White Mare and Other Stories*, op. cit., 95-104.
6   H D Thoreau, *Walden: or Life in the Woods*, 1854; New York (pbk.) 1960, 10. Used by Daniel Corkery as epigraph to *The Threshold of Quiet, Dublin*, 1917.
7   "Moonshine," op. cit, 35; "The Poteen Maker," *Collected Stories*, 155.
8   ibid., 37-8; *Collected Stories*, 157-8.
9   "Becalmed," *Capuchin Annual*, 1940, 209-18.
10 Kuno Meyer, *Selections from Ancient Irish Poetry*, London, 1928, xiii.
11 Richard Rowley to McLaverty, 1 September 1942. Letter in possession of McLaverty family.
12 Unsigned review in possession of McLaverty family.
13 St John Ervine, "Mr McLaverty's Clocking Hen," *Belfast Telegraph*, 10 August 1945.
14 "The Road to the Shore," op. cit. See also *Collected Stories*, 160-172.
15 McLaverty to Daniel Corkery, May 1949. Letter in possession of McLaverty family.
16 "The Road to the Shore," 21-2; *Collected Stories*, 164.
17 ibid., 22-3; *Collected Stories*, 166-7
18 ibid., 26; *Collected Stories*, 172.
19 McLaverty to Julie Kernan, 17 February 1941. All letters in this

correspondence in possession of McLaverty family.

20 McLaverty to Julie Kernan, 5 June 1942.

21 McLaverty to Julie Kernan, 3 June 1943. See *In Quiet Places*, 91-2.

22 McLaverty to Julie Kernan, 4 May 1944; See *In Quiet Places*, 100.

23 Correspondence with Cape and Longmans, 12-14 September 1944. Letters in possession of McLaverty family.

24 Julie Kernan to McLaverty, 23 October 1944.

25 See *In Quiet Places*, 102-3 for McLaverty's reaction to Longmans' proposed change to *In This Thy Day*.

26 Mc Laverty to Jonathan Cape, 27 November 1944; See *In Quiet Places*, 100-02.

27 Publicity enclosure, 27 November 1944; See *In Quiet Places*, 101-02.

28 *In This Thy Day*. London, 1945, 200; Poolbeg (pbk.) edition, Dublin, 1981, 200.

29 Copy in possession of Sophia King.

30 Cape to McLaverty, 30 November 1944. Letter in possession of McLaverty family.

31 McLaverty to Julie Kernan, 15 December 1944; See *In Quiet Places*, 103.

32 Julie Kernan to McLaverty, 11 January 1945.

33 Herbert Weinstock (Alfred A Knopf) to McLaverty, 23 February 1945. Letter in possession of McLaverty family.

34 McLaverty to Houghton Mifflin, 5 March 1945. Letter in possession of McLaverty family.

35 McLaverty to Cape, 6 March 1945. Letter in possession of McLaverty family.

36 Mary B Catherwood (Houghton Mifflin) to McLaverty, 18 April 1945. Letter in possession of McLaverty family.

37 *In Quiet Places*, 155, 163.

38 Rev Eugene Molloy, *Brooklyn Eagle*, 27 April 1947.

39 Kathleen Hoagland, *Sun*, New York, 1 March 1945.

40 Richard Church, *John O'London's Weekly*, 13 July 1945.

41 Oliver St John Gogarty, *Inquirer*, Philadelphia, 20 April 1947.

42 Roy McFadden, *Dublin Magazine*, October-December 1945.

43 St John Ervine, op. cit.

44 Cape to McLaverty, 7 September 1945.

45 See *In Quiet Places*, 100-3, 107, for McLaverty's views on the ending of *In This Thy Day*.

46 *In This Thy Day*, op. cit., 5. Poolbeg ed., 5.

47 See *In Quiet Places*, 83; "Six Weeks On and Two Ashore," *Irish Writing*, 4 (April 1948), 36-45; *Collected Stories*, 182-93.

48 *In This Thy Day*, op. cit., 68; Poolbeg ed., 68.

49 ibid., 171-2; Poolbeg ed., 171-2.

50 ibid., 83; Poolbeg ed., 83-4.

51 See *In Quiet Places*, 114-6; 117-9; 122-4; 131-5; 142-8; 152-8; 162-3; 168-72; 177-8; 185-8 for McLaverty's view on the moral obligation of the writer.

CHAPTER FIVE

THE TETHER OF GOD

THE GAME COCK AND *THE THREE BROTHERS*

Although the "quiet desperation" of the characters Ned and Mary, in *In This Thy Day*, is sacrificed by the author to the exploration of hardness of heart in Mrs Mason, McLaverty did not abandon his study of the daily but desperate struggle of ordinary people in difficult situations. The last three stories written before his abandonment of the form reflect this concern. Two of them, "The Mother" and "Six Weeks On and Two Ashore," seemed to suggest a new direction for his short stories, exploring as they do the dilemmas of the unhappily married or recently bereaved. The third, "Father Christmas" reflects the same concern, though in a minor key.

The first of these, "The Mother," appeared in the anthology *Irish Harvest*, edited in 1946 by Robert Greacen. It concerns a widow with two small sons who is torn between her love for them and her attraction to a man who wants to marry her and send the boys away to school. This is no saintly Irish mother keening over her lost child. The woman in "The Mother" is young, lonely, often impatient but devoted to her children, and, truest detail of all, extremely concerned that the neighbours should not think badly of her. The fact that she has had to place her father in the workhouse because of financial constraint is a source of worry to her and is one of her main reasons for wishing to remarry. McLaverty paints with feeling her loneliness and frustration in the heart of the city:

> ...some day, please God, she'd get away from all this roughness, away to the fringes of the city where she'd have a house with an extra room, and, maybe, bring her father home again where he could sun himself in a patch of garden at the back, and maybe see the whins in bloom on the mountain and hear the larks singing. "O God," she said aloud, "if one had to live one's life again!"[1]

Into this house comes at regular intervals the person referred to by her little boys as "the man." He is older than she is, and the aggressive intimacy suggested by his "putting his arm round her waist" as soon as he enters the hall, emerges as one of his chief characteristics. The menace of the man is shown in small things, such as the waving of a harmless table knife; but the threat is present. Mary's nervous listening for a hint of softening, her careful attendance on him at table and her uncharacteristic threat to the boys show without the need for further explanation her strain in the situation, her anxious hope that everyone will be content in the new relationship and an understandable desire to avoid the displeasure of an overbearing companion:

When they were seated at the table and she was helping him to some salad there was a rumble of a cart outside, and then another pad of feet overhead and a laugh from the two boys.

"Aren't they the devils," she said.

"Wait and I'll go up to them, Mary."

"No, no, Frank, you might frighten them."

"Frighten them!"

"Well, I didn't mean frighten—I meant; how will I explain it."

"Aye, just how will you explain it! Look," and he shook his knife in the air, "them two boyos is playing on you. I know what I'm talking about and if you take my advice you'd pack them off to the country."

"Och, after all, Frank, they're only children and I often think if I could get one of the new houses at the outskirts of the city they'd get as much of the country as'd do them," and looking up at the ceiling she shouted: "Get into bed there, and go asleep or I'll go up with the strap."[2]

Frank, at this point, asks her to come for a walk with him; she is tempted, but does not dare leave the children alone; and so affairs move to a crisis. He delivers an ultimatum: either she meets him on Sunday at eight o'clock for a walk in the country, or, although there is no threat made as such, she knows he will leave her. All this takes place on Friday night; on Saturday, one day before the walk is to take place, she goes to visit her father, "her head high" as she sees the neighbours peering curiously. They do not know her secret, "and she'd make sure they'd never know it." Her father feels acutely the shame of his position and pleads with her to take him out, before he is sent back, well and fit, "to the body of the house—amongst the derelict, the nameless and the shameless." She has no reply to make.

Thus burdened, she goes through many changes of mind in the next twenty-four hours, her strain showing itself in her reluctance to leave the children alone, even when she has decided to do so. As she goes, the change in narrative point of view, which disturbs the rhythm of some of the earliest stories, serves here to strengthen the reader's understanding of the woman's dilemma. The guilt which assails her is intensified by a favourite device, a symbolic blacking out of the friendly moonlight:

> She reached the road and just missed a tram, and while waiting for another, a massive cloud trailed across the moon and scooped the light from the street. And then there came into her mind the sight of the boys' room, the moonlight slipping from it, leaving nothing only the slanting light from the street lamp and the shadow of the window-sash on the ceiling.[3]

She goes home, vents her frustration on the boys by destroying the chestnuts they have gathered, regrets it, and sits down to wait for her final confrontation with Frank. This is as unpleasant as it can be, and they part bitterly. Mary, left alone with the two boys, goes up to them, and despite their childish jubilation and eager demands, the reader knows the extent of "the great stillness" which she feels. In the tears flowing unchecked after such effort and control, McLaverty shows with sensitivity the price she must now begin to pay.

The poet, Padraic Fiacc, writing to McLaverty after the publication of "The Mother" in the 1947 collection *The Game Cock and Other Stories,* praised the story in these terms:

> I'm just after reading your "The Mother"—no wonder they
> compare you to Tchekhov! You have his attitude of mind
> which saves and transcends your Turgenev instinct from
> becoming banal or style for style's sake. How you can do
> all that with poetry alone never ceases to marvel me.[4]

A lighter, but no less considered study of the shifting relationships between married people is found in the story "Father Christmas."[5] This is an account of a day in the life of an unemployed man, urged by his wife to apply for a position as Father Christmas in a large department store. He secures the job, and struggles through the day to maintain some semblance of dignity, despite the crippling pain of tight boots and the potential embarrassment of the costume. His only comfort lies in growing indignation towards his wife for having placed him in this position.

His ill-humour is shamed out of him when he goes home, and his wife tends to his needs; in an interesting shift in perspective, the reader is told that the wife, noticing "the hard ring in his voice," keeps the children out of his way. Although McLaverty does not always succeed in shifting his point of view from one central character, the success of it in this case depends on the humorous comparison between the man's perception of his own nature, and the somewhat different view of his wife. The revelation of character, the loss of self-esteem and its gradual rebuilding through the subtlety of the man's wife, make this a good example of craft in McLaverty's work. This man does not know that his wife is in control of him and his life; the humour and irony rest in his delusion of mastery of the home, and her skilful preservation of the myth:

> She handed him a pair of warm socks from the line and a pair of old slippers that she had made for him out of paste board and a piece of velours.
>
> "I've a nice bit of steak for your tea," she said. "I'll put on the pan when I get these ones into their beds."
>
> He rubbed his feet and pulled on the warm socks. It was good that she hadn't the steak fried and lying as dry as a stick in the oven. When all was said and done, she had some sense in her head.[6]

The last of the stories in which McLaverty concerns himself with power, control and their bearing on human relationships is entitled "Six Weeks On and Two Ashore"[7] and is undoubtedly the finest of that group. It is probably among McLaverty's best. Apart from its literary quality, it is significant as the last story McLaverty wrote before deciding that he would abandon the shorter form. In fact he did publish at least seven more over the next twenty years, and unfinished fragments exist of others but this is the last story before his dedication to the novel of morality. McLaverty's own judgement on this story is worth mentioning; he has written of it in recent years as "one of the best I ever wrote. It is to my mind very sensual, very subtle."[8]

The story takes place on the day that the elderly husband of Mrs O'Brien goes back to take up his position as lighthousekeeper, where he works six weeks in every eight, as in the title of the story. The atmosphere in his house that day is charged with bitterness, expressed by the couple in alternating silence and sarcasm. This is set against the happy expectation of the homecoming lighthousekeeper's wife, newly married and obviously content as she prepares for her husband's return. By means of a cold, bitterly stormy night, McLaverty establishes the wintry chill that pervades the atmosphere of their home; and in the dog he provides a substitute for the wife's care and attention. Such characteristic touches have not until this story been used with this single-minded intensity. It is indeed an intense story, the exchanges or lack of them taking place between two characters only, commented on mainly by the reactions of the unfortunate dog. Loveless though the couple's relationship clearly is, there is a half-hope in Mrs O'Brien's mind that the weather will be too stormy for him to go. Even as she packs his clothes with care—saying that he will not be able to "cast it up to her" if all is not done properly— she wonders if the boatman will find the weather too stormy to bring him out; she hopes the rain will help her out of a difficult situation. The morning brings a sky of "washed blue," and she hears "the hollow tumult of the distracted sea." Immediately, her eye is drawn to the house of Delia Coady, wife of the other lighthousekeeper. Everything in Delia's bearing, and in the very aspect of her house, speaks of joy and expectation:

> The door was open to the cold sun and Delia Coady was on her knees freshly whitening the door-step that had been streaked in the night's rain. All her windows were

open, the curtains bulging in the uneasy draught. Delia raised her head and looked round but Mrs O'Brien withdrew to the edge of the window and continued to watch her. Delia was singing now and going to the zinc tank at the side of the house for a bucket of water.[9]

Her furtive spying, for so it seems as she draws her head back, suggests a kind of voyeurism on the part of the lonely, embittered Mrs O'Brien. She has not ceased to care for her husband, for even if she tells herself that she makes his clothes ready to keep criticism at bay, it is clear that she takes more than perfunctory care in their preparation, as if her former expressions of affection through such care had been translated into a barrier against reproof. When Tom, her husband, stirs into wakefulness, their first conversation of the day is sharp and unfriendly, full of unaired grievance and a weary tension, "one remark following another, spreading out and involving them, before they were aware, in a quarrel of cold cruelty." In counterpoint to these bitter exchanges, Delia Coady sings merrily outside on her freshly-whitened doorstep. She is wearing the dress in which she was married, a fact which sparks off yet another argument, and leads to an outburst on the part of Mrs O'Brien, in which she accuses her husband of neglecting her, of using the excuse of fatigue to neglect her and avoid her company; she calls her state one of "married widowhood," reproaches him about his age and leaves in anger. Her husband, equally unhappy and disappointed in his marriage, sees nothing in the neatly folded clothes, the "cold starched shirt," and the polished brass buttons on his jacket, but evidence of fussiness. She, in the meantime, regrets having made disparaging comments about his age and appearance, but does not know how to bring about an apology. Thus they try to keep to neutral topics but the only one available being Delia Coady, they soon tumble into verbal abuse, and the real cause of their tension spills into Mag's head:

> "She has plenty of paint on, this morning," she added to restore ease.
>
> "Who has?"
>
> "The old boat, I mean," she flashed back.
>
> There it was again: they were back to where they started from—chilling one another with silent hostility or with words that would spurt in lancing fury. Oh, she thought, if only he had shown some of his old love for her during the past two weeks they would not now be snapping at one another, and there would be ease and satisfaction and longing in this leavetaking.[10]

Nothing is made explicit; McLaverty does not state what he believes to be the obvious, so at this point, as "a shadow passed the window" the boatmen arrive to take Tom to the Rock. Mag makes one last attempt at reconciliation, the nearest she comes to physical contact, and is brushed off, as he leaves without farewell. No indication is given that O'Brien is upset by the nature of the parting, except that he slips when leaping into the boat, misjudging the leap and placing himself in the undignified position of having to be hauled out of the water. A minute before, Delia Coady's husband Frank has made his leap "as lightly as a ballet dancer." Mag, left out in the cold, is truly alone.

She scanned the rock and the white path down to the sea. If only he saw her and came out on the parapet as he used to do and signal to her she'd be content—her mind would be eased. She sat down on a green slope and waited. There was no stir about the rock, only a gull or two tilting and gliding above the sea. She got up and waved her hand. The dog scratched at the ground, leapt sideways, impatient to be off. She waved again—still there was no sign that she was being seen. [11]

This was one of the stories included in a second selection of McLaverty's stories, *The Game Cock and Other Stories*, published by Jonathan Cape in 1949. It had not been included in the American edition of 1947, published by the Devin-Adair Company, as it did not appear in print for the first time until April 1948 in *Irish Writing*. In a letter to Vivian Mercier, on 27 November 1949, McLaverty wrote of "Six Weeks On and Two Ashore":

...I feel it is one of the best of my short stories so far. I must add, though, that only a few critics noted it when reviewing *The Game Cock*; I don't blame them: for in these days of rapid reviewing and rapid reading one can't always expect them to respond to that "which is felt upon the page without being specifically named" (Willa Cather). It had no luck with the overworked American editors, and I suppose I should have given it a sexual title to induce the proper response.[12]

Reviews of *The Game Cock* were generally favourable, even enthusiastic. *The New Yorker* called it "Twelve tales of Irish country life, by a writer with a good eye and a good ear for the singing Irish speech." This reviewer found "The Game Cock" and "The White Mare" "altogether delightful." (A note on this review in McLaverty's own hand reads "a bit patronising.") *Facts*, of Redlands, California, noted McLaverty's "unfailing eye for the plausible and telling detail," and the *San Francisco Chronicle* found the stories "delicate, sensitive and lyrically beautiful" marked by "the same gifted writing that characterises Mr McLaverty's novels." *The Times Dispatch* of Richmond, Virginia believed that McLaverty was heading a "literary renaissance of minor proportions" and Carl Lewis of the *Indianapolis Star* remarked that "McLaverty is concerned primarily with people and their reactions to simple, everyday things," but had the curious impression after reading "Pigeons" that "a dirty, domineering England leers always in the background of the North Irish countryside." The last observation apart, there can have been little for McLaverty to object to in his American reviews. His reviews for the Cape edition of 1949 were equally favourable. *The Observer* described him as a "writer who strikes a single note with elegant precision," and who "evokes his chosen aspect of Ireland with unfailing skill."

In the midst of such international recognition for his work in the short story, McLaverty took the decision to abandon the form in favour of the novel. In fact, by 1949, he had already done so, staking his reputation on his first specifically "Catholic" novel, *The Three Brothers*. His journals and correspondence underline the fact that the short story was no longer of primary importance to him, and his chief concern was now the writing of moral fiction and the education of younger writers.[13] Throughout his work,

McLaverty's concern for the consequences of right or wrong-doing, fundamental to his writing as far back as "The Wild Duck's Nest," runs like a recurrent theme. It is this basic concern, overlaid with a specifically Catholic morality, which characterises this fourth novel (published in 1948). In a supposedly anonymous epigraph which, in fact, he wrote himself, he encapsulates its theme and tone:

> Sorrow and suffering and joy are three strands in the tether of God; sorrow and suffering strengthen fervour, and joy strengthens hope. Without fervour and without hope the spirit breaks loose, and when the spirit breaks loose from the tethering, Man roams like an animal without a home.[14]

In its moral attitude, *The Three Brothers* is close to the strict code of the last chapter in *In This Thy Day*, where Mrs Mason is punished for her wickedness. In the later novel, the hand of God is a merciful one, but it is no less strict in its justice. An interesting review of the novel for *The Irish Times*, by Temple Lane, noted the similarity in tone between McLaverty's epigraph and William Blake's:

> Joy and woe are woven fine
> A clothing for the soul divine
> Under every grief and pine
> Runs a joy with silken twine.
>
> It is right it should be so.
> Man was made for joy and woe;
> And when this we rightly know
> Safely through the world we go.[15]

Temple Lane concluded that McLaverty was "a writer of great promise as well as past performance" whose "work has the element of goodness, the purity of heart one often seeks in vain, and having found, is immediately at home and at peace." The search for goodness, and the attempt to retain the purity of the heart, represent not only the intention of this novel, but the reason for the author's rejection of anything, literary or moral, not dedicated to these ends.

McLaverty probably started work on this novel soon after the completion of *In This Thy Day*, as he was able to promise a completed manuscript to Jonathan Cape by September 1947, and to keep his promise at the beginning of October.[16] When Cape replied, McLaverty was delighted to know that he planned to publish the novel in 1948, and the *Game Cock* volume in 1949. Yet, he was still concerned about the epigraph, wanting to be sure that it included all his intentions:

I was in two minds about the quotation on the title page: wondering if I should dispense with it altogether or substitute one from Eliot's *Family Reunion*:

> I believe the moment of birth
> Is when we have knowledge of death
> I believe the season of birth
> Is the season of sacrifice

A quotation that would be congruent with the characterisation of John and Nelly and in negative manner with the tattered rag of life that was the old country draper's.[17]

It is possible to discern, in this concentration on suffering as the only means to salvation, an extension of the moral concern begun, and defended, in the controversy surrounding *In This Thy Day*. Having won that battle, McLaverty seems to have directed his energies towards his development as a moral writer. This concern is evident, here as in the previous novel, in his list of projected titles, sent to Jonathan Cape on 18 December, 1947. They included: *The Dew Shall Weep; A House By The River; The Frost Will Melt; Chaff in the Wind; The Tether of God; Disturb Thy Ease; Untie the World*.[18] None of these titles, with the rhythm and biblical echo of *In This Thy Day*, seems to have pleased either Cape or Macmillan, and McLaverty wrote to Cape on 6 January 1948 that he was prepared to stay with his first suggestion, *The Three Brothers*, for want of a better.[19] The moral preoccupations which had been exercising him since the time of *In This Thy Day* were leading him inexorably into yet another role, that of Catholic writer. Despite the misgivings of his publishers and some of his reviewers about its literary truth, *In This Thy Day* had been one of the monthly selections of The Catholic Literary Foundation. In 1948, their August selection was *The Three Brothers*. The foundation's journal, *Forecast*, described it in enthusiastic terms as:

A Beautiful Book, Signposting Life By Showing the Duality of Existence, the Sorrow in Joy, the Bitter in the Sweet, the Unexpected in the Planned as It Discloses the Spiritual Crises in the Lives of Three Brothers, Commonplace but Very Real People.[20]

In the same issue, anxious perhaps not to be misunderstood as he felt he had been over *In This Thy Day*, the author contributed an article entitled "Michael McLaverty Explains His Methods in Writing as He Sketches Background of *The Three Brothers*." Although this was not the first time McLaverty had set down his thoughts on writing or even the first time he had written or spoken publicly on topics related to the craft, it was his first expression of a personal philosophy of writing. As such it bears investigation, dealing as it does directly with the novel *The Three Brothers*, and indirectly with the major change of direction taking place in his career at the time. His opening paragraph is interesting in itself, showing that he did not agree with those critics who felt that his love of detail, so successful in the short story, could not be transposed to the novel:

> I write each novel as carefully as I write a short story, endeavouring to make each sentence and each passage of dialogue carry their full complement of meaning, and trying also to sketch the background which forms and has formed the lives of the characters in my books.[21]

To those who accuse him of failing to put enough emphasis on background, he answers that the background is to be found in the detail. Through detail and careful description, McLaverty believes he approaches the inner thoughts and motivation of his characters. He recommends that writers, readers and critics consider a work of art with great care before passing final judgement on it, urging, as he did in his letter to John O'Connor, careful "contemplation," without which "there can be no real art." Approaching the heart of his philosophy, he rejects the idea of the obvious and the startling, and his favourite quotation from Kuno Meyer finds its way into the text.

> I am not interested in the abnormal or violent—violent men are usually weak men and those writers who follow that incline usually lose themselves in a maze of melodrama by an insistent emphasis. It is the half-said thing that produces intensity of expression. "To be told nothing and yet to hear and feel everything," Coleridge said of Shakespeare.[22]

McLaverty then reaches the central idea of his message: he proposes not only to relate a story, but to use the consequences of his characters' actions not only for literary, but for moral purposes, informing and elevating the reader's consciousness. Thus the awareness of moral responsibility, dating from as far back as "The Wild Duck's Nest" in 1943, finds its fullest expression yet. *In This Thy Day* having pointed him in the direction of moral fiction, *The Three Brothers* confirms his dedication to it. No longer a short-story writer but a novelist, he was, moreover, no longer merely a writer of novels: his function from this time, beginning with *The Three Brothers*, was to be a writer of conscience. He would be, like Mauriac or Graham Greene, but in a specifically Irish way, a Catholic novelist.

The three main characters in *The Three Brothers* appear almost like figures from a morality play. The good man is John; the selfish one is Bob; and the wilful, misguided one is DJ, who tries the patience of the other two. Their faults and strengths are reflected in a weaker form in the next generation; there is a good son, Brendan, a trainee librarian; and a careless, deceitful son who wastes his time and his father's money at the university. There is a discontented teacher daughter, Anne, deliberately ignoring her father's advice to "fall in love" with her vocation, and a good daughter, Eileen, who in the course of time falls in love with a decent young man, Philip Doran. The good-hearted but slightly jealous Aunt Nelly is attracted to Doran herself but renounces him for the sake of her niece. Finally, there are several minor characters who seem, like similar tantalising characters in *In This Thy Day*, to deserve stories of their own; these include the old man Johnny PM; the teacher; and a librarian. They do not receive detailed treatment because, as in the third novel, their presence and undeniable vitality cannot be allowed to disturb the overall importance of the moral lesson. The "curious quietude," mentioned by Edwin Muir in his review of *Lost Fields*, has become by the time of the fourth novel a hush of deadly seriousness, as if the dedication of the author to his deeper purpose must of its nature preclude lightness of tone or touch. According to McLaverty's stated intention, joy prefigures sorrow, and even in sorrow there is the promise of future joy; yet to this end he sacrifices the rich and unpredictable life of the short stories and the two earliest novels.

There is, of course, much writing of the very highest quality. The opening, like that of *In This Thy Day*, is both satisfying in itself and promising for the novel. McLaverty does not set the scene, but enters immediately the mind and concerns of the good brother, John Caffrey:

When he was half-way up the street after getting off the tram he saw a light in his own parlour window. His two sons would be studying, he thought, or maybe Eileen practising at the piano. He stood for a minute in the cold silence of the street and inclined his ear towards the house, but nothing came to him except the receding hum of the tram as it sped towards the terminus. Hm! he said, those fellows aren't in so great a hurry to get you to your business in the morning: sitting parked at the terminus and drinking tea out of thermos flasks till you'd think they had taken root; and then at this time of night they'd drive past your stop if you weren't careful.[23]

Perhaps the difficulty with the novel rises from the fact that the figure of Bob is, like that of Mrs Mason in *In This Thy Day*, too representative of his prevailing vice. He never stops being mean, selfish and grasping, unlike, for example, Alec in *Call My Brother Back*, who acts selfishly towards Colm but is still capable of kindness towards him. In the incident where Bob refuses to accept a dirty ten-shilling note offered to him in payment for goods by a ragged child, his meanness is cruel, but this is not one aspect of a balanced character. It is the character; he has no other side. In incidents such as this, and in the terrible retribution suffered by the wastrel brother, who is beaten senseless by thugs after one of his very few acts of unselfish honesty, the delicacy of observed detail and the relief of gentle humour cannot be given their due attention by the reader.

In the undoubted darkness of the novel there is a fine, memorable central image. In this, the aunt, Nelly, younger half-sister of the three brothers, lies awake on the night that she has given up her hopes of marriage with Doran, the man she loves, in order that her niece may be happy with him. The night of her loneliness is suggested by the fearful cries of cattle, rattling by train to the slaughter house through the cold light of early morning:

For a while she did not sleep as she went over the events of the day, and then when sleep did come she was awakened out of it by the cry of cattle passing on the road. Ever since she was a child these herds of cattle moving through the night to the waiting wagons at the station had always wakened her, and their crying and their breathing and their shuffling huddled through her mind in a terrifying mystery to which she could give no name. They always come in the semi-darkness, in the cold no-light of the predawn; they are driven from wide flat fields where mists make light of night; their dew-wet hoofs lift the dust on the road and swirl it into their gaping eyes and on to the low-hinging leaves on the trees. They brush and lurch against the hedges, and the thorns grasp hair to stream in the daylight's wind. They cry, and their calls are echoed by distant cattle lying in the warm nests of their own sweat. A crack from the drover's stick sends them leaping forward; they steam and sweat and make the road a river of mist. They cry again, and strings and clots of froth fall from their mouths on to the thirsty road. They reach the village, and windows rattle in the pad-pad of their hoofs. Their gasping breaths and their crushed and driven roughness are narrowed into an intense shadow of sound. At the station there is the shunt of wagons, then the thump of harried feet on bare boards, and, at last, the

rick-rick of wheels as the train rattles with its terrified load
into the cold light of dawn. Outside on the road and over
the fields the silence falls, and falling into Nelly's mind
come fear and mystery and sorrow—life approaching
death.[24]

In that passage, McLaverty's stated intention and his gift
for precise and evocative prose combine most happily.
Indeed the sad and heroic character, Nelly, is the great
triumph of the novel.

The reaction of reviewers to the novel was mixed. None
doubted the sincerity of the author or the quality of his
writing but, time and again, after initial enthusiasm,
reservations are expressed. Nancy Ayer in the *Detroit Free
Press* praised McLaverty's "artistic reticence" but regretted
the "lack of humor and of action." McLaverty himself
considered the novel relatively full of humour, writing in
June 1948 to Jonathan Cape: "On rereading the novel after
an elapse of nine months I was struck most of all by its
humour."[25] Edward McSorley in the *Providence Sunday
Journal* felt the novel was too restrained, not strong enough,
and Harriet Zinnes in the *St Louis Post-Dispatch* accused
McLaverty of sentimentality.[26] It was unusual, indeed, for
McLaverty to be branded sentimental, and he is unlikely,
too, to have welcomed the judgement of his novel as a
"little simple story" in a review in *The Republican*. This
reviewer was not the only one to think the quality of the
writing superior to the plot and characterisation. The
reviewer in the *St Louis Star-Times* considered McLaverty "a
deft stylist, although his characters appear somewhat stilted
at times. *The Three Brothers* is possibly more enjoyable for

its places than for its people." Not all critics were negative. *America* felt the novel improved on acquaintance,[27] while Orville Prescott, in the *New York Times,* concluded that the novel was "not a memorable, moving or important novel...(but) an interesting, mature and adroit one." Like other reviewers, he praised McLaverty's gift; unlike some, he commended his characterisation and use of humour, commenting that "in every Irish writer, it almost seems, whether a crude and sentimental one or a finished and objective one, there is born a deep awareness of sorrow and suffering."[28] A reviewer in *Time and Tide,* thought by the author to be LP Hartley, agreed that McLaverty's humour illuminated the novel, considering him to be "in the best tradition of Irish comic writers."[29] In Ireland, the playwright Teresa Deevy, champion of McLaverty's works, and later a friend, reviewed the novel with unreserved enthusiasm:

> The smooth strong swell of a rising tide, a sense of being carried forward by it, a sense of rest so absolute, so complete that one's faculty of perception deepens and grows rich,— this was my experience when reading Michael McLaverty's latest book...Perhaps McLaverty's greatest gift is ironic humour blended with reverence for all creatures...In Ireland we do not rush out with open arms to greet a genius. We are, I think, slow to acclaim, but once awakened we do not forget. There are some of us who notice a slowness in this country with regard to Michael McLaverty. America—through leading critics—has acclaimed him. I think we will not much longer lag behind.[30]

In her review Teresa Deevy refers to an image which, with

that of the cattle in the night, is central to McLaverty's stated purpose. This is the image of a peacock, wrought in stone by Philip Doran's father for the Caffrey brothers' father, outside the door of the Caffrey shop. Bob rips it out in favour of more modern design, showing his contempt for craft, neighbourly feeling and aesthetic pleasure. Through the story of the peacock, McLaverty the craftsman tells the reader all that is necessary about Bob, rendering unnecessary many of the other anecdotes and illustrations of his unattractive character. All that Teresa Deevy perceives is accurate. She understands the author's conception, and is capable of explaining it in a few words. There is no doubt that it is a quiet, calm, contemplative novel and that it repays rereading. The author takes his reader through each season of the year with careful attention to detail and symbol, observing the ebb and flow of human relationships. The whole is underlined by the message that only charity, patience and forgiveness will bring any understanding of true happiness. Such patent sincerity, combined with an unobtrusive, quiet tone, caused the *Catholic World* to notice it but it is interesting to note its reviewer's comment on it in relation to *The Game Cock*, which is recommended as "probably Mr McLaverty's best published work." Similar sentiments were expressed in the review which was to be McLaverty's favourite. Written by Horace Reynolds in *Detroit Free Press*, it was generous in its praise of specific qualities, but recommended the reader to look at McLaverty's short stories.

...McLaverty hates to find evil in a man, because he realises the unhappiness the possession of evil is sure to bring that man.

It is McLaverty's love of his fellow-man which has made Bob not a monster but an erring man into whom the tenderness and compassion of his creator have poured something of all of us. Deep down Bob knows himself for what he is. Twice, when greatly shocked by the dramatic contrast of his evil with the good in Nelly and John, he cries, "Forgive me!" as he struggles with the black devils in him. They strip the man naked to the agony of his struggle.

All this is the quiet work of a sensitive and perceptive artist...One can only urge those who care for simplicity and truth in their fiction not to overlook both McLaverty's short stories—and novels such as this one.

The Three Brothers did not elicit the response for which its author must have hoped. Neither sentimental nor humourless, he was accused by reviewers of both sentimentality and lack of humour. A perfectionist in planning and execution, he was accused of having produced a slight book. These adverse criticisms could not be eliminated even by the praise of those who perceived his purpose. The poet, Padraic Fiacc, an enthusiastic supporter of McLaverty's work, had written to McLaverty on this topic as far back as 1946:

May I write now that I wanted to say to you when we met that apart from the fact that you are a Greek for concentration might you not be crossing over from the short story to the novel and a little scrupulous in your "unity?" The Irish temperament, being Byzantine, looks for detail. Then again, children are intolerably literal-minded apart from their sense of wonder. You are pastoral and mild and single to create a literature for children. You are also very wise to be true. All the same, there was, when I read your books in America, a concealed distinction, a restraint, the very feature of Padraic Colum, but if I may say it—torment and evil, much as it is generally lacking in the terrible morality of the Irish, if you could make sin a theme with the correct perspective, would be of more appeal in England and America. Because the civilizations of these countries are so miserably complacent they turn and devour the work that has struggle in it. Of course I have not read your latest novel, and I have only read *Lost Fields* and your first. I believe very strongly in your short stories.[31]

McLaverty himself no longer believed in the short story, except as relief and background to his real work, the representation of morality through his much-practised observation and imagery. The decision seemed irrevocable, and, although he was to publish over the next twenty years four more novels and several more short stories, he did not modify his philosophy beyond this point. Having arrived at acceptance of his role, McLaverty set his mind to reinforcing his position as a writer of conscience, first, and a writer of lyrical prose, second. The decision to be a moral writer was not easily taken, as can be seen by his many letters and journal entries dealing with his dilemma. Having decided, McLaverty could not then in conscience withdraw from what he perceived as his artistic responsibility, and if the price to be paid was a reduced output of the kind of work for which he had received most praise, then he was prepared to pay it, without counting the cost. Thus, in effect, McLaverty put behind him the years of acclaim and began the difficult task of writing the kind of work which would satisfy not only his aesthetic, but also his moral sensibilities.

REFERENCES

1   "The Mother," *Irish Harvest*: A Collection of Stories, Essays and Poems, ed., Robert Greacen, Dublin, 1946, 106; *Collected Stories*, 135-6.
2   ibid., 105; *Collected Stories*, 139.
3   ibid., 114; *Collected Stories*, 149-50.
4   Padraic Fiacc to McLaverty, 25 July 1947. Letter in possession of McLaverty family.
5   "Father Christmas," *The Game Cock and Other Stories*, London, 1949; *Collected Stories*, 230-1.
6   ibid., 54; *Collected Stories*, 230-1
7   "Six Weeks on and Two Ashore," *Irish Writing*, 4 (April 1948), 36-45; *Collected Stories*, 182-93.
8   Written by McLaverty on his copy of unpublished thesis, "An Ulster Novelist: Michael McLaverty," presented to Université de Lyon, 1960, for Diplôme d'Études Supérieres, by Mme Raymond de Micheaux. MS in possession of McLaverty family.
9   "Six Weeks On and Two Ashore," op. cit., 37; *Collected Stories*, 184.
10 ibid., 41; *Collected Stories*, 188.
11 ibid., 45; *Collected Stories*, 193.
12 McLaverty to Vivian Mercier, 27 November 1949. Letter in possession of McLaverty family.
13 See *In Quiet Places*, 136-7; 141; 142-8 for McLaverty's views on the short story form.
14 Epigraph to *The Three Brothers*, (London, 1948) attributed by the author to anonymous source, but written by himself. Recounted in conversation between McLaverty and Sophia King.
15 William Blake, "Auguries of Innocence," (1802) in *William Blake*, ed., Michael Mason, Oxford Authors Series, Oxford, 1988, 27-31.
16 McLaverty to Jonathan Cape, 7 September and 6 October 1947. Letters in possession of McLaverty family.
17 McLaverty to Cape, 4 November 1947. See *In Quiet Places*, 108-9.
18 McLaverty to Cape, 18 December 1947. Letter in possession of McLaverty family.
19 McLaverty to Cape, 6 January 1948. Letter in possession of McLaverty family.

20 "Michael McLaverty Explains His Methods of Writing as He Sketches Background for *The Three Brothers*," *Forecast*, Milwaukee, Wisconsin, 1948, 6-7. See *In Quiet Places*, 122-3.

21 *In Quiet Places*, 122.

22 ibid., 123

23 *The Three Brothers*, London, 1948, 13; Poolbeg (pbk) edition, Dublin, 1982, 13.

24 The Three Brothers, op. cit., 154-5; Poolbeg edition, 154-5.

25 McLaverty to Cape, 27 June 1948. Letter in possession of McLaverty family.

26 Harriet Zinnes, *St Louis Post-Dispatch*, 18 October 1948. This review and *Providence*.

27 *America*, 18 November 1948. Review in possession of McLaverty family.

28 Orville Prescott, *New York Times*, 25 August 1948. Review in possession of McLaverty family.

29 LP Hartley, *Time and Tide*, 6 November 1948. Review in possession of McLaverty family.

30 Teresa Deevy, *Irish Writing*, July 1949. Review in possession of McLaverty family.

31 Padraic Fiacc to McLaverty, 27 March 1946. Letter in possession of McLaverty family.

SECTION III

JOY AND WOE

1950-78

CHAPTER SIX

"SINS OF THE MIND"

TRUTH IN THE NIGHT AND *SCHOOL FOR HOPE*

A decision had been taken: a new road lay ahead. McLaverty had withdrawn, in effect, from the public world of writing but he retained a reputation as a generous author, so that younger authors looked to him for example and advice. Over the next decade and a half, he would develop his role as mentor to the young. He was no longer searching for a satisfactory literary form because he believed that he had found it. The Catholic moral novel was, to his mind, the vehicle most suited to his moral and aesthetic sense. He ended the Forties with lectures on Mauriac and Hopkins and with a declaration of his intention to renounce the short story in favour of the moral novel.[1] Three novels were published between 1951 and 1958: *Truth in the Night*,[2] *School For Hope*[3] and *The Choice*.[4] All of these develop in theme and tone the moral concerns expressed by McLaverty towards the end of the crucial decade of the Forties. In each the author investigates the effects of spite, selfishness or impatience on human relationships, and advocates the healing power of charity, patience and Christian acceptance.

These are his novels of "joy and woe"; and it is clear from his letters and journal entries that, while the writing of them often cost him dearly in terms of mental and physical strain, he remained unshaken in his conviction that he must persevere.[5] Moreover, despite his determination in 1949 to give up writing short stories, he published during the Fifties three fine examples of the shorter form: "A Half Crown,"[6] "Uprooted"[7] and "The Circus Pony."[8]

Short stories were not uppermost in his mind, however, after his decision to abandon the form. He was finishing his fifth novel, published in 1951 as *Truth in the Night*. A letter of 20 November 1949 to Cecil Scott, his editor at Macmillan in New York, shows him immersed in the new novel:

Since the beginning of September I have worked steadily at it in my free evenings, and as it grows apace I feel a greater love for it than I did previously...I have well over forty thousand words of it written but at the moment I'm bogged in a time-gap which I want to bridge artistically: to present it as time lived and not as time stated—it is, I think, the most difficult task that confronts any novelist.[9]

Clearly, work began to go quickly, for by 13 November 1950, Scott wrote to tell McLaverty that corrections had been received and would be inserted in the manuscript.[10] By the autumn of 1951 it was published in America and Jonathan Cape brought out the London edition in 1952.

Truth in the Night is a novel quite unlike any other by McLaverty. Although, like *Call My Brother Back*, it is set on Rathlin Island, the tone and mood of this novel are quite different, as though the author had deliberately introduced an element of evil into his childhood paradise. In *Truth in the Night*, the integrity of the island is embodied in the character of an old lady, a former teacher named Mrs Reilly. Her daughter-in-law, Vera, widowed and with a young daughter, is negative to her positive, night to her day, and it is Vera who introduces the oddly discordant note into this tale of island life. Bitter and discontented as the Mauriac heroines she most closely resembles, she causes unhappiness to her child, her first husband's family, and, ultimately, her second husband, Martin Gallagher, a gentle and well-meaning young man. Her first husband's brother and sister, Pat and Sarah Reilly, bitterly resent her for her reserve and distance from them, and for what they perceive as neglect of their brother's memory, even before she marries Martin Gallagher: after the wedding many opportunities exist for reciprocal expressions of meanness and spite. The combined efforts of old Mrs Reilly and Martin Gallagher cannot halt the inevitable movement towards disaster as Vera, pregnant with Martin's child, ignores the obvious signs of her first child's illness, and necessitates a hazardous journey through storm-tossed waters to reach a mainland hospital in time. The little girl dies; the unborn baby dies; and finally Vera, facing her own death, realises too late what she has done:

> "I was spoiled. I was bitter and heartless, but if God allows me to live for a while I'll try to undo it all...I lived for what was to come, and in my foolishness didn't know that this was it. ...We must do our best, enjoy our bit of home and our bit of life now. To live for the future is to live for the fog. Now's the time—now!"[11]

In the journals of the late Forties and early Fifties, McLaverty returns repeatedly to the works of Mauriac, clearly fascinated but apparently baffled by the fact that there is in his work "no Laetare Sunday." Instead, he finds "a stifling depression, a preoccupation with the forces of evil" which are never "offset with analogous effects of joy, charity, kindness and humour."[12] Yet it is hard to find much alleviation in *Truth in the Night* of Vera Reilly's dark and troubled mood. Here, if ever there was one, is a character born to "endless night." It is tempting to see a similarity between McLaverty's title and that of Mauriac's sequel to his novel *Thérèse Desquéroux*, *La Fin de la Nuit*. In his preface to that novel, Mauriac explains his attitude to his troubled heroine, Thérèse, in terms which seem equally applicable to McLaverty's Vera:

> She took form in my mind as an example of that power, granted to all human beings—no matter how much they may seem to be the slaves of a hostile fate—of saying "No" to the law which beats them down...But she belongs to that class of human beings (and it is a huge family) for whom night can end only when life itself ends. All that is asked of them is that they should not resign themselves to night's darkness.[13]

Vera Reilly belongs, with Thérèse, to that family "for whom night can end only when life itself ends." Like Thérèse, in spite of herself, she contrives to "poison and corrupt the lives around her." She deliberately destroys the little model boat made by her first husband, holing it with a red-hot needle so that it sinks in its first race after his early death.

Watching it sink, she knows a terrible moment of retribution, horror and foreboding as she sees her brother-in-law, looking in his desperation like one drowned, struggle to recover the last reminder of his dead brother:

> He swam with bent head; his trousers filled up like sacks of coal and his shirt bellied out and then collapsed like a fallen parachute...He reached the spot and stood for a moment treading water. He breathed deeply and dived, and in a few seconds he emerged, his hands twined with long green leaves, his black hair covering his eyes. He tossed back his hair and dived again, but when he rose once more with a net of weeds about his head the people shouted and waved to him to come in...
>
> Mary was crying and her mother gripped her hand so firmly that it hurt her. She looked at the bobbing head in the water and then turned away. "God!" she said, "what have I done!"[14]

She does not repent, however. As her brother-in-law rejects her offer of her house, that he may dry himself after his soaking, she "cast a look of tight scorn at him and turned away without speaking."[15]

Similarly, Vera feels bound to reject the advances of all those who feel affection for her—her mother-in-law, her second husband, and her own daughter. She tells the young boy whom Martin has adopted that he is illegitimate, causing him to leave the island when Martin is most ill and in need of him. So thoroughly is her character made vitriolic and unyielding that it is difficult for the reader to feel any sympathy for her at all, although her cruelties seem outside her, imposed upon her against her volition. In this, too, she resembles Mauriac's Thérèse. She reaches a kind of repentance in the long night of truth but is not permitted to live.

There are many memorable images and vignettes in the novel, such as the little chestnut tree planted by Vera's daughter, Mary, which she hopes to see grow "like a tent: a green tent in the daytime and a black tent at night," but which outlives her.[16] The island itself is memorably evoked, as here, in the opening paragraph of the novel:

> The L-shaped row of houses above the concrete pier gathered its armful of morning sun, and on the scuffed grass in front of the doors lay a few geese as white as the gables of the houses and whiter even than the stone walls that curved across the flinty fields of the island.[17]

Into this setting comes Martin Gallagher, returning from some unsatisfactory years in Belfast, where he had gone against the pleadings of his elderly parents, now dead. There might have been story enough in Martin's guilty need to farm the land he once rejected, and in his attempts to make welcome, and adopt as a son, the young boy Jamesy Rainey, whom Vera later drives away. There is much in the quarrel between Martin and Vera's brother-in-law, Pat Reilly, precipitated by Vera, to concentrate attention on the necessity for the two young men to learn to live in harmony on the small island, without complicating it even as far as Martin's curiously lukewarm decision to marry the virago Vera. The quiet rhythm of the island is well suggested, and McLaverty's deadly accuracy for language gives him more than one opportunity to bring his people wickedly to life. Here are two island women, gathering their washing, and discussing the likelihood of Vera's bearing more children:

"She's still fresh."

"She is just."

"And Martin's no weakling. He's as broad as the gable end of that house."

"Poor Tom. He was the colour of that sheet you have in your hand."

"But he was kind. Young Mary's the dead spit of him."

"Vera's hard."

"This might soften her. It might indeed...There's a cold snap in that air."

"I think I'll go in with these clothes. The dew could fall on them even when you're holding them in your warm arms."[18]

Reviews of *Truth in the Night*, particularly in America, were very favourable. Indeed Macmillan's publicity director, Virginia Patterson, wrote to him in September 1951: "It is a pleasure indeed to send you the enclosed batch of very good reviews. (I am not withholding unfavourable ones— there are no unfavourable ones!)" Reaction on this side of the Atlantic was more muted, and one or two of the reviews caused the author some concern. One of these appeared in *The Irish Times* on 15 March 1952, commending the author's "vivid prose" and the "remarkable precision" with which he observes "the habits and conventions of a devoutly religious and closely-knit community." This reviewer considered that "the author's picture of the tension between Vera and her dead husband's jealously proprietorial family is the most significant aspect of the story" but that "its success as a novel is impaired by the sudden gallop at which Mr McLaverty takes its ending." It was by no means a bad review, but it elicited the following vehement entry in the author's journal:

> One wonders what is the reviewer's function. Surely he should get below the surface outline, "the story," and ask himself what is the theme—and having possessed the theme he should go on to elucidate it for the ordinary reader. In my case he should have realised that the book was written to uncover a moral truth, viz. that hate and spite and anger (Vera's character) disrupt the individual soul and the soul of a small community.[19]

A sense of disappointment characterised many of the reviews. The *Sunday Times* began by describing McLaverty as "a writer with a fine power of recording the colour and movement of sea and sky, of rain over the hills or sun on the fields" but felt that the novel lacked the "spark of gaiety" and concluded that "a story which might have risen to genuine tragedy remains merely doleful." Even David Marcus, staunch supporter of McLaverty's short stories, felt "a small reservation" and gave only muted praise to the novel in comparing it with Sam Hanna Bell's *December Bride* for *Irish Writing*, in March 1952:

> Mr McLaverty's material somehow seems unequal to his great powers...[and]...one feels that despite the expert achievement of effect and the master-craftsman's

reproduction of detail, Mr McLaverty's picture suffers from
too small a lens and too rigid a focus.[20]

McLaverty's response to this review is not recorded but it
is reasonable to assume from his journal entry after *The
Irish Times* review that he must have been cast down. In
fact he had much on his mind in late 1951 and early 1952,
because his wife was very ill for some months, following
peritonitis, and, although he was already at work on the
novel which would be published in 1954 as *School For Hope*
he found it difficult to concern himself with external
matters. He did not stop thinking about *Truth in the Night*
but seems to have resigned himself to what he perceived as
wilful misunderstanding by the critics. This belief, dating
from the difficulties over the publication of *In This Thy
Day*, seemed to grow stronger with the passing years, and
the journal entries reflect his increasing determination to
write in his own way, however isolated this might make
him.[21] Writing in January 1954 to an American critic,
Blanche Mary Kelly, who had praised McLaverty's work in
a volume entitled *The Voice of the Irish*, McLaverty confirmed
his sense of isolation and resignation:

> I didn't mean it to be the "horribly tragic" book most of
> them made it out to be. I wished to show by Vera's actions
> how hate and spite and anger disrupt the individual soul
> and how this rebelliousness is battered into wisdom only
> by the purgative power of suffering. As a foil to Vera was
> the old woman whom you admired so much: her charity
> harmonised and held things together, love nourishing love
> and fulfilling itself.[22]

Kelly had said, in her article, that in *Truth in the Night*, "it is impossible not to be struck by the resemblance between Vera's experience and the dark night of the soul".[23] Because her understanding of the novel came so close to his intention, McLaverty was able to write to her in a spirit of gratitude, without abandoning his growing sense of isolation as a writer.

He was not unhappy in this self-imposed detachment. His journals of the years 1951 and 1952 reflect a quiet contentment despite the grave worries in his domestic life. Phrases recur, familiar since the late Forties, but crystallising now into a determined philosophy: "Suffering and pain and disappointment are used to keep the soul awake"; "Suffering is the prelude to a deeper and fuller life." Mauriac, whose spirit pervades the atmosphere of *Truth in the Night*, is completely out of favour, as is seen by this entry for 1951: "From a reading of Mauriac one would never conclude that there is a God of love. His work is *stratified* with thick layers of lasciviousness." Instead, writing in 1951, he quotes St Thomas Aquinas: St Thomas: "Sins of the flesh are less grave than sins of the mind, than pride and hatred and despair'".[24]

Though Mauriac was now to be left behind, he had left his mark on McLaverty's work. In *Vera*, the author had fashioned his own Maria Cross, woman as temptress and potential salvation, his own tortured Thérèse, waiting for the end of the night. He had developed his own idea of the stranger, the person apart who could not fit in with the others, and if it was too strong for his usual meticulous style, he had still achieved life and great force in that terrible woman. Without her, he might have written a gentler story but the effort of calling her into being changed his writing, for better or worse, and he would never again be free from the theme of the stranger. Nor would he be free from the sense of exile which he imposed upon himself as a writer and upon his protagonists in their struggle for survival. It is interesting to note that it was then, in 1951, that he jotted down an idea for a novel which has at its heart the kind of joy in renunciation and the necessity of expiatory suffering which so links his work of this time with that of Francois Mauriac:

A man of forty-five has one "shady" incident in his life: an unsuccessful love affair with a married lady whose husband takes an action against our hero. It is published in the paper.

When the novel opens we have him far away from the scene and 20 years ahead of it. He has tried to live it down; he is good at heart—he falls in love with a girl of good family ; she knows there's something on his mind but she can never get to the bottom of it. When out with her mother she visits the town where our hero used to live. Mother tells of her daughter's forthcoming marriage. To whom? To a man called Joseph Doonin—"Joe Doonin"—he seems to recollect, then remembers the incident, says nothing, but leaves mother and daughter worrying.

Into their place arrives a teacher. He meets Joseph and Joseph knows he knows, and knows also that he will tell. To ask him not to would be dishonourable. Arrives one evening and sees the teacher in the home of the girl he loves—the strange silence, strange looks, knows by the looks that the truth has been told about him. At the door the girl hesitates, walks with him; the truth he tells himself—the girl in tears; her love can't beat her pride—they part—he leaves but he's happy, happy in the happiness that revealing his past has given him.[25]

Fourteen years before the publication of *The Brightening Day*, he had scribbled down the outline in this extract. It might have been a most Mauriac-like novel if written in the mood of the early Fifties, but its time had not come and the book which emerged in 1965 is very different from that planned in the excitement of this fruitful phase.

For this was, indeed, a most creative time for him, seeing the beginning of a new novel, and the production of a fine short story, "A Half-Crown," published in *The Bell* in August 1951. This is a very typical McLaverty Belfast story, veering from third person narrative into the grieving memory of an old, lonely woman who accuses her son, wrongly, of stealing a paltry sum, and loses him forever. The theme is not new to McLaverty's writings, variations on it appearing in *Lost Fields*, "Look at the Boats," *The Three Brothers* and, most recently, in the story of the orphan boy in *Truth in the Night*. Sometimes the lost one is guilty; more often not, but always, the grief and regret outweigh whatever indignation may have been felt at first. "A Half-Crown" is a quiet, understated and moving story, and McLaverty handles with skill difficult movements from first to third person. He enters the mind of the old woman with ease, and expresses her plight with compassion devoid of mawkishness. In this extract, young boys collecting the old woman's unwanted sofa for a Fifteenth-of-August bonfire have found embedded in it a half-crown. Its loss, years before, caused her to join with her daughters in accusation of her only son, who then left the house for ever. As she tries to recollect the events of the evening, McLaverty catches unerringly the rhythm and cadence of Belfast speech, encapsulating in the well-worn phrases her unspoken grief for her favourite child:

> ...My mind's wandering on me again. Where was I? Yes, Jimmy washed himself in the scullery and I boiled a fresh egg for his tea. He didn't want any hot water for shaving for he said he wasn't going out. Merciful God, he wasn't going out! He said he was in no hurry for his tea and he'd wait till Mary and Anne had got theirs. He lay on the sofa—his shirt was open at the neck and his face was red and fresh after the good washing he gave himself. I handed him his slippers that I had warming at the side of the hob and I lifted his working shoes to give them a brush or two for the morning. And then when the girls had finished their tea I cleared away the soiled dishes and asked Jimmy to sit over to the table.[26]

It is a story in the same elegiac mood as McLaverty's earliest stories and his first novel, *Call My Brother Back*, in which he recreates the same world of hard-working men and women, expecting little, but appreciative of the fruits of their labour. He conveys too the pride of his people, which could cause a young man to leave like that and never darken again his mother's door. Within the context of the story, and the society of which it is so accurate a mirror, it is entirely, poignantly credible.

McLaverty's gift for the short story had not been lost for lack of use but there was no indication that he would turn back to it. As the judge of a short-story competition run by Queen's University's then student magazine, *Q*, he exhorted the entrants to become "artists of the normal...[for] it is the normal that survives, and it comes from exploring the resources of your own people and your own environment." He suggested, too, that a spell of apprenticeship at the short story would "help the growing writer to find his own personal quality of perception."[27] He had not lost faith in the short story as a form: indeed in December 1951 he wrote, apologising for doing so without introduction, to Mary Lavin, telling her that her collection, *A Single Lady*, "contains, to my mind, a half dozen of the greatest short stories that I have ever read."[28] By 1952, McLaverty believed that he had found his "own personal quality of perception" and the small canvas, however naturally its execution came, was no longer for him. His new novel, interrupted by his wife's illness, was proving difficult but he was determined to proceed with it, and his mood, as he wrote to Daniel Corkery at the Christmas/ New Year period of 1951/2, was contented and optimistic:

I was at work on a new one, but since my wife's illness I had to put it aside. I tried to go back to it last week, to seize it, but, alas, nothing would come that satisfied me and I knew I must wait till I am seized by it. I am more content when I am writing—but I'll have to get back to it soon or turn completely to a new theme. I am more content when I am engaged in a bit of work. My wife, thank God, is now up and around, and the whole house is drifting back to normal.[29]

Corkery had been a potent influence on McLaverty in the latter's early writing years, and it is clear from their correspondence that at that time McLaverty valued the older man's opinion. McLaverty gave Corkery much valuable advice in dealings with the American publisher, Devin-Adair, with whom both were connected in the late Forties, and from this beginning a tentative literary friendship began. Yet Corkery never unbent from his position as mentor and this was to have unfortunate consequences for McLaverty some years later, as Corkery's opinions mattered much to him. Indeed, Corkery's praise of McLaverty's work was genuine but reserved, as when he wrote to him in 1949 about "The Game Cock": "Only for your gift of intimacy, hardly one of them would carry itself through—they are so slight."[30]

Meanwhile, McLaverty was trying to revive his new novel. Writing it proved no easier throughout the first half of 1952, but in September he noted in his journal:

Have taken up my novel again after a long lapse of two months. Convinced, now, that novelist needs quiet so that his people grow according to their nature and not to contrivance. When I have thought out a scene, feel it and hear it, then I am ready to write it.[31]

However, he was not yet quite ready to write it. In a letter of June 1953 to Cecil Scott he regrets that he cannot have the book ready before his vacation at the end of the month, "and my chief delayer in this respect is my own desire for

perfection: perfection of phrase and consistency of mood."
He had seventy thousand words written, however, and these
he sent to Scott, but with an unmistakable air of weariness
over the whole project:

> At times I have misgivings that I am too restrained and
> the style too bare to produce the effect intended. I try to
> suggest, to hint rather than make things obvious. The
> long apprenticeship I spent at the short story because of
> its brevity induces a slow and relaxed response on the
> part of the reader, a response that the same reader seldom
> gives to a longer work written with the same compression
> of style.[32]

In November 1953 McLaverty sent on the remaining nine
chapters. "No book," he wrote to Scott, "ever gave me so
much trouble," and he explained how he had "cut out
thousands of words in an effort to preserve unity of scene
and to use nothing that did not give point and piquancy
to the main theme." Tellingly, he noted that he had
"created" each of his chapters "with the same meticulous
integrity that I'd expend on a short story."[33] Yet, though
Scott liked the novel, and considered it "your best book, I
think," McLaverty was vaguely dissatisfied with it, and
clearly expected little from the unseen enemy, the reviewer.
On 6 December 1953, he wrote to Scott that Cape did not
like his working title, then *Gables of Light*, and proceeded
to explain the place of this difficult book in his moral
canon:

Primarily it's a novel of conscience: the conflict of conscience with desire. But there's much more in it than that because the group counts as much as the individuals. And figuratively the title stands for the core of meaning in all my books: the white and the black, the joy and sorrow in life—and in this book light shines sharply out of it; this is especially true in the character of Mary. I loved writing of her and only wished she could have appeared oftener.[34]

The new title did not please Cape any more than the original, and his firm came up with their own suggestion— *School For Hope*. By the end of December Scott had accepted this, even though he felt that the original *Gables of Light* "is one of your very individual titles; people who like and read your books will recognise *Gables of Light* as the new book by you."[35]

Although the new title was accepted by publishers and author, McLaverty wanted no-one to be in doubt about his commitment to this as a novel of conscience. So, again, on 31 December 1953, he sent to Scott a copy of his summary of the book, prepared to help Cape with the "blurb" for the book's cover:

Is it true that conscience does make cowards of us all? Should a sensitive young girl, who has come to teach in an Irish village school, allow the fact that her mother and sister have died in a sanatorium to dominate her life? Should she obey the dictates of conscience by telling what might ruin her chances of marriage?[36]

It is a good summary of the plot and of the author's overriding concerns at that time. The integration of opposites, and the necessity of suffering as the means to redemption, were his themes but he did not and could not bank down his lyrical gift. It is shown particularly in the opening chapter of the novel, published as "The Miss Devlins" in *The Bell* in February 1953.[37] Here, as completely as in any of his short stories, he suggests the life and even tenor of the ways of the two spinster Devlin sisters and Johnny, their yardman. Through their work and conversation, the dip and sway of their moods and their reluctance to change in any fashion the rhythmic security of their lives, McLaverty brings them to life:

In the mid-summer evenings when they had tidied away the tea-things in the kitchen the two old sisters retired to the sitting-room and there, with the two windows open to the long-legged sun, they sat in front of the pansy-leaf firescreen that hid the empty grate. Some years ago, Elizabeth, the elder of the two, had wrought the firescreen with beads no bigger than a pin-head, but failing eyesight had enforced her to desist from work of such intricacy and, as she was not one who could sit idly in a chair, she was now crocheting a surplice for the foreign missions. Mary, the younger by two years, was sitting with her hands folded in her lap, resting from the day's housework and thinking of tomorrow's, and wondering what she could do now that she wouldn't have to do then. She had no need to worry about the outhouses: their yardman, Johnny, saw to that: the cows milked, the eggs collected from the fowl-house, and the yard swept clean as they had always insisted.[38]

Their days are full of detail and tidiness, small tyrannies and concessions the stuff of their existence. Yet, they are contented and do not welcome the suggestion by the parish priest that they take into their homes a young teacher who has been appointed to the school. Over fifteen pages they agonise and discuss, the thoughts of one sister in counterpoint to those of the other, while the wily Johnny tries to wheedle them out of any plans that might impose extra work on him. It is a scene that would not be out of place in a novel by Jane Austen, because the author employs restraint and a gentle, mocking humour. It has all the qualities of his best short stories, bearing out his claim to Cecil Scott that he had expended on each chapter the same attention normally given to a short story. It stands well on its own: yet it is described, not as a short story, but as "an extract from a new novel." As part of the novel, this lovely vignette has to extend itself into the author's larger purpose, and before long Elizabeth and Mary are drawn into the drama of conscience.

The novel depends for its dramatic and psychological impact upon the love-affair of the young teacher, Nora Byrne, and the headmaster of the school, Peter Lynch. He is forty and she is an unworldly twenty-five; both have lived quiet, uneventful lives and are eminently well-suited. Apart from Nora's morbid—and unfounded—fear that the tuberculosis which killed her mother and older sister will also claim her life, nothing stands between them. It is clearly a groundless fear, as the author makes it clear from the outset that she is a fine, healthy girl:

"Oh, mercy on us!" Nora sighed; and though she seldom indulged in over-eating she forced herself to sample everything she was offered. Mary was delighted for there was nothing she hated more than cooking a meal that wouldn't be eaten, and she was convinced now that a girl like this with such a healthy appetite was sure to be a healthy girl in spite of Elizabeth's anxiety.[39]

Probed by the elder sister about her background, she is understandably reticent, for Elizabeth's questions are searching to the point of rudeness. When questioned about her mother with curiously Dickensian insensitivity—"Forgive me, Miss Byrne, for my carelessness, but I forgot to ask about your dear mother"—Nora replies that she is dead, and that she does not know the cause. It is an understandable riposte but the novel centres on the consequences of this untruth. As the oddly calm, dispassionate romance between Nora and Peter Lynch progresses, the nigglings of conscience felt by the girl assume gigantic proportions. Near the end of the story, she misses by a few minutes the dreadful revelation of her secret by Lynch's bitter sister, who is reminiscent of the sister in McLaverty's first story, "The Green Field." Here is Nora's confession—in every way like one made, not to a lover, but a priest:

> Her moment of truth had come; she bowed her head, and as her fingers picked the white petals off the stem she strove to efface from her soul every lie or half-lie, every concealment of the truth, that had lain so heavily upon her. He listened to her like a priest in the confessional.[40]

Nor does Lynch tell her immediately that this is of no moment to him. His first question picks up her reference to the doctor's examination: "And he discovered nothing, Nora?" Only when reassured does he tell her that she is all to him. He is caution incarnate. She is shriven, and the reconciliation that follows her forgiveness is as passionless for the reader as it appears to be for the participants.

The novel is undoubtedly weakened by the necessity to make central this confession. Nora and Peter are not memorable lovers, though Helen, the bitter sister, has a demonic energy which can cause the reader to be quite sorry for her when, at the end, like the sister in "The Green Field," she is clearly about to be supplanted in her own home by the young teacher. It is difficult not to side with her when Nora, mildly and piously, expresses her hope that they can all be reconciled when she marries Helen's brother:

> "I believe in miracles. And I believe we could all be happy together. It's what I live for. Never in my life have I felt so strong and so convinced that this will be for Peter's happiness, for yours, and for mine."
>
> "For my happiness! What do you know about me— nothing!" She gripped Nora's wrist and Nora felt the pincers of her fingers squeeze numbness into her arm. She saw the ugliness of anger in the face uplifted towards her. She saw particles of food in the crevices of her teeth and caught the unwholesome smell of her breath.[41]

Helen tells Nora to leave, because she will not be welcome when the truth of her past becomes known, and suddenly, inexplicably, Nora agrees. Quickly—too quickly—Helen softens, and immediately Nora returns to her former piety, forgiving Helen, though unable to resist pointing out that "no-one can hold it against you except your own conscience."

These passages, unlike the author's lyrical descriptions or his disturbingly accurate renditions of local speech, do not ring true. Perhaps the novel was difficult to write because McLaverty was somehow conscious of the frailty of the central theme. In fact, he knew when he was writing the novel that the heart of it lay, not in the romance of the young teacher and her headmaster but in the character of the kindly Mary, dominated by her sister, bullied by her neighbour, Helen Lynch, but fulfilled by the surrogate daughter whom she finds in Nora. Clearly, she could not appear more often because of the overmastering necessity of making a moral novel. Yet the story belongs to her, and she deserves more than to fade from it, leaving the room and the stage to the uninspiring lovers and the bitter Helen

It is Mary, not Nora, who is remembered after the novel is closed. It is the school, and the vivid, often frightening descriptions of the realities of teaching unwilling children day after day, which is recalled rather than the teachers. It is only when he writes of the countryside, of teaching, or of his favourite, Mary, that McLaverty finds his natural rhythm. Here, providing Nora with an objective correlative for her dilemma, he is at home:

Around her were the harvest fields, the stooks standing on their shadows, and children's voices carrying far as in the stillness of an evening. But at a turn in the road she

> halted, gazing at a stream that tumbled into a pool as
> brown as a chestnut; a bramble branch arched into it and
> she noticed one thorn wrinkling the water with lines as
> fine as on a snail's back.[42]

Writing almost twenty years later of this passage, in an article appropriately named "Michael McLaverty: The Thorn in the Water," Benedict Kiely described this as one of many such "intimate moments " in McLaverty's work, "when the person and the landscape melt into one another." He concludes that an awareness of Irish society's underlying worries and "ghosts," such as TB, characterises his best work. Yet, surely, there is sufficient thorn in the calm water of Mary's lonely life, or in the inevitable parting of Mary and Nora when Nora marries Peter, or in the equal loneliness of the bitter Helen, without the introduction of the superimposed crisis of conscience over the initial lie.

Reviewers on both sides of the Atlantic were mixed in their reactions to the novel. Some were unqualified in their praise and headings for American reviews include: "A Real Old Fashioned Novel"; "Graceful Writing with Irish Setting"; "Ireland's Poetry Found in Story." The reviewer in *Time*, wrote: "In its quiet, pastoral way, it celebrates nature as well as human nature. No more pretentious than a mousetrap, it captures the novelist's most elusive mouse— a little bit of life." The *Catholic Free Press* of Worcester, Massachusetts, felt that "the steely strength of the book is found in the author's probing of character, his exposition of the impact (sometimes the clash) of life on life, his illumination of the common experience of people no different from one's everyday associates." William B Hill,

S.J., of Scranton, Pennsylvania, was disappointed, considering the novel "a rather tired piece of work, lacking in the animation and consistency necessary for a good novel." To him, the author failed to "make the struggle vivid" but he softened the harshness of this by describing the author as "one of that rare breed, a novelist who combines genius with good taste," and acclaims his "ability to reproduce the beauty that he sees in abundance." Orville Prescott, in the *New York Times*, found the novel, "disappointing, because of the author's excellent earlier works," and considered it an "artfully written but drably uninteresting novel." The reviewer for the London *Times Literary Supplement* was more damning:

> To be successful, this kind of story requires a Chekhovian pathos which Mr McLaverty does not achieve...In the end a reader feels that Irish charm, unharnessed to a solid theme, fails of its effect.[43]

In the *Dublin Magazine*, Teresa Deevy praised the novel unreservedly, while acknowledging that "it still escapes the attention of many."[44]

The author's faith in his novel was not shaken by adverse reviews, and while he welcomed favourable notices, they served only to reinforce his belief in the truth of his mission as a moral writer. In August 1954, he wrote in his journal:

> I use words for their associative subtlety and depth, the exact word, the fresh word, but it must not draw attention to itself. I try to find the "objective correlative" that would evoke the mood I desire or bring out by implication the

inward mood of my characters.[45]

It is not clear whether this entry was made before or after the receipt of a letter from one who had read the book "with full attention." Daniel Corkery wrote to McLaverty on 3 August 1954 the following, shattering judgement:

You must be surprised at my delay in thanking you for your book. I have been having some visitors—in spite of the horrible weather. But I also wanted to get away from the book for I had an uneasy feeling of thinness as a characteristic of it whilst reading it. And to out with an unpleasant impression, distance does not dissipate that feeling.[46]

It was by no means an unkind letter but Corkery felt quite clearly that the novel had failed. No amount of analysis or suggestions for future work could take away that bitter message. Indeed the last words of the letter are: "I fear you will never forgive me for all this."

That McLaverty bore no rancour towards Corkery is evident in the draft of a reply to this letter:

I read your kindly letter (and how well-wishing it is)—not once but many times, and when *you* say my book is thin that is enough for me and I strike it off as a failure. Not that I thought it was that when I had written it. But you made me see why and where. The book in its original form was about twice its published length but I slashed at it in revising it, hoping to make it taut, actionless, but realise now I must have choked the life in it.[47]

This letter, never posted, shows that Corkery could do what reviewers could not, and the author's faith in his own work, and indeed in his ability, was greatly shaken. Meekly agreeing in his projected letter to read Conrad, wondering tentatively whether he might attempt a play, or even turn back to the form he had so confidently rejected, McLaverty seems at his lowest ebb. Not even over the disagreement about the ending of *In This Thy Day* was there ever this note of despondency, of loss of direction.

One thing was certain: however strong his influence may have been in the late Forties and early Fifties, François Mauriac was no longer a model for McLaverty. Yet, with Hopkins, he had been a powerful influence during a time of great crisis, and the result had been one dark, stormy novel and one so closely pared that it had lost much of its action. Now, the tempest over, it was time for the author to take stock and decide what, if anything, was left after "wrecking and storm."

REFERENCES

1   McLaverty to John Pudney, 31 December 1949. See *In Quiet Places*, 141.
2   *Truth in the Night*, New York, 1951, London, 1952.
3   *School for Hope*, New York and London, 1954.
4   *The Choice*, New York and London, 1958.
5   Journal 1952-9. See *In Quiet Places*, 168-94
6   "A Half-Crown," *The Bell*, XVII, 5 (August 1951), 25-33.
7   "Uprooted," *Dublin Magazine*, XXXI, 3 (July-September 1956), 22-35.
8   "The Circus Pony," *Dublin Magazine*, XXXII, 4 (October-December 1957), 23-35.
9   McLaverty to Cecil Scott, 20 November 1949. All letters in this correspondence in possession of McLaverty family.
10 Cecil Scott to McLaverty, 13 November 1950.
11 *Truth in the Night*, New York, 1951, 215; Poolbeg (pbk) edition, Dublin, 1986, 251-2.
12 See *In Quiet Places*, 117-9; 131-5; 150-8; 162-3.

13 François Mauriac. *Thérèse (Desquéroux)*, translated by Gerard Hopkins, Harmondsworth, 1983, 161 (Penguin edition).

14 *Truth in the Night*, 71; Poolbeg edition., 85-6.

15 ibid., 72; Poolbeg edition, 87.

16 ibid., 59; Poolbeg edition, 73.

17 ibid., 1; Poolbeg edition, 7.

18 ibid., 154; Poolbeg edition, 182.

19 Journal, 1952-4; *In Quiet Places*, 162.

20 David Marcus, "From Joyce to Joyce," *Irish Writing*, 18 (March 1952), 44-9.

21 Journal 1952-4; *In Quiet Places*, 162-3; 168-72, 177-8.

22 McLaverty to Blanche Mary Kelly, 27 January 1954. Letter in possession of McLaverty family.

23 Blanche Mary Kelly, "Michael McLaverty," *The Voice of the Irish*, New York, 1952. MS in possession of McLaverty family.

24 Journal 1951; *In Quiet Places*, 155.

25 ibid; *In Quiet Places*, 151-2.

26 "A Half-Crown," *The Bell*, XVII, 5 (August 1951), 25-33. See also *Collected Short Stories*, Dublin, 1978, 122.

27 "Commentary on Short Story competition," op. cit.; *In Quiet Places*, 166.

28 McLaverty to Mary Lavin, 5 December 1951. Letter in possession of McLaverty family.

29 McLaverty to Daniel Corkery, Christmas/ New Year, 1951/2; *In Quiet Places* , 60.

30 Corkery to McLaverty, 21 May 1949. Letter in possession of McLaverty family.

31 Journal 1952; *In Quiet Places*, 168.

32 McLaverty to Scott, 19 June 1953; *In Quiet Places*, 173-4.

33 McLaverty to Scott, 2 November 1953; *In Quiet Places* , 174.

34 McLaverty to Scott, 6 December 1953; *In Quiet Places*, 175

35 Scott to McLaverty, 29 December 1953.

36 McLaverty to Scott, 31 December 1953; *In Quiet Places*,175-6.

37 "The Miss Devlins," *The Bell*, XVII, 9 (February 1953), 529-43.

38 ibid, 529.

39 *School for Hope*, New York, 1954, 34

40 ibid., 205.

41 ibid., 226.

42 ibid., 6.

43 *Times Literary Supplement*, 2 July 1954. Other named reviews in possession of McLaverty family.

44 Teresa Deevy, *Dublin Magazine* (New Series) XXX, 4 (October-December 1954), 79-80.

45 Journal (1954); *In Quiet Places*, 177.

46 Corkery to McLaverty, 3 August 1954. Letter in possession of McLaverty family.

47 McLaverty to Corkery, 9 August 1954 (draft of unsent letter); *In Quiet Places*, 179-80.

CHAPTER SEVEN

THE CHOICE

Corkery's rejection of *School For Hope* was a blow to McLaverty but he recovered. He may have been helped by proofs of faith from other quarters, such as a letter in July 1954 from David Marcus, asking him for a contribution to *Irish Writing*. Marcus, on the point of resigning his editorship of that valuable periodical, wrote: "We are very anxious to have you in our pages before we give up."[1] There is no record of McLaverty's having contributed to *Irish Writing* in that year but he was already recovering from Corkery's criticism by September 1954, when he wrote in his journal: "If a novelist has an attitude to life and the book unfolds this the critics say he is a novelist with a 'message' and proceed to condemn him." He was not prepared to change his view of what was fit material for fiction, for he writes at about the same time in the journal: "Sex: an innate modesty prevents us from speaking in detail about this in our own life. Why then, should a novelist *usurp* this inborn tendency and write in detail in a book?"[2]

Throughout late 1954 and all 1955 McLaverty was engaged in re-assessing his literary position. It is significant that there is no reference to novel-writing during this period, for he was concentrating his energies on two of his early models, Katherine Mansfield and Anton Chekhov, and, significantly, turning again to the short story. By 1956 he would have published two of his finest: "Uprooted" and "The Circus Pony." He resisted, also, the efforts of the BBC to turn some of his short stories into plays, since he felt that one such adaptation, of his story "The Mother" (broadcast by the BBC in 1952) had been a failure. John Gibson, Drama Producer at the BBC in Northern Ireland, sorry that McLaverty had not liked the production, invited him in December 1953 to write "a full-length play specially for radio" as he was "very anxious to get the best writers in Ulster interested in play-writing."[3] McLaverty was not interested, but replied courteously to Gibson's letter, concluding with the words:

> I appreciate your sincere interest in trying to promote radio-drama here, and I should like to be in a position to help you. But since finishing my last novel I have turned to the short-story again and so the writing of a radio-play would not appeal to me at present.[4]

Of more interest to him at that time were his articles on those he considered master-writers. The first, on Katherine Mansfield, was published on 15 January 1955, in *The Belfast Telegraph*. The second, on Anton Chekhov, appeared in the same newspaper on 5 November 1955. Indeed, these two articles stand like protective reinforcement at either end of a year of reflection and decision.

Writing of Katherine Mansfield, he relates her problems of finding her voice to his own conviction that it is only the transcendence of suffering that finally releases a writer to produce his best work. He writes of her last meeting with her brother, soon to be killed at the Front and of the turning-point in her life brought about by his death: "Sorrow releases in her the hidden springs of true feeling, and with love and reverence and humility she decides to write about her own country." He identifies strongly with her, and it is interesting to note that the direction in which he thinks she might have moved, had she lived, is not very different from that taken by himself in 1948:

> She is not everybody's writer. Her stories are almost plotless, concerned with mood rather than incident, with subtlety rather than the obvious, with sensitivity rather than the bareness of fact. if she had lived longer she would, I feel, have probed deeply into the corrupting influences of petty jealousies and hates and absences of love that surround ordinary lives.[5]

Throughout 1955, McLaverty's entries in his journal show his deepening faith in his chosen vocation as moral writer. Added to it is a sense of indignation, almost of anger, that he is so consistently misunderstood. In this extract, dated April 1955, he may be referring, obliquely, to Corkery's criticism:

> I can't understand how it is that in some quarters my novels are regarded as thin and insubstantial. Is that the fate of all artists who hint and suggest rather than state and state concretely and abundantly? To be popular, a writer must leave nothing to the reader's imagination—

give the reader everything and tie everything in a neat
parcel. Leave nothing in doubt. Write always on the
surface.[6]

By May 1955 he echoes again the theme of Donat
O'Donnell's study, *Maria Cross*, writing: "Man's unhappiness
is due to his failure in understanding the meaning of the
Cross. He cries out against disappointment, against suffering.
If he would only accept it..."[7]

In the Chekhov article as in his piece on Katherine
Mansfield, McLaverty feels a close identification with the
subject, and the sober sadness of his introduction sits well
with the stoicism of his own outlook at the time:

> "Life has gone by as though I hadn't lived." That sober
> reflection, one of the saddest Chekhov ever penned, forms
> one of the concluding sentences of his play, *The Cherry
> Orchard*.
>
> It is a sentence that distresses many a man as he realises
> that the years have stolen on him and all the things that
> he intended to do are left undone.[8]

Later, the characteristic McLaverty note is sounded, as he
writes: "A play like his *Three Sisters* or his volumes of short
stories will never be popular: for he writes with compactness,
writes by the line and not by the chapter, making no
concessions to the skimming reader." He praises, too,
Chekhov's "moral involvement, the touchstone of the
greatest fiction, that makes his stories so difficult to
summarise or retell orally." Most of all, he celebrates the
writer's "innate gift for selecting the right incidents to

counterpoint his theme." It is not hard to see McLaverty's own sense of loneliness and isolation as a writer in his comment on Chekhov's gift:

> This gift he would have generously presented to other writers if he had been able. But it was, I suppose, a mystery to himself as it is even to those who read him with the same care and attention by which he wrote.[9]

McLaverty was one such careful reader, and now, once more, he was a short story writer. In January 1956 he wrote to the editor of an American journal, *The Sign*, to offer him "a new short story." Modestly, he describes it: "I think it is a good one, 't least it's as good as anything I have written."[10] Even more modestly, he urges the editor, Fr. Gorman, to send it back if it is not suitable. By 21 February, Fr Gorman had not only accepted the story, named "Uprooted", but had sent a cheque, and McLaverty was furnishing him with minor changes in the manuscript. In this letter, too, there are more stirrings of creativity:

> I am engaged on a novel at present but I have some notes jotted down for short stories and when I get time off I'll see what I can do with them.[11]

So, once again, a novel was forming in his mind, and his return to the short story was to be only a temporary one, something for the rare occasion when he had "time off." Nonetheless, "Uprooted," published in summer 1956 in *The Dublin Magazine*, was a very good one. Set during the Second World War, it is the story of an old man, forced with his family to leave his County Down farm because of compulsory purchase by the government. It awakens echoes of the old man Craig in *Truth in the Night*, especially when the old man surveys the familiar countryside which he must now leave:

> The larks would be free in the sky, but soon there wouldn't be the bark of a dog in the fields, and where children once played there would be nothing but huts peopled with strangers who had no wish to be there.[12]

There is no mistaking the sureness of touch, the precise detail evoking the characteristic elegiac note. Nor can the reader miss the echo of the other earlier story of uprooting, "Stone," when the old man finally struggles back to his home place. Like the grasping Jamesy Heaney in "Stone," this gentle old countryman finds his only security gone; and McLaverty leaves him, like Jamesy, in the moment of his terrible realisation:

> ...Then he stopped and gazed towards the place where his house should stand. But it was no longer there, not a stone of it to be seen. There was nothing but a windy plain with neither tree, nor bush, nor cow, nor sheep upon it...He trembled and gripped the stick in his hand, his eyes resting on the church and the white headstones in the graveyard.[13]

It is a masterly story. No matter how drawn he was to the novel, McLaverty never lost his feeling for the form of the short story. Indeed, despite his avowed intention of abandoning the form, the work of this period shows that this was an impossibility for him. He was constantly drawn back to the shorter form. Certainly, another story was in preparation in 1956 and it was ultimately published in the *Dublin Magazine*, under the title "The Circus Pony" in the autumn of 1957.

Before that, however, grief was to come to the author, for 1956 saw the death of a valued friend, Dan Clarke, headmaster of the school in which he had taught since 1929. A short, poignant entry in the journal marks this break:

> For Dan:
>> From Heraclitus: "I wept when I remembered how often you and I/tired the sun with talking and sent him down the sky."[14]

On 27 July 1957, Teresa Deevy, by then a regular correspondent and family friend, wrote to McLaverty of Dan Clarke's death, incidentally giving some indication of the way in which it had influenced McLaverty's thinking about his future plans:

> You sent me a truly *grand* letter some weeks—or months ago, for there was much in it that appealed to me, moved me deeply. I felt we were very near to one another—you spoke of the loss of your dearly-loved friend. (I had *not* known of this). You apparently had been with him at the end.—This was largely what brought about your application for this responsible position—Michael, may all go well now. I will not forget this in my prayers—Mollie, I'm sure,

is heart and soul with you—I know so well *now* the longing
to be of use—in this very fleeting life...I do social work
now, and find a happiness in it that *strengthens* me—and
yet sometimes I reproach myself saying, "this is an excuse.
Better stick to your own job of writing—that, offered, is
the best of endeavours. Making the most of gifts given is
surely the thing we were meant to do." But I think a time
comes when this gift is benefitted by other useful work,
and that work may take a larger part of our lives in future—
It is a personal matter—a question each must decide...There
now, I hope I haven't been boring and prosy...[15]

The "responsible position" for which McLaverty had applied
was the headmastership of a new secondary school for
boys. Named St Thomas's, and situated on the north side
of Belfast's Whiterock Road, it opened on 2 September
1957. It was an extremely large school, and, as only the
third Catholic secondary intermediate—which meant that
pupils did not have to pass the qualifying Eleven-plus
examination to enter it—it would clearly be of great
importance to the community. To be its headmaster was a
great responsibility. Teresa Deevy, writing in September
1957, comments on the opening, and on the welcome
news that McLaverty had, by working through the summer,
completed a new novel:

That's splendid!—about the novel. I'll be looking out so
eagerly. Yesterday I read *proudly* the accounts of the new
school opened in Belfast—the account in Irish Press...
Michael—this is grand that you worked through the
summer and got the novel finished—How happy you must

feel. And now this new school. I prayed for it, and for you
and Mollie and all...[16]

So, by September 1957, the novel that was to become *The
Choice* was drafted; McLaverty was established in a
prestigious, if demanding new position; and in the autumn
of the same year, "The Circus Pony" appeared in *The Dublin
Magazine*.

This is a story worthy of Chekhov. Four children:—a
boy, Kevin, and his three sisters, Eileen, Rita and the
youngest, Joan—wait for their father to come home. In the
opening sentences of the story, their security, the comfort
and ease of their lives is suggested by the contrast of warmth
inside and the wintry wind outdoors:

> The four children were in the sitting-room, warmly
> sheltered from the cold wind that was sweeping up in
> gusts from the lough. Now and again it flung handfuls of
> hailstones against the window-panes and bumped like a
> mattress against the gable of the house. Kevin, a boy of
> ten, was standing at one of the windows gazing out at the
> dry hailstones as they bounced on the lawn and combed
> through the chilled trees in the orchard. And with each
> shower that passed he saw the hailstones gather in the
> hoof-marks in the fields and lie white as snow on the road
> that switch-backed across the hedgy countryside.[17]

Writing almost twenty years later, Seán O'Faoláin was to
comment: "In a (perhaps over-written) story, 'The Circus
Pony,' winter is handed to us in nine visual words:
'hailstones gather in the hoof-marks in the field.'"[18] Whether

or not it is over-written, and it does not seem so, it is true of McLaverty's gift that in his short stories he can, with startling economy of phrase, suggest in a very few words a mood, a season, or a lifetime's grief.

This is seen not only in the phrase noted by O'Faolain, but in the scraps of conversation between the likable but somewhat spoiled children, who want from the pony (borrowed by their father from a circus until Easter) instant gratification in the form of tricks and performances. To this end, the boy, Kevin—who could be any of the boys of the earliest stories—boasts to his friends of the pony's achievements, and suffers shame and humiliation when the pony does not oblige. One of Kevin's sisters, taunted by the local children, climbs on the pony's back, tapping him lightly with a stick. When the startled pony gallops away, she is thrown and dragged. Hurt in her pride more than her person, she lashes out at the pony, discovering, accidentally and with bitter shame, how to make the pony do his circus tricks:

> And suddenly the pony rose up stiffly on its hind legs, grimaced horribly, the silver bit in its mouth and grass between its teeth.
>
> "Rita! Rita!" Eileen yelled as she and Kevin ran down to her. Eileen snatched the stick and broke it in two, the pony still pirouetting, and breathing with a fearful sound.[19]

The Chekhovian note is sounded in that moment of revelation, and in the sight of the poor animal, standing "subdued, motionless with expectant fear." Nothing is overdone in this revelation of the pony's appalling life, and McLaverty, in a master-stroke, ends the story with a glimpse of the boy Kevin, who knows he has learned a terrible lesson but is too shocked and baffled by the experience to understand it:

> Kevin stared dumbly, now at the pony, and now at the broken stick lying at Eileen's feet. He was thinking of something, something that puzzled him. But what it was he did not know.[20]

This ending was chosen, in fact, after the story had already been published. Originally, in the version which appeared in the *Dublin Magazine*, there was an additional paragraph:

> "Get him to do it again!" came a prolonged shout from the roadside. "Get him to do it again!" But none of the four children seemed to hear what was shouted up at them.

The effect of this pruning underlines the difference between the writing of novels and short stories, since it was to a too drastic cutting of *School For Hope* that McLaverty attributed what Corkery felt to be its "thinness." There is no thinness in the revised ending of "The Circus Pony." Very much aware that, in the short story, so much depends on what is not stated, McLaverty deemed the last paragraph unnecessary: so it was cut for the inclusion of the story in the 1976 volume, *The Road To The Shore*.

This would be the last short story for several years, as the work of the school and the preparation of his new novel occupied him fully. By 23 February 1958 Teresa Deevy was writing to him: "Very exciting about proofs etc.", which suggests that he was nearing publication date. A letter from her, dated 7 May, indicates the extent to which the new duties of the school were occupying McLaverty when she writes: "Michael, do not grow anxious if your school work keeps you from your *own* work.. I know what it is to *burn* for time to give towards creation—but these obstacles, these delays, can, and I think *do* enrich the work later."[21] The novel was published in June by Macmillan in New York, and on 27 July, Teresa Deevy recorded her delighted impressions of *The Choice*:

> Oh! *thank* you—and again thank you. It is good to have an author, today, who writes as you do…That is one strange thing about it—so beautifully simple a story that "excitement" is scarcely to be coupled with it—and yet, to me, this was one of the most *exciting* experiences I've had for a very long time. And *that* lay in discovering the way you *revealed* life of the most ordinary people as a thing of *wonder*, a *thing to be reverenced*. That has always been, to my mind, your aim (as it is mine, in plays). But never before have you done it in so *masterly* a way…Does Mollie agree with me—that this is the *best* of all your novels?— *Three Brothers* comes second with me…[22]

The Choice is a very quiet, understated novel, lacking the fire and storm of *Truth in the Night*, but deeper and truer to human experience than *School For Hope*. Its hero, Tom Magee, faces the choice of the title when he has to decide after his wife's death whether to stay with his grown-up family or follow his long-felt wish to return to the home of his boyhood. The plot is well summarised in a review published in the *Times Literary Supplement* on 29 August 1958:

> ...Tom Magee, a railwayman in the small Irish town of Rockcross, is faced with an important decision when his wife dies. Should he apply for a transfer to his native town, Monabeg, or remain in Rockcross with his children, who want him to stay? He is a gentle, sensitive man with a strong awareness of family ties and the choice causes him great anxiety, particularly on account of his spoilt and selfish daughter, Julia. He finally moves to Monabeg but finds himself there unjustly suspected of informing on a neighbour who has been illicitly distilling whisky. The pace is quiet, the heightened moments are those to be expected in the life of any family...

This reviewer identifies the essential strength of the novel, for here, more surely than at any time since the second novel, *Lost Fields*, McLaverty finds a confident voice, or, as the reviewer puts it, "an emotional key neither too sharp nor too flat." In the four novels between *Lost Fields* and *The Choice*, there is always some note which is too strident for the necessarily low-paced, understated theme. In *In This Thy Day* and *Truth in the Night*, it lies in the intransigence of the two main women characters, Mrs Mason and Vera Reilly, who overmaster the other characters and disturb the balance of the novels. In *The Three Brothers* and *School For Hope*, it is not the characters who are overbearing (for in fact the characters in both these novels are, at times, almost too understated to keep the interest of the reader) but the moral themes themselves which threaten to choke the life of both characters and story. In *The Choice*, the balance is maintained. McLaverty's themes are familiar from the earlier novels: charity—*caritas*—makes life endurable and its opposite, intolerance, expressed in jealousy, spiteful gossip or xenophobia, is death to the individual and to society. Added to this is a Hopkins-like recognition of the necessity of expiatory "wrecking and storm" in the life of the individual; and a Jansenistic feeling, reinforced by Mauriac, that sin is very close to the nature of man, and that at any moment it could swamp the good and destroy it.

In *The Choice*, all the strands of McLaverty's repeated pattern are finally woven smoothly, and emerge from the story rather than sitting heavily on its delicate frame. In Tom Magee, a man whose age corresponds roughly with that of the author, we have a mature hero. Unlike an earlier older hero, the father in *The Three Brothers*, Tom Magee has very difficult problems and decisions to make: he is stretched to the limit. With the death of his wife, he must risk censure from his children if he follow his heart's desire by going home; having decided to go, and carried all the problems of his children with him, he is ostracised as a stranger and an informer by those among whom he hoped to find peace and rest at the end of his days. In a poignant scene, at the beginning of the novel, knowing that his wife must soon die, he settles her for the night:

> He put his arms around her, and with one slow but gentle movement he turned her as she had wished, and as he did so the thinness and lightness of her body struck him with real sorrow, sorrow for the absence of relief and

comfort no one could give her. In the presence of others he could never exhibit his love for his wife but now that they were alone he stroked her head, the thin hair dry to the touch as withered grass. He kissed her on the cheek, and as he made the sign of the cross on her forehead she raised her emaciated hand and stroked his. Neither of them could speak, but each at that moment felt the unhealable break that was coming into their lives. He lay down beside her on the eiderdown, not knowing what to say or what to do. All he desired for her was a sound, deep sleep, a sleep free from one stroke of pain.[23]

Thus, the man who refuses, out of delicacy and reticence, to write about sex, here writes with tenderness and authority of its raison d'être, love. In that passage there are deftness and confidence, qualities absent from his descriptions of the lukewarm courting couple in *School For Hope*.

McLaverty seems to have found in this novel the ability to transpose his gift for the writing of short stories to the different task of novel-writing, and whether or not Corkery's words still affected him, he neither over- nor under-emphasises his theme. Perhaps the best example of this is in his choice of central image. He wants to show the effects of xenophobia, of distrust and spite, and he expresses this in a powerful image of a diseased pike, brought in triumph from the water, then rejected in revolted horror:

A cheer went up as the enormous pike lay choking on the bank, its spiky fins raised like a fan. People pressed close and then stepped back, repulsed by what they saw. On its under-jaw, swollen like a balloon they saw a huge pink growth, wrinkled and layered like fungus, and embedded in it was the glittering spoon-bait streaked with blood.

"Cancer!" somebody said and spat out.[24]

The cancers in the novel, calumny and detraction, are here condensed into one powerful, distressing image. As the story progresses, the notion of disease is evoked from time to time, as when, discovering that his spoiled and spiteful daughter Julia has taken it upon herself to refuse the first offer of a transfer made to her father by the railway company, he gazes at the disturbed waters of the lake, objective correlative for his own mind:

> He came out by the lakeside, now deserted, where a squally wind scattered handfuls of shadow on the water, and coots, disturbed by his presence, jerked like wound-up toys towards the shelter of the reeds. He tried not to think of the letter in his pocket, tried not to accuse Julia, and as he did so the image of the cancerous pike filled his whole mind.[25]

Less successfully, the image recurs in conversation between Tom and his clerical student son, Christy, a curiously lifeless character whose main function seems to be as a mouthpiece for orthodox piety. Here, as he lands a fish, Tom remembers the diseased pike and comments to his son, for the second time, that ugliness stays in the mind longer than beauty. Christy's reply reads like one of McLaverty's journal entries on moral topics: "It's the old warp in our natures hankering to be made more crooked. We remember them in spite of our better natures. And that struggle will go on till the flesh withers away from us."[26] Coming from a young man, not yet ordained, the remark strikes a false note, though his father's reply: "Our natures are warped and bent as you say—there's no doubt about that"—sounds natural, because the speaker is older and knows something of life and human nature. If Christy were the protagonist of this novel, it would surely fail, for he is not a real person; but because the hero, Tom Magee, is a man flawed and imperfect, tempered by hard experience and unwilling to be crushed by the cares of his difficult life, it is possible to identify with him and to wish him success and happiness. In Tom, McLaverty embodies the nature of the struggle to live with the extremes of "joy and woe" and consequently, there is a real sense of grief when, harassed and unable to leave his station long enough to attend his son's ordination, he dies of a heart attack, brought about by the shock of finding that his little fishing boat has been wantonly destroyed by the townspeople. Fortunately, the final elucidation of the moral theme is given, not to the young priest, Tom's son, but to an old man, the parish priest, who might be expected to speak from experience, echoing the author's candid faith:

This man that we pray for this morning is the last of his generation. He loved you too much and that was his undoing. He had respect for what you thought of him and his family, and out of that respect and in order to clear his good name he did not go to his son's ordination. He has cleared his name. But the cost, my dear people, was very high.[27]

The novel ends a few lines later, with the chastened people of the town following the coffin, which is carried by those who accused Tom Magee in the wrong. The last line of the novel, faintly reminiscent of the style of old folk-tales, reads: "And to this day in that countryside a small cluster of people lying among the fields is called Mageestown."

The strength of the novel lies in the fully realised portrait of Tom Magee and in the reader's comprehension of his great loss, suggested most effectively in the short but moving evocation of his love for his wife, quoted earlier. Because of this unity of theme and characterisation, some weaker characters can be carried. These include the drunken son-in-law, given to a swaggering and inexplicable use of nautical terms on all occasions; the shrewish daughter, who reforms so completely after her threatened miscarriage that she is almost a new character in the novel, and is by no means as interesting; and the colourless young priest. One minor character, subject of an interesting sub-plot, is Tom's sister-in-law, Brigid, who, like Nelly in *The Three Brothers*, yearns to be married to the hero but is forced to renounce her hopes. It is her declaration of love to the amazed and confused Tom that causes him, finally, to decide to move away:

"I love you!" broke from her again, but perceiving the crumpled expression on his face she plucked at the dog's leash and fled from the bridge. He stared into the tunnelled road between the moonlit trees. Above the noise of the wind he heard the dog's bell for a moment, and then heard it dwindle and vanish in the distance.[28]

Brigid is a sad character, like Nelly, and McLaverty makes no attempt to alleviate her lonely distress. Like the women in "The Green Field," *The Three Brothers* and *School For Hope*, she exists as an example of the spinster sister in Ireland at that time—lonely, faintly derided by both sexes, and with little to look forward to but an increasingly bitter, solitary old age. Moreover, unlike Tom, she has no choice in what she does. McLaverty, no feminist, nonetheless records faithfully what he sees, and her future is a bleak one.

Reviews of the novel were generally very favourable. Critics noted "the luminous quality of the writing" and "a simple directness whose truth of portrayal stimulates the mind and reaches the heart." McLaverty was acclaimed for his "old fashioned virtues." Several reviewers compared his work with that of Turgenev, one in particular noting that:

> Michael McLaverty has a wonderful feeling for his life in that part of Ireland where traditions still predominate, and he has written a tragedy as true to life, as simple and moving as one of Turgenev's stories. The setting is Ireland: the material is all of human nature.

Others, while praising the novel, thought it "more a long short story than a novel" and that the "episodes of domestic discord and misunderstanding are set forth at inordinate length." The reviewer for the *Catholic World* felt that the end of the novel "seems rather hasty and fortuitous, as though Mr McLaverty were anxious to make an end before he found he had a plot on his hands."[29] Yet each of these, thought it, "a superior novel—unpretentious, appealing, illumined by a haunting and melancholy vision of experience" with a story "real and compelling." No-one thought it thin: McLaverty had rediscovered his voice.

REFERENCES

1 David Marcus to McLaverty, 5 July 1954. Letter in possession of McLaverty family.
2 Journal 1954; *In Quiet Places*, 177-8.
3 John Gibson to McLaverty, 4 December 1953. Letters in correspondence in possession of McLaverty family.
4 McLaverty to Gibson, 13 December 1953.
5 "A Note on Katherine Mansfield," *Belfast Telegraph*, 15 January 1955. *In Quiet Places*, 181-4.
6 Journal, 1955; *In Quiet Places*, 185.
7 ibid.; *In Quiet Places*, 186.
8 *In Quiet Places*, 189-193.
9 ibid; *In Quiet Places*, 193.
10 McLaverty to Fr Ralph Gorman CP, 23 January 1956. Letters in correspondence in possession of McLaverty family.
11 McLaverty to Fr Gorman, 21 February 1956.
12 "Uprooted," Dublin Magazine, XXXII, 4, (October-December 1957), 22-35. See *Collected Short Stories*, Dublin, 1978, 74.
13 ibid.; *Collected Stories*, 81
14 Journal 1956; *In Quiet Places*, 194.
15 Teresa Deevy to McLaverty, 27 July 1957. Letters in correspondence in possession of McLaverty family.
16 Teresa Deevy to McLaverty, 3 September 1957.
17 "The Circus Pony," *Dublin Magazine*, XXXII, 4, (October-December 1957), 23-35. See *Collected Stories*, 267-278.
18 Seán O'Faoláin, "A Northern Laureate," *Irish Press*, 13 March 1976.
19 "The Circus Pony," op. cit.; *Collected Stories*, 277
20 ibid., *Collected Stories*, 278.
21 Teresa Deevy to McLaverty, 7 May 1958. Letters in this correspondence in possession of McLaverty family.
22 Teresa Deevy to McLaverty, 27 July 1958.
23 *The Choice*, London, 1958, 36-7; Poolbeg (pbk) edition, Dublin, 1991, 36.
24 ibid., 54; Poolbeg edition, 54.
25 ibid., 120; Poolbeg edition, 120
26 ibid., 203 Poolbeg edition, 203.
27 ibid., 238-9; Poolbeg edition, 238-9.
28 ibid., 100; Poolbeg edition, 100.
29 *The Catholic World*, August 1958.

CHAPTER EIGHT

THE STRANGER

By 1958, it seemed that McLaverty had regained his confidence. Having steeped himself in the work of his early influences, Chekhov and Katherine Mansfield, he had recovered enthusiasm for one of his first themes, that of exile. No longer reflecting on the concerns of the very young or the very old, he began to concentrate his attention on the particular loneliness of the stranger among friends. Essentially it forms the theme of *The Choice*, but McLaverty did not feel he had exhausted his exploration. Still unwritten, for example, was the projected story of the middle-aged man who had had a guilty affair. A journal entry dated 24 July 1959 shows the theme of exile to be uppermost in his mind:

> On re-reading some of Chekhov's stories I notice the pang
> of exile, of homesickness in many of them. This recurring
> theme gives a poignancy to the stories, an emotional
> compulsion that stirs one almost to tears...And it is this
> homesickness that makes K.M. an artist.

Co-existent with his preoccupation with exile was his

belief—reiterated in a journal entry of 1 January 1959—
that "You can't dissolve suffering but you can transfigure
it." It seemed that McLaverty was now in an ideal position
to explore these themes in the story of the man whose past
would always haunt him.

However, he was not yet ready to do so. Increasingly,
the work of the school took up his time, and in a letter to
a young English author whom he encouraged, Mary Harris,
McLaverty displays a genuine anxiety beneath his usual
self-mocking humour:

> I didn't want you to know that I was a writer, and that's
> why I signed myself "M.F."—a thing I never do. But now
> that you've puzzled out my identity I'm pleased. Like
> yourself I've little or no sales. I just about finger-tip the
> two thousand mark for Cape and in U.S.A. I manage to do
> somewhat better, and as I am not a prolific writer I couldn't
> live on my scant earnings on that line. And what's more
> I haven't written a line for the past eighteen months, for
> I became headmaster of a large intermediate school and it
> absorbs all my time and thought and leaves me fagged
> out at the heel of the day. I haven't even time to read:
> except for re-reading some stories of Chekhov and Tolstoy,
> whom I love, your *Julie* was the first new novel I have
> read in the past year.[1]

This letter indicates two new features of his life—that he
was, willy-nilly, a headmaster first and writer second and
that, perhaps as a consequence of this, he felt the encouragement of the young to be of more urgent importance than
the pursuit of his own work. It is significant that the note

of anxiety is overlaid with one of resignation.

Yet, he was not to be allowed to give in to the pressure of school work. In early 1959, another young writer received encouragement from McLaverty, and the short but intense correspondence which resulted seems to have given McLaverty the energy to resume work. The young author in question was John McGahern, who wrote first to McLaverty on 13 January 1959 to tell him how much he had enjoyed his work. He praised in particular *School For Hope* and had enjoyed *Truth in the Night* and *The Choice*, but felt that "The Circus Pony"was better than anything else McLaverty had written, as it reminded him of Corkery's "Vision" and Katherine Mansfield's "The Young Girl." This letter pleased McLaverty greatly, and he replied on 23 January, thanking McGahern, and setting out for him a programme of further reading—listing such familiar names as Chekhov, Katherine Mansfield, Tolstoy and Mary Lavin. As in his letter to Mary Harris, he notes sadly that he has no time to write:

> I don't teach any more and I regret that greatly. This past eighteen months I'm head of a large secondary school in the city and though the salary is good the administrative work is unrewarding and it leaves me with no time and no energy at the end of the day. *The Choice* was finished two weeks before the school opened and except for a little story, not a good one, written during the Christmas holidays I haven't had time to write or even think of writing, and the thinking is more important than the actual labour of writing. But as each week passes I always hope that the burden of school will lighten and leave me

time to follow the heart's desire. Strange to say my literary work has no following in Ireland, and the novel about the school sold poorly here and yet was a success in Italy where it still sells moderately after two or three years in print. But of all my books I have the deepest affection for *The Three Brothers* and *In This Thy Day*.[2]

Again, the tone of acceptance and resignation is very marked, as though he feels himself to be exiled from writing and in some unfathomable way unable to return to it. Nor does the writing of the "little story," which is not further identified, seem to bring him any satisfaction in its creation. His encouragement of McGahern, however, was of as much benefit to him as to the younger man. Discussion of other writers with a mind so similar to his own stimulated him. McLaverty also encouraged the younger man to make the acquaintance of Mary Lavin, who received him warmly. Meanwhile, McGahern sent McLaverty an extract from a novel on which he was working. On 21 September 1960 he told McLaverty that he would be published in a London quarterly named X in the following spring, and the letter expressed his delight that McLaverty, despite the demands of the school, was working at a new novel. McLaverty's reply contains the generous but precise criticism which is typical of his letters to younger writers:

Your work afforded me the same rush of delight that used to come over me when I saw my algebra teacher write on the board Simplify. To read your work and Chekhov's and Tolstoy's is to convince me that simplicity is the finest ornament of any style; the few words, the right words, chosen for point and propinquity. It was this fine control that fascinated me, for the young are too prone to have the loud-stops full out. Not so with you: each sentence was sharp and effective, each incident achieved without fuss, intimate without being laboured.[3]

By June 1961 McGahern was writing to tell McLaverty that he had withdrawn his first novel from the publishers, but that his work in progress would be published by Faber when it was finished. In July they met in Belfast, and in a letter thanking McLaverty for his hospitality, McGahern expressed the hope that the novel which McLaverty has begun will continue to go well. This is the first indication that a new novel was in progress.

During 1962, McLaverty sent some manuscripts of his early stories and novels to a firm named Hamill and Barker, who were very pleased to purchase them, with a view to placing them in a university. McLaverty made later presentations of his work to Boston University but this seems to be the beginning of his own retrospective view of his work—as though, while still struggling to regain the will to write, he regarded his work as belonging already to the past. It seems to have been part of his sense of resignation to critics' reception of his work. In 1960, he had been extraordinarily helpful to an Irish woman, married and living in France, who was anxious to make him the subject of a thesis for her *Diplome d'Études Supérieures*: again, this suggests a retrospective view, which he had no obvious desire to contradict.

Despite an attack of influenza in September 1962, McLaverty made time to write to John McGahern about an extract from his work which he had read in *Dolmen Miscellany*. His criticism, as before when writing to McGahern, is careful and considered but there is the first trace of disapproval of McGahern's writing:

> There were one or two places where my Northern eye or ear stumbled, found the rhythm upset, or the object blurred. I tripped on "blinded windows" and would have preferred "that beat on the slates and on the windows". And in the dialogue found that the addition of "on us" knocked off balance the line "rich Americans didn't run off with a girl like you."And a point that seemed to me to lack *general* truth was Regan's use of "bejasus" in front of his children.[4]

McGahern thanked him courteously for his careful reading, noting that all his masters, one of whom he considered McLaverty, had written with care. He also rejoiced at the prospect of McLaverty's finding leisure to do what McGahern considered his proper work, his writing, adding that he must not waste his unique gift, even in a good cause.

One or two fascinating references are made in letters to a story which is almost certainly that eventually published as "After Forty Years." Teresa Deevy, in what was to be her last letter to McLaverty before her death in early 1963, mentions such a story in a letter dated 8 November 1962:

> But not one word of the placing of your short story. Have you sent it anywhere. The pair of travellers—just perfect...[5]

A letter from John McGahern at Christmas 1962 also makes reference to a story which reminds him of Joyce's "The Dead": "After Forty Years" shares its central theme of a long dead love who comes between an apparently happy couple. McGahern does not care for the use of the word "flared" used in conjunction with the word "whistle." This seems to be a direct quotation from "After Forty Years" which in its published form contains the sentence: "Then the guard's whistle would flare into the night." There is no record of the story's publication at this time, but the story which was eventually published in 1976 seems to have existed as early as 1962 and is evidence of McLaverty's extrication from the despondent silence which had overtaken him with the onslaught of the work at St Thomas's.

In September 1962 a new English teacher arrived at the school. Writing to McGahern on 26 May 1963 McLaverty mentions this man:

> There's a chap on the staff I'd like you to meet. He has a first class hons in English and though that may suggest to you that he hobbles through literature it's not so in this case. He is creative and is endowed with good taste and discernment and has read and reread passages in your book with unstinted admiration for its style and quiet power. In September he leaves us and goes to the training college as lecturer in English.[6]

This was Seamus Heaney, and his one year in St Thomas's was to brighten McLaverty's life more than anything had done since his arrival at the school. A picture of that year emerges from Jack Holland, a pupil at the time, who

describes Seamus Heaney talking about their headmaster's
literary importance:

> Michael McLaverty was our headmaster...I had no idea of
> his literary eminence until our English teacher, Seamus
> Heaney, explained that in a university in Boston, America,
> his books—which included by then seven novels and two
> collections of short stories—were on display. Until that
> time McLaverty was merely the man who led the morning
> prayers in school assembly, who had a passion for geometry
> and for the poems of Gerard Manley Hopkins and Edward
> Thomas and who occasionally took his long, lithe cane
> out of the glass case in his office to punish refractory
> pupils.
>
> ...It was a rough, violent school, but one unusually
> blessed in teachers of English. McLaverty taught
> occasionally, passing on—at least to this pupil—his love
> of Edward Thomas's work. For one year, Heaney took my
> class (4B) and once brought us on an excursion to
> Carrickfergus to visit the places referred to in MacNeice's
> poem of that name.[7]

Heaney's impressions of McLaverty as a teacher are memor-
ably recorded in his introduction to McLaverty's *Collected
Stories*. His first meeting with him is celebrated in his poem,
"Fosterage", which captures the essential rapport that existed
between them from the beginning, and shows, too,
McLaverty the teacher, guiding the younger man:

"Description is revelation!" Royal
Avenue, Belfast, 1962,
A Saturday afternoon, glad to meet
Me, newly cubbed in language, he gripped
My elbow. "Listen. Go your own way.
Do your own work. Remember
Katherine Mansfield—*I will tell*
How the laundry basket squeaked...that note of exile."
But to hell with overstating it:
"Don't have the veins bulging in your biro."
And then, "Poor Hopkins!" I have the *Journals*
He gave me, underlined, his buckled self
Obeisant to their pain. He discerned
The lineaments of patience everywhere
And fostered me and sent me out, with words
Imposing on my tongue like obols.[8]

Everything that was McLaverty at this time in his life is suggested in that poem—his desire to pass on knowledge, generously and urgently; his abiding faith in his own early models, Katherine Mansfield and Chekhov; and his unconscious revelation to the perceptive young poet of his own "buckled self," tortured and scrupulous as Hopkins himself. It was McLaverty who first introduced to Heaney the excitement of Kavanagh's poetry, and he gave him also, as Heaney mentions in the poem above, his own copy of Hopkins's *Journal*. Always generous with his library as with his time, he made with this gesture a gift of more than usual significance, for McLaverty felt then, as now, that Seamus Heaney was "the only genius I ever met," and it is doubtful that he would have given his copy of Hopkins's *Journal* to anyone else.[9]

This professional collaboration lasted only one year, though the friendship then begun has endured; but, with Heaney's departure to St Joseph's Training College in 1963, McLaverty felt even more the difficulties of running St Thomas's. In the autumn of 1963, he took, finally, the decision to retire as headmaster, and, although the cutting of this tie cost him much anxiety, he felt relieved when the decision was made. On 6 December 1963, he wrote to Cecil Scott:

I sent in my resignation to the Board of Governors a short while ago and they pleaded with me to withdraw it but I didn't, and I won't. I have agreed to stay until the end of the school-year viz. June 30th 1964. It will be a great relief for me to get away from it. It was slowly killing me, and to stay any longer would not only destroy the good health that God has given me, but would also thwart the creative spirit left in me.

...Meanwhile, at home, my novel was in full spate, and for the first time for two years I foresaw it in its completed state. It has suffered a set-back in the last two weeks, but as I am now, I may say, my old self, a free man, I'll be back at it shortly. I have about 17 chapters finished and have about 4 to go, and recently when I read it aloud to my wife she said it was the most interesting of all my books, one that would hold a reader.

...Half a dozen of my stories which I wrote years ago are still going the rounds here and on the continent and that gives me quiet confidence in the novels for they are all written with the same care as the short stories and with the same regard for the truth.[10]

Slowly, imperceptibly, confidence returned, as he began to see the end of the drain on physical and emotional energy which St Thomas's had become. It shows itself almost immediately in a note dated 29 November 1963 to another young writer, Brian Friel, about his play *The Blind Mice*, which had been broadcast on radio:

> I wrote a note to you today in school, but with the constant interruptions that are now my daily round that note has gone astray.
>
> What I want to say is this: your play last night moved me as no other play since hearing *Autumn Fire* broadcast from Dublin, a few years ago. There were many beautiful touches in your play: the birds alighting on the roof of the cell, the yelp of the dog that was kicked, the tin plate pushed under the door, and the Burmese face at the grille—this last touch emphasised for me Hopkins's line: "To the Father through the features of men's faces." The ending of your play was as poignant as Murray's *Maurice Harte*, a play rarely seen nowadays.[11]

He was to resign at the end of the school year, and gradually his confidence and energy seemed to return. In an entry in his journal dated 5 May 1964, he reminds himself of the need to persevere with his art:

> One has arid periods: better, then, to seek bright companionship.
> "If you leave your art for a day, it will leave you for three."

> Don't wait for inspiration—sit down and write and
> the ideas will flow. After wakening in the morning after
> a long sleep begin to think about what you will write that
> day. Keep going. Sometimes what you re-read of your
> own seems dull and insipid. Don't destroy it—read again
> in a better mood.[12]

These words seem intended as a reminder to himself, in his
new-found buoyancy, of the depths to which his spirits
had sunk. In the letter to John McGahern dated 26 May
1963, in which he had spoken so warmly of Seamus Heaney,
he had also recorded his deep despondency at his failure to
work at the novel: "I have typed nothing at the novel for
the past months and won't be able to look at it till August.
I just can't write while I'm harnessed to the school." Now
that he was so nearly free, all seemed possible once more.

Yet, his transition was not entirely straightforward. He
had looked forward to his retirement and planned that his
long delayed return to writing should be as joyous as it
would be fulfilling. Unfortunately, he had reckoned without
the inevitable droop in spirits so often attendant upon a
major change, and, at first, he could not write at all. Roy
McFadden, his friend since the early Forties, records in his
poem, "D-Day," the flat disappointment of the beginning
of McLaverty's retirement:

> The family grown, his pension was enough
> For careful husbandry.
> Waspishly he swept aside
> Gnats of accountancy,
> Released to write his masterpiece for love.

He groomed his desk, dusted with deference
The touchy typewriter;
Discharged and fuelled fountain pen,
And tapped the paper square:
Adjusted to celestial audience.

But it was not compelling. Undismissed,
The centipedal street
Occluded with occurrences.
While he, irresolute,
Contended with the self's recidivist.

Collapsed tweed hat askew, dismissed, he stole
Out to the urgent air;
Reviewed the beans and lettuces,
The slugs' gelatinous spoor;
And combed and petted the ecstatic soil.[13]

This poem, poignant and precise, refers to an incident told to McFadden by McLaverty himself. He sat in his accustomed place, ready to write, but was distracted by the sounds of children on their way to school. The long days of summer had not worried a man accustomed to annual weeks of leisure but now it was September, and, for the first time in thirty-five years, he was not going to school. The silence, broken by the children's noisy passing, was no longer peaceful and, to escape it, he walked about his garden. When he returned, however, the page remained blank and the house lonely. He could not write.[14]

Now, if ever, he needed to spur himself into action. Always before, there had been some definite obstacle between him and his writing: now there was only himself. Perhaps a realisation that he would have to take time to adjust was the reason for his advice to John McGahern to rest before undertaking another project: "Watch your health and take a long breather before embarking on new work."[15]

However, there were signs of hope. Macmillan in New York had taken his new novel, at this stage entitled *The Stranger*, and McLaverty had signed the contract in July, adding in a note to Cecil Scott: "I do hope you'll have good luck with this book."[16] Scott was in no doubt, feeling that the book was "a quiet book, of course, but...also an extremely good book."[17] In a letter to John McGahern, dated 15 January 1965, McLaverty reveals much about his life at the time, less hopeful than earlier about his new novel, and voicing also his disquiet at what he hears of McGahern's next work:

> I got your very welcome letter before Christmas and would have answered it before this only I was laid up for a short spell, and when I was on my feet again the proofs arrived from New York and I worked hard at them and returned them to Scott in record time. The book is to be called *The Brightening Day*, Cecil Scott having discovered that there was already a book published in the States with the title *The Stranger*. The new title seems to me a better one: it's an optimistic one that may attract a few extra readers. I told you in a previous letter that Cape turned the book down, and now that my staunch friend Jonathan Cape is dead his successors reminded me that my last four books were remaindered and didn't think the new book would do any better. I don't blame them one bit and we parted

good friends and still correspond with one another. After receiving Cape's decision I offered the English rights to Macmillan in New York; their London office will distribute it over here. It may not have been a wise move on my part but it's done now and I needn't grumble.

...I really haven't settled down yet since I retired and find it no easy thing to do. I'm told it takes a year or more to adjust oneself to a new routine.

John, the few sentences you wrote to me about your new novel have saddened me. More anon when I hear from you.[18]

Cape's rejection had undoubtedly disappointed McLaverty, and contributed to his low spirits. By autumn he was ill and, as he wrote to McGahern, roused himself only sufficiently to correct the proofs of the novel. On 26 April he wrote to Cecil Scott: "...I hope the novel will pay its way and not let you down—one never knows."

Macmillan's publication date was set for 24 May 1965. On 23 May, he wrote to John McGahern, trying as honestly and sincerely as he could to indicate his very mixed feelings about McGahern's new novel, *The Dark*:

I have read your new novel and was greatly impressed by its painful sincerity and its pared-to-the-bone style, a style that has caught the essentials and has left the verbal flotsam and jetsam to the best-selling novelists...The book rings with truth at every turn and it must have been a heartbreaking and exhausting book to write. I recoiled from one or two pages (a priest's thoughts) and wished they hadn't been there though I realise that not a line of it was written out of a weakness to shock or degrade. The final chapters, which I found compassionately moving, do justice to Mahoney as a father and as a man and demonstrate that you have the maturity and fairmindedness of a true novelist.[19]

The measured criticism of this honest letter indicates most strongly the predominance in the writer's head of moral responsibility: in tone it resembles Corkery's equally strained letter to McLaverty himself, after the publication of *School For Hope*. Nonetheless, when McGahern's novel, scheduled to go on sale in Ireland in May, was held by customs and subsequently banned by the Irish Censorship Board, McLaverty wrote warmly and encouragingly to McGahern, who was then living in Spain. Thus their correspondence continued, sporadically, over the years; but, although affection and regard have remained, the two men's writing paths diverged sharply at this point and their fruitful correspondence was effectively ended.

By 9 June, McLaverty, writing to Cecil Scott, was in buoyant mood:

Thank you very much for your cablegram and good wishes on the day of publication of my novel. I haven't seen any reviews of it yet and I am hoping that it will receive some good ones.

In this hope he was to be disappointed. Reviewers noted his style and lyrical power, but no one praised the novel. A review published in *The Belfast Telegraph* on 2 September summarises the plot, adding a thinly-veiled comparison with McGahern's banned novel:

The claim on the blurb that Michael McLaverty is an Irish writer of the stature of Frank O'Connor invites the keenest criticism of the Belfast author's latest novel, *The Brightening Day*.

For beside an O'Connor story this is mild fare. A young school teacher has fled his home town after a scandal in which, needless to say, he was totally innocent. He settles in a remote Northern village, in an isolated cottage.

He earns his money by giving private lessons to the crippled son of a widowed mother in the local big house. He gradually establishes himself; there is a delicate suggestion of romance with his pupil's elder sister, home on holiday from a Scottish university.

Then his "secret" threatens to upset everything. He is tempted to run again. He stays, pupil passes all his exams, and all ends well, as we always knew it would. The story moves along on a cosy cushion of sentiment. The atmosphere is nineteenth century.

But perhaps the blurb comparison to O'Connor should not be taken too seriously. It also describes the village as being on the west coast, whereas it can hardly be anywhere else but Strangford. For those who are prepared to accept *The Brightening Day* as a simple sentimental tale, it is well told and satisfying as such.

Not for nothing have four of Mr McLaverty's books been selected by the Catholic Literary Foundation. He is in no danger of being banned in the Republic.[20]

Not all of the reviews were as crude or as cruel. The reviewer of the *Irish News* compared the author, favourably, with Kickham, and concluded:

> Mr McLaverty is not to be tempted into forbidden ways either in his description of love-making or into the more subtle methods used by some modern fictionists. Four of his novels have been selected by the Catholic Literary Foundation. He gives us a readable, pleasant story of people one might meet at home or at the seaside, acting in ways that neither excite our passions nor induce overmuch surprise. In short, he presents us with a racy, interesting novel of Irish middle-class life today.[21]

Kindness, too, can be harmful, though the reviewer clearly does not intend to damn with faint praise. Yet this is the effect of such reviews, in their way more damaging than the *Telegraph*'s heavy derision.

Nor was this merely a local reaction. McLaverty's novels had always been well received in America but in this case, the reviews were poor. Mairin Elias in *Best Sellers*, dated 1 June 1965, called it "a slow-paced novel about some rather dull people in a peaceful setting on Ireland's sea-coast" which rather takes away from her later well-intentioned but clichéd observation that "the Irish setting is picturesque and the simple life in a country village is real and enchanting." The *Library Journal*'s reviewer considered the novel "in general a saccharine and superficial book" and concluded that "this is one title which the American public can easily dispense with." Nor was the author's attention to scrupulous morality to escape the notice of American reviewers. Martin Levin, writing on 18 July 1965 in the *New York Times*—a newspaper which had in the past given McLaverty some of his best reviews—virtually dismissed the novel:

> The Erotic Revolution has evidently not yet touched Northern Ireland, of which Michael McLaverty writes with the moral certainty of a Victorian novelist...There is a fresh regional piquancy in the author's visions of small-town life.[22]

The Brightening Day was a failure. What had happened to make it so, from its first inception in the author's mind as the story of a man who had had an affair with a married woman and, guilt-ridden, tried to forget it in the love of a young girl? This, as far back as 1951, was the genesis of the novel. This hero, a man of mature years, was to renounce his love for the girl when she discovered his guilty secret and be glad and grateful for the chance to expiate his sin in the act of renunciation. Apart from the unusual complication of a guilty affair, this would have been familiar McLaverty territory; and even the guilty affair would not have been out of the question in 1951, as he worked through his preoccupation with Mauriac. Somewhere, in the years between, a shadow had fallen between ideal and reality, and what was left was a dim reflection of the original idea. Moreover, just as *Lost Fields* was influenced and strengthened by the author's reading of Duhamel's *Le Notaire du Havre*, so was this novel coloured and possibly weakened by McLaverty's reading, in 1961, of Turgenev's *A Month in the Country*. That nineteenth-century play is transposed to late twentieth-century Ireland, and the result is a static, anachronistic tale.

The young hero, Andrew Wade, leaves his home because of an unjust accusation of flirtation with a married woman, a friend since university days. The young man is patently innocent, and consequently the obloquy that is heaped upon him and the relentless pursuit of him throughout the novel—because of what becomes his guilty secret—simply hangs upon too thin a pretext. Had he been guilty in thought or word, let alone deed, there might have been justification for his mental torture and the righteous indignation of those who become his friends in his new home. Yet, all that anyone can accuse him of is having reversed his Christian names, so that he becomes John Andrew Wade instead of Andrew John; he has been wrongly accused and sued for damages following an incident so trivial as to be unbelievable. Into this, there falls the plot of *A Month in the Country*, in which a young tutor inspires the love and desire of the mature woman who is his charge's mother. In *The Brightening Day*, Andrew Wade becomes tutor to a young crippled boy, Philip Newman, whose mother becomes attracted to Andrew. This causes her much soul-searching, and indeed could have been a strong point in the novel, as Nelly's love for her niece's suitor strengthens and humanises *The Three Brothers*. Mrs Newman's mild infatuation does not strengthen the novel but stretches it thin because the woman has no cause for self-accusation. The mother in Turgenev's play has already one guilty liaison behind her but Mrs Newman's life is an open book. Her searching of conscience, then, as she reflects on Andrew's revelation of his relatively blameless past and her own unwitting attraction to him, seems singularly overscrupulous and joyless.

Seán O'Faoláin, writing in 1976, noted this tendency, marking it as McLaverty's one essential weakness:

> ...The only quarrel I have with Michael McLaverty is that being so extremely Catholic (with the capital "C") he has limited the universality, the catholic (small "c") element we expect from every writer of fiction. He tends to take refuge too often inside the cloistered, conventual, doctrinal, even theological hermitage of his Church.[23]

The central idea of renunciation, of privation as a means of expiation, is rooted in McLaverty's literary sensibility, and it is because of this that he requires that Mrs Newman renounce her feelings for Andrew in favour of her daughter; that her daughter Anne, who has suffered already one broken engagement, should now be rewarded by the love of a good man; and that her son, Philip, should give up his position as Andrew's friend and confidant in order to make way for his sister. Equally, it is necessary that Andrew suffer torment and be sorely tried, before being judged worthy of the prize of the young, innocent Anne. Whether or not this is true to human experience is irrelevant, because in this novel the moral purpose, which threatens to overmaster all the novels from *The Three Brothers* onward, finally accomplishes its end. Consequently, much that is strong in the novel is sublimated beneath the overriding and insistent doctrine of renunciation and expiation. Because of this, the reader cannot fully savour the precise and evocative descriptions of Strangford; the character of the

Newmans' grandmother, who is worthy of a story to herself, as she flees the imagined persecutions of the Jews; and the two central dramatic conflicts—that of Andrew as he tries to rise above the ruins of his past, and that of Mrs Newman as she struggles to suppress feelings for a younger man. It was this relentless insistence on the moral import of the novel which caused O'Faoláin to take the author to task. McLaverty, with his gift for the "catholic," the universal, captured in Blake's "grain of sand," chooses instead to compel his gift in another direction and force it in ways it would rather not go. That is why the original idea of 1951 for a novel of conscience, of a man regretting his folly and living with the consequences, becomes refined out of existence in this work. Even as it occurred to him in 1951, McLaverty was already transcribing in his journal the words of the Dominican scholar, Fr Gerard Vann, on Mauriac.

> And what of the other problem: the harm that may be done to the reader? Here again a certain robust good sense is needed. Ethics is not an exact science: if every artist waited for an absolute guarantee that this work would have ill-effects on nobody, nothing would ever be done...Incitement to sin is, like modesty, a relative term...but though it is not the office of the novelist to teach, the fact remains that he does imply and inculcate a view; he does affect the minds of his readers...[24]

The influences exerted upon McLaverty by Hopkins and Mauriac in the Forties changed his course as a writer. Almost thirty years afterwards the effect remained and McLaverty remained bound by his own conscience. Consequently he sacrifices to his moral theme the lost undeveloped story of the old grandmother and her canary:

> The canary cheeped, stretched out one wing and then the other, and beat an arpeggio on the perch as if in time to the music of the piano. The old lady smiled at its antics and poked the temples of her spectacles between the bars of the cage, watching the canary grow thin and cock its head to the side.
>
> Mary slipped away from the room, and the old lady joined her hands; drowsy from the heat and the softly playing piano, she closed her eyes and turned her mind back to the days when she was young and hunted with the hounds across the frosted fields.[25]

Even the central symbol of the little homemade boat which is ritually burned each Christmas in the Newman family is imbued with extra significance but fails to match the stark poignancy of the other symbolic model boat in "The Schooner," or the bitter sadness of the sabotaged model boat in *Truth in the Night*. Instead, the precise and evocative description of its funeral pyre gives way to a tableau, pointing out Andrew's symbolic position as the man of the family:

> The top of the oil bowl was removed and Andrew struck a match and lit the wick that projected from a metal disc based with cork. The light shone red on his face as he crouched on a little platform of stones and pushed the boat into the pond. Its bow wrinkled the water like a concertina. Andrew stood up, Anne beside him; Philip stood with his mother, her hand resting on his head in

the darkness.[26]

What is saddening about *The Brightening Day* is that it contains in its pages vivid images and deftly drawn characters, all swamped by its overstated moral theme. It is a pity that the hero could not have been the flawed middle-aged man he was originally intended to be, so that his love for the young girl might have had in it an added poignancy and his planned renunciation of that love an extra dignity. What a pity, too, that it could not have been this older man that Mrs Newman came to love, for then there might have been further conflict in her realisation of both his in erest in her daughter and his unsuitability for either of them because of his past.

The blameless youth of *The Brightening Day*, who thinks and responds like an older man, does not awaken sympathy. He is not, as the originally planned protagonist might have been, the stranger of McLaverty's original title, and the prototype of Mrs Newman would have been in no danger from him. In effect, the author "purifies the source" beyond recognition and, in so doing, removes much of the original's vitality. The moral tone of the book is beyond reproach but it lacks human conflict.

More than ever, it was McLaverty himself who was now, in the world in which he launched forth this work, a stranger. To an extent, he had felt this sense of distance since his declaration of independence over the ending of *In This Thy Day*. It had grown through the later Forties and, particularly, in the Fifties, as he became aware of the difference between his world view and that of others. Yet, he had always believed that, given time and leisure, he could write the novel that would prove to the world the rightness of his moral position. With his resignation from St Thomas's, it seemed that that time had come and it was a matter only of waiting for the success of *The Brightening Day* before he could renew his career as a writer. Now, instead of acclaim, he received rejection. It had happened before: but after the difficulties of *In This Thy Day* he had had *The Game Cock*'s success; and after Corkery's dismissal of *School For Hope*, he had had the warm reception of *The Choice*. And always, when writing failed him, he had had the school. Now, in 1965, he no longer had even the school and his sense of exile was complete.

REFERENCES

1 McLaverty to MK Harris, 12 April 1959. Letter in possession of McLaverty family.
2 McLaverty to John McGahern, 23 January 1959; *In Quiet Places*, 195-6.
3 McLaverty to McGahern, 23 March 1961; *In Quiet Places*, 200-1.
4 McLaverty to McGahern, 27 September 1962; *In Quiet Places*, 205.
5 Teresa Deevy to McLaverty, 8 November 1962. Letter in possession of McLaverty family.
6 McLaverty to McGahern, 26 May 1963; *In Quiet Places*, 207-8.
7 Jack Holland, "Clinging to Old Pieties," *Fortnight*, 280, January 1990, 26-7
8 Seamus Heaney, "Fosterage," *North*, London, 1975, 71.
9 McLaverty in conversation with Sophia King, 1982
10 McLaverty to Cecil Scott, 8 December 1963. Letter in possession of McLaverty family.
11 McLaverty to Brian Friel, 29 November 1963; *In Quiet Places*, 208-9.
12 Journal 1964; *In Quiet Places*, 209.
13 Roy McFadden, "D-Day," *A Watching Brief*, Belfast, 1979, 33-4.
14 Roy McFadden in conversation with Sophia King, January 1991.
15 McLaverty to McGahern, August 1964; *In Quiet Places*, 210.
16 McLaverty to Scott, 29 July 1964. Letters in correspondence in possession of McLaverty family.
17 Scott to McLaverty, 7 December 1964.
18 McLaverty to McGahern, 15 January 1965; *In Quiet Places*, 210-1.
19 McLaverty to McGahern, 24 May 1965; *In Quiet Places*, 217-8.

20 Dennis Kennedy, "Is This Man as Good as O'Connor?" *Belfast Telegraph*, 2 September 1965.

21 CH, "An Ulster Novel of Today," *Irish News*, 24 August 1965.

22 American reviews collected in *Book Review Digest 1965*, ed. Dorothy P Davison and Josephine Samudio. New York, 1966, 819.

23 Seán O'Faoláin, "A Northern Laureate," *Irish Press*, 13 March 1976.

24 Journal 1951; MS in possession of McLaverty family.

25 *The Brightening Day*, New York, 1965, 111; Poolbeg (pbk) edition, Dublin, 1987, 111.

26 ibid., 141; Poolbeg edition, 141.

CONCLUSION

THE SILKEN TWINE

Joy and woe are woven fine,
A clothing for the soul divine.
Under every grief and pine
Runs a joy with silken twine.[1]

It seemed to McLaverty, in 1965, that critics and the reading public had failed to comprehend his purpose in *The Brightening Day*. This was no surprise to him, for he had believed since the mid-Forties that his work would not be understood. There is no doubt that he was grieved by what seemed the public's indifference. Indeed, a letter from Cecil Scott, dated 18 February 1966, shows that McLaverty had declared to him his unwillingness to write any more novels. Yet, though this letter displays the extent of his disappointment, it also reveals a joy beneath McLaverty's sadness. To his great delight, he had been invited to teach part-time at St Joseph's Training College, where Seamus Heaney was then a lecturer:

You sound so happy in getting back to your teaching, and
I could not help thinking of that earlier letter when you

were obviously unhappy. I am glad that things have worked
out so well for you.

You say in your letter that you do not intend to write
another novel. Well Michael, I do not believe you. I think
I shall be getting another novel from you, and no-one will
be happier than I when the manuscript reaches my desk.[2]

McLaverty's reply, dated 13 March 1966, indicates the extent
to which he had thrown himself back into the profession
which he had earlier wanted to leave:

I have been very busy and very happy lecturing on the
teaching of English to the postgraduates in the College.
They are now out in the secondary schools in the city
doing their practice of teaching, a practice that will last
four weeks and keep me busy from nine until four each
day supervising their work...

But this is really what I wish to say. Would you think
of publishing a volume of short stories? I know that
publishers hate the sight of them arriving in their office
for they scarcely ever sell more than 2000 copies.[3]

Once again McLaverty had found new vigour and hope, in
teaching and the short story. One of the stories he sent to
Scott for the projected anthology was "After Forty Years"
which had existed as early as 1962 but seems not to have
been published at that time. Although Scott decided,
reluctantly, that a volume of short stories would not sell
sufficiently to make it profitable, he told McLaverty, in a
letter dated 19 April 1966, that all the stories sent him
were "first rate" and that "Uprooted" and "After Forty Years"

were "great stories." He suggested instead of a volume of McLaverty's stories an anthology of the author's own favourites, including "Chekhov, de Maupassant and other English and French writers in it." Scott felt that McLaverty would "find real joy in roaming over literature" and that the finished product, with an introduction and some critical commentary from McLaverty, would "be a most distinguished book."[4] He also thought it would sell well. Sadly, although McLaverty and Scott planned the anthology together over the next two years, it did not materialise, partly because of McLaverty's poor health during the late Sixties, and partly because of the death of Cecil Scott.

What emerges from the proposal is the idea of a new anthology of McLaverty's stories—an idea which he had rejected in the late Forties in the rush of enthusiasm to write the moral novel and forget the shorter form. In the late Sixties his own interest resurfaced, perhaps as a result of his disappointment following *The Brightening Day*. A letter from John Boyd, dated 18 July 1966, confirms that the novel's failure still distressed McLaverty, despite his new-found satisfaction in teaching at St Joseph's:

...You are a writer like Forrest Reid: after all, the best-sellers of last week are forgotten the week following. I certainly don't think you should be discouraged after the poor sales of *The Brightening Day*. I remember that *Following Darkness* received very poor sales to begin with and only came into its own twenty years later when it was re-published as *Peter Waring*. You must go on despite the indifference at the moment. Again remember Henry James...[5]

Boyd also warned McLaverty, at least half-seriously, not to let his teaching work become "too absorbing." Yet, something was needed to absorb McLaverty's energies, for there was little hope at that time for his novels. He had considered trying to have *Call My Brother Back* re-published, and to this end had submitted it to Mercier Press in 1964. Nothing came of this, as McLaverty himself withdrew the offer, because he felt the shipwreck scene in Part I was "false and untrue to the decent people of Rathlin Island" and because "much of Part II is also out-of-date and belongs to bitter history."[6] The novel would not be reprinted until 1970 and until McLaverty had endured as many rejections as he had for *In This Thy Day* in the Forties. Through the Sixties it was turned down by Faber, Gill and Macmillan and Dolmen, before being printed by Allen Figgis in 1970.

If *Call My Brother Back*, the novel that made its author's name, could not find a publisher in the Sixties, there seemed little hope for the subsequent novels. His London publishers, Jonathan Cape, who had declined to publish *The Brightening Day*, gave him very little cause for optimism about the others, as is seen in a letter from G Wren Howard, chairman of Cape, dated 7 November 1967:

> You have every right, as provided in the various contracts, to claim back all the rights you originally gave us in respect of the seven titles listed in your letter, and to this I willingly agree. All the books are, as you well know, out of print, and it would not be economically possible to reprint them in present circumstances.[7]

By 19 May 1968, McLaverty wrote to a Sister Marian

Dominic, in answer to a query about his work, that "my writing mind has deserted me or I've deserted it. I've written nothing only a shorty story or two during the last two years."[8]

One of these "shorty" stories was "Steeplejacks," about which he had expressed reservations to Cecil Scott when they were thinking of a collection of McLaverty's stories. On 10 August 1968, "Steeplejacks" was published in *New Irish Writing* in the *Irish Press*. This was a new but prestigious forum for new writing and, from its beginning in April 1968, its editor, David Marcus—who had also edited its important predecessor, *Irish Writing*—had made it clear that he wanted to include the best writers, new and established. Mary Lavin had already written for it, as had John McGahern, Edna O'Brien, Julia O'Faolain, Maurice Leitch and John Banville. When McLaverty's story was published, David Marcus in his usual biographical paragraph accorded McLaverty his place as "one of the most distinguished of contemporary Irish writers."

The story is a fine one, taut and controlled, about the art of the steeplejack, seen through the eyes of an experienced professional and a boy of eighteen whose nerve fails him. The seasoned climber looks down with calm contentment at the town spread out below him as he reaches the top of the brick chimney which dominates the story:

From the broad lip of the chimney he hauled out abandoned jackdaws' nests and flung the bundles of sticks into the air, and after putting his hammers in a straw basket that was suspended from a pulley block he plucked at the rope and signalled to his men to lower away. He watched the basket move to the ground in short, irregular jerks, and before descending the ladder himself he looked across the fields to the houses at the edge of the town where smoke rose untroubled from the chimney pots and freshly washed shirts hung limp from the lines in the backyards.[9]

McLaverty rediscovers here the confident style of his best short stories: if one did not know that this was his work, the "freshly washed shirts" on the line and the smoke from the chimneypots would give a very strong clue. Similarly, by describing the landscape as seen through the young man's eyes, he conveys terror and consequent unreadiness for the task of climbing the chimney:

He paused, frightened. Above him he saw the ladder converge at the top like railway lines. He had a long way to go yet, and on looking down to measure his distance from the ground he saw, in one swaying moment, the old drying sheds buckle and stretch like an accordion. [10]

The point is not overemphasised. The youth is rescued by Rooney, the experienced steeplejack, and recovers, slowly, with encouragement from the other men; but his hand shakes as he accepts a cup of tea. Then, the focus of the story is changed, skilfully, as the reader notes the reaction of Rooney and the frightened young man to the sight of a small boy climbing the unattended ladder. John, the eighteen-year-old, is terrified and runs in panic for the fire-brigade. Rooney watches the boy, coolly, knowing that he has it in him, not only to climb to the top, but to become a steeplejack when he is grown. Not only does the boy go to the top, but he comes half-way down, and climbs up again, strolling round the lip of the chimney like Rooney himself and touching the lightning conductor. When, called by his mother, the child shoots down the ladder, the reader feels the unspoken contrast with the older John's blind panic.

The story ends with a somewhat comic meeting between Rooney and the child's mother. Rooney tells the astonished woman of her son's exploit, and the boy, like many a McLaverty boy before him, hangs his head and "pluck[s] at a loose thread on his jersey." Rooney tells her he is "a born climber, a born steeplejack" and her reply, as she contemplates her "heartscald" of a son, is that "he'll not be able to climb into bed when I'm done with him." Rooney leaves as the bell of the now unnecessary fire-brigade is heard in the distance, mentioning casually over his shoulder that "there's good money in it." McLaverty knows the people of whom he writes and he is well aware of the different complexion which the prospect of a good job in the future might place upon the child's escapade.

After a disappointing series of rejections of *Call My Brother Back*, McLaverty tried Allen Figgis of Dublin, although he was so lacking in optimism that he asked Figgis to send it on to the Dolmen Press if he did not want it, as "this would save it another trip across the border." He also described it as "my most popular [novel] but not my best."[11] His luck had turned however, for Figgis was prepared to publish it. McLaverty wrote to him, in glad mood, on 27 May 1970:

Yes, the terms and conditions are o.k. The book will be a
success—I'm sure of that. Seamus Heaney says you'll never
regret it...Good luck. I'll do something I never did in my
life: boost a book of mine round the schools.[12]

The novel was a success. By March 1971 it had sold over
two thousand copies, and was soon being used in schools
as a textbook. It is a pity that Figgis, who had expressed
interest in seeing other novels of McLaverty's with a view
to publishing them, was unable to do so. However,
McLaverty was no longer dependent on him. The re-
publication of *Call My Brother Back* had brought his work
to the attention of a new generation of readers, and people
wanted to see more of his work, all of which was then out
of print. David Marcus, who had known of McLaverty's
gifts for almost thirty years, was engaged with Philip
MacDermott in the setting up of a new publishing house—
Poolbeg Press. By 1975, ten years after the idea had first
been discussed by McLaverty and Scott, Marcus was
planning, with McLaverty, a Poolbeg collection of the
author's short stories, to be called *The Road to the Shore*.

This was a happy time for McLaverty, ushering in what
was to be an unexpected late flowering of his work. Since
1970, having left St Joseph's, he had been teaching part-
time in St Dominic's High School, one of Belfast's best-
known grammar schools for girls. He enjoyed the work
and the ambience of the school, talking to the senior pupils
of Chekhov, Tolstoy, Katherine Mansfield and Hopkins.
This meant that he had the double satisfaction, throughout
the Seventies, of knowing that he could teach again, and

that people once more wanted to read his work.

For suddenly his writing had a new public. Reviews of *The Road To The Shore* were very good, and it was on this occasion that Seán O'Faoláin published his review on McLaverty—"A Northern Laureate"—in which he said that the author was too "Catholic" to be "catholic." His prime example for this was *The Brightening Day* but he felt that this obtrusive Catholicism was leavened, and even redeemed by "'the life-giving drop'; that is the saving little tinge or smart or sting of reality that salts the lyricism." This O'Faoláin found in "Six Weeks On and Two Ashore," "Stone," "The Schooner" and "that darlint' story 'The Poteen Maker'. "

How does McLaverty suggest the passing of a goods train? By a powerful, long, rumbling, realistic description? He says that a glass tinkled on a dresser. A day after rain? He mentions the wet lobes on the ears of corn in a field of barley. [13]

It was this sense of "the freshness that lives deep down things" that caused people to read *The Road to the Shore*, in, as Dervla Murphy expressed it in *The Irish Times*, "one spellbound sitting." As well as the stories mentioned in the extract from O'Faoláin's review, the collection contained stories long out of print, such as "Evening in Winter," "The White Mare," "Steeplejacks," "The Circus Pony," "The Wild Duck's Nest," "Uprooted" and the title story, "The Road to the Shore." Also included were two of his most recent stories, the 1965 "Mother and Daughter," and, at last, the story discussed as early as 1962 in McLaverty's letters to Teresa Deevy and John McGahern—"After Forty Years."

On the day that O'Faoláin's review of the collection was published, David Marcus gave over his *New Irish Writing* page to "After Forty Years." Nothing could have been more appropriate, for this is McLaverty's "The Dead," at once a celebration and a lament, and a perfect example of the way in which, within the short story, it was possible for him to be both Catholic in the religious sense and catholic in the universal sense.

It is the story of an elderly couple, married for forty years, who are travelling by train to Derry, on their way to Donegal for their first holiday since the husband's retirement. In the course of their journey, they pass through Toome and, oddly, inexplicably, the husband, John, is disturbed by the name—a kind of melancholy Adlestrop. It emerges that he taught there, when he was fresh from teacher-training college and enjoyed an innocent friendship with a young married teacher. Her husband was cruel to her and she looked to him for companionship in the course of the working day. Reluctantly, pressed by his wife's curiosity, he tries to explain the delicate balance of their association and of his conscientious departure from Toome in order to avoid scandal. He pleads with his wife to understand but she cannot, and their peace of mind, their mutual understanding and harmony together, is irreparably broken. The wife suffers the fate of Gabriel Conroy in pressing her spouse to tell her his thoughts, and he, lost in the memory of the young woman's accidental drowning shortly after his departure, is by the end of the story far away from the woman he married:

"Their boat was found capsized. A sudden squall must have struck it. The mainsail, you see, had been tied—it said so in the papers...Her husband's body was washed ashore on one of the islands, but hers was never found...never found...It was probably carried down the river in flood and into the sea...To think she died like that, and she so young, so light on her feet, and so thoughtful of others...God have mercy on her."

He leant back against the headrest and closed his eyes. His wife continued her knitting with grim speed, the train rattling loosely on its journey through the night.[14]

It is a story of the quality of "Six Weeks On and Two Ashore" but its poignancy arises as in "The Dead" from the fact that the revelation is forced from an unwilling teller, who has long ago learned to live with the sadness of lost love. Indeed, the word "love" in relation to his friend of long ago seems not to have occurred to the husband until his wife uses it in bitter accusation. As in "Six Weeks On and Two Ashore," telling detail is used to suggest what is happening. Joyce used snow as his objective correlative: McLaverty uses a train and a pair of knitting needles.

At the beginning of the story the couple are comfortable, attuned to each other's familiar if irritating habits, and content to travel in companionable silence. The train, like a Greek Chorus, marks the changes from happiness to misery. It hisses as it passes the end of the platform where John reads the long-forgotten name of Toome, and while he gazes, dumbfounded, the train leaves the town behind. As he tries to field his wife's questions about his short stay in Toome, the train's movement underlines his awkward but determined attempt to escape from the danger area:

> Over the long flat stretch of land the train stretched out
> eagerly, their shoulders jogged and swayed, and the back
> of the man's head rubbed against the leather headrest.[15]

They are still united, their solidarity threatened only by the wife's curiosity, but this very desire to know leads her, unwittingly, into an area which is beyond her, and from which, once in it, she has no escape. When John describes the teacher's singing of an old melody, they both know that something irreparable has happened, and the train is used to express this break:

> "I knew it couldn't go on...When I saw the tears in her
> eyes it took my whole strength to hold back from lifting
> her hand and kissing it...And the way she could sing. I
> used to pause in my work to listen as she led the children
> through 'The Last Rose of Summer.' That song, God knows,
> is sad enough. But the way she sang it made it the saddest
> of all songs."
>
> The train whistled and the wheels rocking unevenly
> over a road crossing drowned his voice, and he clasped
> his hands and drooped them between his knees and fell
> silent.[16]

When she accuses him of having been in love with the teacher, he rejects the idea with the simplicity of the truly innocent: "Ah, how could I be and she with a wedding ring on her finger?" He tells her that he knew he had to leave "for my own soul's sake." The final-straw is the revelation that a fountain pen of John's was given to him by the young teacher. The fact that he has never used it, and has indeed offered it to his wife for her own use, helps not at all: the bond is broken. She distances herself from him, physically as well as mentally, and as he thinks of the young teacher's lonely death, she knits, as we have seen, "with grim speed" and the train, its rhythm now disjointed as their marriage, continues "rattling loosely on its journey through the night."

It is an ideal vehicle for McLaverty's themes: here is a hero more innocent than Andrew Wade in *The Brightening Day*; more isolated than Tom Magee in *The Choice;* and here the Catholic—in the sense that John must leave to avoid an occasion of sin—merges with the universal, catholic themes of the blurring of love with friendship, jealousy, possessiveness and renunciation. In this he transcends *The Brightening Day*, because he uses his gift to the full. He suggests but does not explain: he depicts but does not underline. It is a story of great delicacy and strength, a powerful, poignant coda to his life's work.

For, with the publication of *The Road To The Shore*, McLaverty's work could be said to be complete. More stories were gathered into the equally satisfying and well received *Collected Stories* which Poolbeg brought out in 1978, and whose contents Walter Allen described as "small miracles."[17] The only previously uncollected story in that volume was "The Priest's Housekeeper," an amusing anecdote based on the experience of a priest of McLaverty's acquaintance but not a story of the calibre of "Steeplejacks" or "After Forty Years."

It was with the publication of *The Road to the Shore* that there began the long-awaited Indian summer of McLaverty's work. In 1978 he was invited to speak at Listowel Writers' Week. Poolbeg brought out *Call My Brother Back* in 1979 and is continuing to reprint all the novels. In 1981 Queen's University, Belfast where he had taken his Bachelor's and Master's degrees in Science in the Twenties, awarded him an Honorary Master of Arts degree. In 1982 Poolbeg published his children's story, *Billy Boogles and the Brown Cow*, described by himself as a story "about the wicked giant Billy Boogles, twins Arthur and Anne Mac Neill and of course Browny the cow with the magic in her tail." In that same year, he won the American-Irish Literary Foundation's prestigious annual award of $10,000, in recognition of his "impressive body of work as a short story writer and novelist." The foundation went further, stating precisely why they found McLaverty worthy of this award:

He infuses his precisely detailed descriptions of the life of a boy on a Belfast street corner or a family on a Co Down farm with a poet's imagination and with piercing insights into the human heart and conscience.[18]

At last, he was recognised. Nor was the American-Irish Foundation alone in seeing him as a poet in prose. Walter Allen, in his review of *Collected Short Stories*, dated 12 October 1978, expands on Seamus Heaney's comparison with Hopkins:

He is a realist, but as Seamus Heaney points out in his perceptive and warmly appreciative introduction, that word alone is insufficient to describe him for at bottom his stories are poetic. Heaney sees parallels between them and the poetry of Gerard Manley Hopkins. These I can see, but for me, McLaverty's stories are much more closely suggestive of Wordsworth's lyrics which anticipate uncannily so much of the manner and the matter of the modern short story. [19]

Seamus Heaney had said in his introduction that "his love of Gerard Manley Hopkins is reflected in a love of the inscape of things, the freshness that lives deep down in them, and in a comprehension of the central place of suffering and sacrifice in the life of the spirit—never in that purely verbal effulgence that Hopkins can equally inspire."[20] Today, reviewing the career of McLaverty, Heaney echoes Allen in his comparison with Wordsworth:

It is a case of a career that has a structure like Wordsworth or Hugh Mac Diarmid—perfectly crystallised occasions of his characteristic genius at the beginning, done speedily and instinctively and apparently effortlessly—followed by an artistic maturity when self-consciousness and the ambition for self-transcendence strain and ultimately impair the original sense of inevitability.[21]

His novels, after the first two, caused severe strain on a nature finely attuned to delicacy and lyricism, as though a painter of miniature water-colours had set himself to cover a vast canvas in oils. For twenty years, from the time of his bid for artistic independence in 1945 over *In This Thy Day*, until the bitterness of the public's rejection of *The Brightening*

Day, he struggled hard to marry his intricate artistic vision with the heavy demands of the realistic twentieth-century novel. He described, from experience, the fine interweavings of Blake's "joy and woe." For a time, it seemed that woe would predominate. Yet, always, at his lowest points—when publisher after publisher rejected *In This Thy Day*, when Corkery told him *School For Hope* was a failure; when *The Brightening Day* failed to bring him the recognition he sought; and when even his first novel, *Call My Brother Back*, seemed doomed to be ignored by a new generation in the late Sixties—there surged Blake's joy, in the form of his short stories. His ability to write them, untouched by the severe moral constraints placed upon himself in his novels, brought him back from these brinks of despair. After *In This Thy Day* he wrote "The Mother" and "Six Weeks On and Two Ashore"; after *School For Hope* he produced "Uprooted" and "The Circus Pony"; after *The Brightening Day* there came "Steeplejacks." All of these grew steadily, almost unnoticed, virtually disregarded by their creator as he forced himself yet again into the difficult harness of novel-writing. Yet, as by a miracle, when *Call My Brother Back* was finally accepted by Figgis for re-publication, a body of uncollected stories had grown sufficiently to form a brand-new book. Suddenly, readers had the McLaverty for whom they had been waiting. It was but a short step from this to the collection of the other stories, long out of print. In writing these stories McLaverty had woven, almost unknown to himself, his silken twine, the joy that would relieve and rationalise the many griefs and vicissitudes suffered by him in his years of servitude to the moral novel.

And what of these moral novels? They were written, as McLaverty himself has said, with the same care and attention which he devoted to his short stories. We remember from them the moments of inscape, the pure epiphanies of his vision—a lonely old woman, dreaming of her youth, riding to hounds; a cancerous pike poisoning the tranquil river; another woman, clutching her rosary but unable to pray as she realises the loss of her only son; yet another, doomed to lonely spinsterhood, listening to the despairing calls of cattle on their way to the slaughterhouse; an old island man, forced to live in the city when his heart and mind yearn for Rathlin; and ever, the thorn disturbing the peace of the calm water. Add to these the clear, spare moments of truth in "Six Weeks On and Two Ashore," "The Circus Pony," "The Wild Duck's Nest" and—perhaps the quintessential McLaverty story— "After Forty Years," and there forms in the mind a composite picture, a symbiotic union of happiness and grief. Together, these images give a sense of McLaverty's legacy to literature: his own, unique auguries of innocence.

REFERENCES

1 William Blake,"Auguries of Innocence," *William Blake*, ed. Michael Mason, Oxford Authors Series, Oxford, 1988, 29.
2 Cecil Scott to McLaverty, 18 February 1966. Letter in possession of McLaverty family.
3 McLaverty to Scott, 13 March 1966; *In Quiet Places*, Dublin, 1989, 218-220.
4 Scott to McLaverty, 19 April 1966. Letter in possession of McLaverty family.
5 John Boyd to McLaverty. Letter in possession of McLaverty family.
6 McLaverty to editor Mercier Press, 27 November 1964. Letter in possession of McLaverty family.
7 G Wren Howard to McLaverty, 7 November 1967. Letter in possession of McLaverty family.

8   McLaverty to Sister Marian Dominic, 19 May 1968. Letter in possession of McLaverty family.
9   "Steeplejacks," *New Irish Writing, Irish Press*, 10 August 1968. See also *Collected Short Stories*, Dublin, 1978, 243.
10 ibid.; *Collected Stories*, 244-5
11 McLaverty to Allen Figgis, 16 February 1970. Letter in possession of McLaverty family.
12 McLaverty to Figgis, 27 May 1970. Letter in possession of McLaverty family.
13 Seán O'Faoláin, "A Northern Laureate," *Irish Press*, 13 March 1976.
14 "After Forty Years," *New Irish Writing, Irish Press*, 13 March 1976; *Collected Stories*, 101.
15 ibid,; *Collected Stories*, 95.
16 ibid,; *Collected Stories*, 97.
17 Walter Allen, "Small Miracles," *Irish Press*, 12 October 1978.
18 Citation of the American-Irish Literary Foundation, June 1982.
19 Walter Allen, op. cit.
20 Seamus Heaney, introduction to *Collected Stories*, 9.
21 Seamus Heaney in conversation with Sophia King, 13 December 1990.

SELECT BIBLIOGRAPHY

PRIMARY SOURCES

NOVELS

Call My Brother Back, New York and London, 1939
Lost Fields, New York, 1941; London, 1942
In This Thy Day, New York and London, 1945
The Three Brothers, New York and London, 1948
Truth in the Night, New York, 1951; London, 1952
School For Hope, New York and London, 1954
The Choice, New York and London, 1958
The Brightening Day, New York and London, 1965

SHORT STORY COLLECTIONS

The White Mare and Other Stories, Newcastle, Co Down, 1943.
Stories included are: "The Game Cock"; "The White Mare";
"Moonshine"; "The Prophet"; "Look at the Boats"; "A School-
master".

The Game Cock and Other Stories, New York, 1947; London, 1949.
Stories included are: "The Game Cock"; "The Wild Duck's
Nest"; "The Road to the Shore;" "Father Christmas"; "The
White Mare"; "The Mother"; "The Prophet"; "Aunt Suzanne";
"The Poteen Maker"; "The Schooner"; "Pigeons"; "Look at
the Boats". The London edition includes one extra story not
found in the New York volume: "Six Weeks On and Two
Ashore".

The Road to the Shore, Dublin, 1976. Stories included are: "The
Road to the Shore"; "The Poteen Maker"; "Uprooted"; "Six
Weeks On and Two Ashore"; "The Wild Duck's Nest"; "The
Circus Pony"; "Mother and Daughter"; "The Schooner"; "After
Forty Years"; "Stone"; "Steeplejacks"; "Evening in Winter";
"The White Mare".

Collected Short Stories, with an introduction by Seamus Heaney, Dublin, 1978. Stories included are: "The Prophet"; "Pigeons"; "Aunt Suzanne"; "Stone"; "The Priest's Housekeeper"; "Uprooted"; "The Game Cock"; "After Forty Years"; "The White Mare"; "A Half-Crown"; "Evening in Winter"; "The Mother"; "The Poteen Maker"; "The Road to the Shore"; "A Schoolmaster"; "Six Weeks On and Two Ashore"; "The Wild Duck's Nest"; "Look at the Boats"; "Father Christmas"; "Mother and Daughter"; "Steeplejacks"; "The Schooner"; "The Circus Pony".

PUBLISHED ARTICLES BY MICHAEL M^CLAVERTY, IN CHRONOLOGICAL ORDER

"The Young Poets," *The PEN in Ulster*, Belfast, 1942.

"Michael McLaverty explains his methods in writing as he sketches background of *The Three Brothers*," *Forecast*, Milwaukee, Wisconsin, August 1948, 6-7.

"Letter to a young novelist," *The Key*, London, 1948.

"Commentary on short story competition," *Q*, 1952. (Q was at that time the name of the students' magazine at Queens University, Belfast.)

"A Note on Katherine Mansfield," *Belfast Telegraph*, 15 January, 1955.

"Anton Chekov—a man of sympathy and a gentle, ironic humour," *Belfast Telegraph*, 5 November, 1955.

UNPUBLISHED ARTICLES AND LECTURES BY MICHAEL M^CLAVERTY

"Irish Fiction," lecture to Young Ulster Society, 27 February, 1940.

"The Irish Short Story,", lecture to Belfast branch of Irish PEN, March 1940

"The Novel," unpublished essay, 1941.

Lecture on Gerard Manley Hopkins, to Belfast branch of Irish PEN, 1944.

"Night and Day; A Note on Literature," text of talk delivered to Queens University English Society, 2 December, 1949.

(Texts of the above, with the exception of *The Irish Short Story*, are in *In Quiet Places: the Uncollected Stories, Letters and Critical Prose of Michael McLaverty*, ed. Sophia Hillan King, Dublin, 1989.)

SECONDARY SOURCES

ARTICLES ON MICHAEL M^CLAVERTY, IN CHRONOLOGICAL ORDER

McFadden, Roy, "A Note on Contemporary Ulster Writing," *Northman*, XIV, 2, (Winter 1946), 20-26.

Fiacc, Padraic, "Good and Evil: Prolegomenon to a Study of McLaverty's Work," *Irish Bookman*, I, 5, (December 1946), 37-41.

Hoehn, Rev Matthew, OSB, *Catholic Authors: Contemporary Biographical Sketches*, (First Series), 1930-1947, Newark, New Jersey, 1947.

McCarthy, Abigail Q, "Catholic Literature—and Two Irishmen," *Today*, Christmas 1947, 16. McLaverty is one of the authors discussed in this article.

Boyd, John, "Ulster Prose," *The Arts in Ulster*, ed. Sam Hanna Bell, Nesca Robb and John Hewitt, London, 1951, 99-130. McLaverty is one of the writers discussed in this article.

McHugh HA, CSSR, DCL, "Michael McLaverty, Novelist," *The Redemptorist Record*, XV, 4, (July-August 1951), 98-100.

Kelly, Blanche Mary, Litt D, "Michael McLaverty," *The Voice of the Irish*, New York, 1952.

Brian, Sister Mary, OP, "The Stories of Everyman," *Today*, (January, 1959), 32-35.

Martin, Augustine, "Inherited Dissent: The Dilemma of the Irish Writer," *Studies*, 54, (Spring 1965), 1-20.

McMahon, Sean, "The Black North: Prose Writers of the North of Ireland," *Threshold*, 21, (Summer 1967), 158-174. McLaverty is one of the authors discussed in this article.

Kiely, Benedict, "Michael McLaverty: The Thorn in the Water," *Hibernia*, 34, (17 July 1970), 11.

Foster, John Wilson, "McLaverty's People," *Éire-Ireland*, 4, (Fall 1971), 92-105.

Donnelly, Brian, "Michael McLaverty: An Appraisal," *Irish Press*, 2 March, 1974.

Heaney, Seamus, Introduction to *Collected Short Stories*, Dublin, 1978, 7-9.

King, Sophia Hillan, "Conscience and the Novelist: Michael McLaverty's Journals and Critical Writings of the Forties," *Studies*, 78, No. 309, (Spring 1989), 58-71.

King, Sophia Hillan, "Quiet Desperation: variations on a theme in the writings of Daniel Corkery, Michael McLaverty and John McGahern," *Aspects of Irish Studies*, edited by Myrtle Hill and Sarah Barber, Institute of Irish Studies, Queens University, Belfast, (Belfast, 1990), 39-46.

ACADEMIC THESES

de Micheaux, Mme Raymond, "An Ulster Novelist: Michael McLaverty," unpublished thesis presented to Université de Lyon, for Diplôme d'Études Supérieures, 1960.

Foster, John Wilson, "Separation and Return in the Fiction of Brian Moore, Michael McLaverty and Benedict Kiely," unpublished doctoral dissertation, presented to University of Oregon, 1970.

Despois, Colette, "Introduction to Michael McLaverty's work with a translation of three short stories and a stylistic comment on the translation," unpublished Travail d'Études et de Recherches, presented to Université de Paris-Sorbonne, 1981.

King, Sophia Hillan, "Explorations of Fictional Form: Michael McLaverty's Stories, Novels and Criticism 1932-1950," doctoral thesis, presented to The Queen's University of Belfast, October 1987.

POEMS DEDICATED TO MICHAEL M^CLAVERTY

Fiacc, Padraic, "North Man," *The Selected Padraic Fiacc*, Belfast, 1979, 8.

Heaney, Seamus, "Fosterage," *North*, London, 1975, 71.

McFadden, Letter to an Irish Novelist," *Flowers for a Lady*, London, 1945, 45; "Second Letter to an Irish Novelist," *Threshold*, 21, (Summer 1967), 82-3; "D-Day," *A Watching Brief*, Belfast, 1979, 33-4; "Reunion," *Letters to the Hinterland*, Dublin, 1986.

OTHER WORKS CONSULTED

ARTICLES

Corkery, Daniel, "Ourselves and Dean Swift," *Studies*, 23, (June 1934), 202-218.

Corkery, Daniel, "The Nation That Was Not a Nation," *Studies*, 23, (December 1934), 610-622.

Shaw, Francis, SJ, MA, "The Celtic Twilight," *Studies*, 23, (March 1934), 24-41.

Shaw, Francis, "The Celtic Twilight: Part Two—The Celtic Element in the Poetry of WB Yeats,"*Studies*, 23, (June 1934), 260-278.

POETRY, PROSE AND LONGER CRITICAL WORKS

Allen, Walter, *The Short Story in English*, Oxford, 1981.

Allot, Miriam, ed., *Novelists on the Novel*, London, 1959.

Bell, SH, Nesca A Robb, John Hewitt, ed., *The Arts in Ulster*, London, 1951.

Blake, William, *William Blake*, ed., Michael Mason, Oxford Authors Series, Oxford, 1988.

Cather, Willa, *Not Under Forty*, London, 1936.

Colet, Roger, trans., *Selected Short Stories*, by Guy de Maupassant, Harmondsworth, 1979.

Friedland, Louis S, ed., *Letters on the Short Story, The Drama and Other Literary Topics* by Anton Chekhov, with a preface by Ernest J Simmons, revised ed., London, 1964.

Garnett, Constance, trans, *Select Tales of Tchehov*, London, 1927.

Connolly, Cyril, *Enemies of Promise*, London, 1938.

Corkery, Daniel, *Synge and Anglo-Irish Literature*, Cork, Dublin, London, 1931.

Corkery, Daniel, *The Threshold of Quiet*, Dublin, London, 1917.

Cowley, Malcolm, ed., *Writers at Work: The Paris Review Interviews*, First Series, Harmondsworth, 1981.

Daiches, David, *The Novel and the Modern World*, revised edition, Cambridge, 1960.

Deane, Seamus, *A Short History of Irish Literature*, London, 1986.

Duhamel, Georges, *Le Notaire du Havre*, Paris, 1933.

Eliot, TS, *After Strange Gods: A Primer of Modern Heresy*, London, 1934.

Fallis, Richard, *The Irish Renaissance: An Introduction to Anglo-Irish Literature*, Dublin, 1978.

Foster, John Wilson, *Forces and Themes in Ulster Fiction*, Dublin, 1974.

Gardner,WH, ed., *Poems and Prose of Gerard Manley Hopkins*, Harmondsworth, 1978.

Gibson, James, ed., *Chosen Poems of Thomas Hardy*, London, 1975.

Harmon, Maurice, *Select Bibliography for the Study of Anglo-Irish Literature and its backgrounds*, Dublin, 1977.

Hayes, Richard J, ed., *Manuscript Sources for the History of Irish Civilisation*, 3, Boston, 1965.

Hopkins, Gerard, trans, *The Knot of Vipers*, by François Mauriac, Harmondsworth, 1985.

Hyde, Douglas, trans, *Religious Songs of Connacht*, Dublin, 1906.

Hogan, Robert, *Dictionary of Irish Literature*, Dublin, 1980.

House, Humphry, ed., *The Notebooks and Papers of Gerard Manley Hopkins*, London, 1937.

Ireland, Denis, *From the Irish Shore: Notes on My Life and Times*, London, 1936.

Joyce, James, *Dubliners*, London, 1914.

Kiely, Benedict, *Modern Irish Fiction: A Critique*, Dublin, 1950.

Kilroy, James F, ed., *The Irish Short Story: A Critical History*, Boston, 1984.

McGahern, John, *The Dark*, London, 1965.

McGahern, John, *Amongst Women*, London, 1990.

Meyer, Kuno, trans, *Selections from Ancient Irish Poetry*, London, 1911.

Moore, Brian, *The Lonely Passion of Judith Hearne*, London 1955.

Moore, Brian, *The Feast of Lupercal*, Boston and Toronto, 1957.

Murry, John Middleton, *Countries of the Mind: Essays in Literary Criticism*, London, 1922.

O'Flaherty, Liam, *Spring Sowing*, London, 1924.

O'Flaherty, Liam, *The Short Stories of Liam O'Flaherty*, London, 1937.

O'Connor, John, *Come Day, Go Day*, Dublin, 1948.

O'Donnell, Donat, *Maria Cross: Imaginative Patterns in a Group of Modern Catholic Writers*, London, 1954.

O'Faoláin, Seán, *A Nest of Simple Folk*, New York, 1934.

O'Faoláin, Seán, *The Short Story*, Cork, 1948.

Rafroidi, Patrick, and Terence Brown, ed., *The Irish Short Story: Studies of Irish Writers and Their Work*, Lille, 1979.

Rafriodi, Patrick, and Maurice Harmon, *The Irish Novel in Our Time*, Lille, 1976.

Skelton, Robin, ed., *JM Synge, Four Plays and The Aran Islands*, Oxford, 1962.

Thoreau, Henry David, *Walden: or Life in the Woods*, New York, (pbk.) 1960.

INDEX

Adelphi, 45

"After Forty Years," 12, 219-20, 241-2, 252, 256
   description of, 248-52

Allen, Walter, 253, 253-4

America, 83, 158

American-Irish Literary Foundation, 253

American Literary Foundation, 22

Aquinas, St Thomas, 176

archives, 218

"Aunt Suzanne," 38, 49, 81
   description of, 58-64
   and *Lost Fields*, 97, 99

Austen, Jane, 185

Ayer, Nancy, 157

Banville, John, 244

BBC, Northern Ireland, 195

"Becalmed," 10, 38, 67, 92-3, 113

Belfast
   blitz, 14-15, 109-10
   in McLaverty's work, 50-1, 53, 58-9, 81-2, 83, 178
   in "The Game Cock," 69, 71

Belfast Telegraph, The, 130, 195, 229-30, 231

Bell, Sam Hanna, 174

Bell, The, 103-4, 178, 184

Best Sellers, 231

Best Short Stories, The, 53

Billy Boogles and the Brown Cow, 253

Blake, William, 13, 149, 235, 255

Blind Mice, The (Friel), 224

Books of the Month, 103

"Boots, The," 59, 66, 67
   description of, 37-40

Boston Post, 103

Boston University, 218

Boyd, John, 242-3

Brightening Day, The, 178, 242, 248, 252, 254-5
   rejected by Cape, 227-8
   reviews of, 229-32
   description of, 232-5

Brooklyn Eagle, 128

Call My Brother Back, 10, 47, 54, 92, 104, 114, 168, 179
   major themes, 35, 74, 77
   characters, 37, 155
   and "Leavetaking," 49, 64, 65
   Belfast in, 51, 59
   published, 76-8
   description of, 79-86
   autobiographical, 83
   reviews of, 83-4
   shortcomings, 101, 102
   republished, 243, 246-7, 253, 255

Cape, Jonathan, 95-6, 147, 157, 182-3, 227, 243
   and *In This Thy Day*, 123, 124-5, 127, 131
   and *The Three Brothers*, 150-1

Capuchin Annual, The, 67, 76, 86, 92, 116

Carnduff, Tom, 2

Cather, Willa, 37

Catholic Authors, 78, 94

Catholic Free Press, 189

Catholic Literary Foundation, 151, 230

Catholic World, 52, 159, 212

Censorship Board, Irish, 229

Chapman and Hall, 64
Chekhov, Anton, 10, 195, 217, 222, 242, 247
  influence of, 12, 30, 46, 214
  McLaverty on, 42, 195, 197-8
Chesterton, G. K., 22
Choice, The, 5, 167, 202, 214, 216, 238, 252
  description of, 205-12
  reviews of, 206, 212-13
Church, Richard, 129
"Circus Pony, The," 168, 195, 200, 202-4, 216, 248, 255, 256
Clarke, Dan, 9, 200
Collected Stories, 221, 252, 253-4
Colum, Padraic, 161
Come Day, Go Day (O'Connor), 19
Commonweal, 84
Conroy, Mary. see McLaverty, Mary
Corkery, Daniel, 96, 117, 208, 216
  influence of, 12, 29, 42, 180-1
  on *School For Hope,* 191-2, 194, 196, 204, 229, 238, 255

"D-Day" (McFadden), 225-6
Dark, The (McGahern), 227-9
"Dead, The" (Joyce), 220, 249, 250
December Bride (Bell), 174
Deevy, Teresa, 158-9, 190, 200-2, 204-5, 219-20, 249
Detroit Free Press, 157, 159-60
Devin-Adair Company, 125, 126-7, 147, 181
Dolmen Miscellany, 219
Dolmen Press, 243, 246
Dublin Magazine, The, 129, 190, 198, 200, 202, 204
Dubliners (Joyce), 74
Duhamel, Georges, 96, 232
Duns Scotus, 16

Elias, Mairin, 231
Eliot, T S, 150
Ervine, St John, 2-3, 115, 130-1
"Evening in Winter," 49, 50-2, 59, 82, 248

Faber, 243
Facts, 148
"Father Christmas," 138, 142-3
Fiacc, Padraic, 18, 142, 160-1
Figgis, Allen, 243, 246-7, 255
Fin de la Nuit, La (Mauriac), 170

Flaherty, Robert, 83
Forecast, 22, 151
"Fosterage" (Heaney), 221-2
Friel, Brian, 224

"Game Cock, The," 49, 50, 64, 97, 114-15, 129, 148
  major themes, 37, 40, 52
  description of, 68-74
  Corkery on, 181
Game Cock and Other Stories, The, 43, 127, 142, 147-8, 150, 159, 238
Gibson, John, 195
Gill and Macmillan, 243
Gogarty, Oliver St John, 129
Gorman, Fr, 198
Greacen, Robert, 1-2, 138
"Green Field, The," 29-35, 186, 187, 212
Greene, Graham, 153
"Grey Goat, The," 37, 40-2, 89, 90

"Half-Crown, A," 168, 178-9
Hamill and Barker, 218
Harris, Mary, 215, 216
Hartley, L P, 158
Heaney, Seamus, 9-10, 220-3, 240, 247, 253, 254
Hewitt, John, 2, 103-4
Hill, William B, S.J., 190
Hoehn, Fr, 94
Holland, Jack, 220-1
Hopkins, Gerard Manley, 13-14, 22, 25, 167, 221, 224, 247
  McLaverty on, 16-17, 24
  influence of, 192, 207, 235
  Journal of, 222-3
  McLaverty compared to, 253-4
Houghton Mifflin, 127
Howard, G Wren, 243
Hunter, Mercy, 114

In This Thy Day, 19, 30, 38, 138, 152, 175, 238, 243, 254, 255
  reviews of, 2-3, 115, 128-31
  moral tone of, 15, 149, 153
  extracts published, 17-18, 115-16
  characters, 34, 154, 155, 206
  early stages of, 120-2
  Longmans unhappy with, 123, 124
  refusal to change ending, 123, 126, 132, 151, 192, 237

description of, 123-7
assessment of, 131-6
McLaverty favourite, 217
Indianapolis Star, 148
Inquirer, 129
Ireland, Denis, 2
Ireland Today, 58, 64, 68
Irish Censorship Board, 229
Irish Harvest, 138
Irish Monthly, 29, 37, 43, 50
Irish News, 231
Irish Press, 244
Irish Times, The, 149, 173-4, 175, 248
Irish Writing, 147, 174, 194

James, Henry, 242
Johannesburg Star, The, 83
John O'London's Weekly, 129
Joy, Fr John, 29
Joyce, James, 12, 74, 220, 249, 250

Kavanagh, Patrick, 222
Kelly, Blanche Mary, 175-6
Kernan, Julie, 77, 94, 97
    and *In This Thy Day*, 120-2, 123, 125-6
Kickham, Charles, 231
Kiely, Benedict, 189
Knopf, Alfred A, 126, 127

Lagan, 116, 133
Lane, Temple, 149-50
Lavin, Mary, 180, 216, 217, 244
"Leavetaking," 37, 49-50, 64-7, 79, 86, 90, 91
Leitch, Maurice, 244
"Letter, The," 37, 42-3, 45, 58, 86, 89
"Letter to a Young Novelist," 21-2
Levin, Martin, 232
Lewis, Carl, 148
Library Journal, 231
Listener, The, 103
Listowel Writers' Week, 253
Little Brown and Company, 126
Longmans Green, 53, 77-8, 121, 123, 126, 135
    McLaverty leaves, 18, 125-6
    Call My Brother Back, 76-8
    Lost Fields, 94-6
    "Look At The Boats" ("The Sea"), 86, 92-3, 114, 115, 178
    major themes, 10
    description of, 90-2

Lost Fields, 38, 64, 114, 120, 123, 124, 161, 206, 232
    major themes, 11, 74, 92, 178
    Belfast in, 59, 78
    description of, 94-103
    reviews of, 103-4, 129, 154

McCloskey, Fr, 6
MacDermott, Philip, 247
MacDiarmid, Hugh, 254
McFadden, Roy, 1, 10, 18, 129-30
    "D-Day," 225-6
McGahern, John, 216-19, 220, 225, 227, 244
    The Dark, 227-9
McLaverty, Catherine, 4-5
McLaverty, Mary, 6-7, 175, 180, 223
McLaverty, Michael. *see also* novels; short stories
    assessments of, 1-4
    abandons short stories, 3-4, 11-15, 17-19, 23-5, 109, 120, 148-9
    as moral novelist, 3-4, 13, 16-23, 135-6, 148-9, 161-2, 167-8, 196-7, 233-7
    early life, 4-7
    early writings, 7-11, 29-30
    journal of, 12-15, 20, 22-3, 170, 175, 176, 190, 196-7, 224-5
    and young writers, 15-16, 21-2, 215, 216-19
    change of publishers, 18, 125-6
    moves towards novels, 64, 76-7
    and American publishers, 126-7
    Forecast article, 152-3
    ignores critics, 175
    sense of isolation, 175-6, 237-8, 240
    on the short story, 180
    re-assesses literary position, 194-5
    at St Thomas's, 200-1, 215-16, 220
    and McGahern, 216-19, 220, 225, 227-9, 249
    archives of, 218
    retrospective, 218
    resigns from St Thomas's, 223-6, 238
    reluctant to write again, 240-1
    at St Joseph's, 240-1, 242
    late flowering of, 247-8, 253-4
McLaverty, Michael Snr, 4-5
Macmillan Company, 127, 151, 168, 173, 205, 227-8

MacNeice, Louis, 2, 221
McSorley, Edward, 157
Mansfield, Katherine, 214, 216, 222, 247
  McLaverty article on, 195-6, 197
Marcus, David, 174-5, 194, 244, 247, 249
Maria Cross (O'Donnell), 22, 24, 197
Marian Dominic, Sister, 243-4
Maupassant, Guy de, 242
Mauriac, François, 21-2, 24, 153, 167
  comparisons with, 170, 172
  influence of, 176-8, 192, 207, 235
Maurice Harte (Murray), 224
Mayne, Rutherford, 2
McGahern, John, 249
Mercer, Vivian, 147
Mercier Press, 243
Meyer, Kuno, 30, 153
"Michael McLaverty Explains His Methods," 22
Micheaux, Mme de, 9
"Miss Devlins, The," 184-5
Month in the Country, A (Turgenev), 232-3
"Moonshine" ("The Poteen Maker"), 15, 109, 110-16, 116, 248
Moore, Brian, 59
Moore, Reginald, 116
"Mother, The," 15, 138-42, 255
  radio adaptation, 195
"Mother and Daughter," 248
Mourne Press, 113-15
Moynihan, John C., 103
Muir, Edwin, 103, 154
Mulcahy, Matt, 2
Murphy, Dervla, 248
Murry, John Middleton, 45

New Ireland Society, 2
New Irish Writing, 244, 249
New Statesman, The, 74
New Stories, 53
New Writing, 11
New York Times, The, 83, 158, 190, 232
New Yorker, The, 147-8
"Night and Day: A Note on Literature," 24
Noeud de Vipères, Le (Mauriac), 21, 24

Notaire du Havre, Le (Duhamel), 96, 232
novels, 64, 127-8, 201-1
  moral tone of, 3-4, 13, 16-23, 148-9, 161-2, 167-8, 196-7
  choice of titles, 122-3, 151, 182-3, 227
  compared to short stories, 129, 131-2
  article on, 152-3
  major themes, 214-15, 233-5
  assessment of, 254-6

O'Brien, Conor Cruise. *see Maria Cross* (O'Donnell)
O'Brien, Edna, 244
O'Brien, Edward, 94, 126
O'Brien, Edward J, 53, 76-7
O'Brien, Kate, 115
Observer, The, 148
O'Connor, Frank, 129, 230
O'Connor, John, 19, 152
O'Donnell, Donat. see O'Brien, Conor Cruise
O'Faolain, John, 129
O'Faolain, Julia, 244
O'Faolain, Sean, 202-3, 234, 235, 248
O'Flaherty, Liam, 12, 30, 40, 67
Oxford Times, 84

"Passing Generation, The," 116, 133-4
Patterson, Virginia, 173
PEN, McLaverty address to, 15-16
"Pigeons," 29, 51, 68, 69, 73, 79, 89, 129, 148
  major themes, 37, 52, 69, 74
  Belfast in, 49, 50, 81
  description of, 53-8
Poolbeg Press, 247, 253, 254
"Poteen Maker, The," 15, 248. see "Moonshine"
Prescott, Orville, 158, 190
"Priest's Housekeeper, The," 252
"Prophet, The," 47, 114, 115
Providence Sunday Journal, 157
Pudney, John, 11, 24

Queen's University, Belfast, 6, 24, 180, 253

"Race, The," 49, 67-8, 89
"Reaping Race, The" (O'Flaherty), 67

Reid, Forrest, 9, 242
Republican, The, 157
"Return, The," 49, 52-3, 87, 90
Reynolds, Horace, 83-4, 159-60
Road to the Shore, The, 204, 247, 248, 252-3
"Road to the Shore, The," 15, 109, 116-20, 248
Rowley, Richard, 2, 113-14

St Dominic's High School, 247
St John's school, Belfast, 7-8, 9
St Joseph's Training College, 223, 240-1, 242, 247
St Louis Post-Dispatch, 157
St Louis Star-Times, 157-8
St Malachy's College, Belfast, 6, 80-1, 83
St Mary's, Strawberry Hill, 6
St Thomas's Boys' Secondary School, 9-10, 215-16, 220, 238
McLaverty appointed to, 200-1, 204-5
McLaverty retires from, 223-6
San Francisco Chronicle, 148
Saturday Review of Literature, 84
School For Hope, 167, 175, 204, 205, 208, 212, 216
early stages of, 181-2
description of, 184-9
reviews of, 189-90
Corkery's opinion of, 191-2, 194, 196, 204, 229, 238, 255
moral theme, 206-7
"Schoolmaster, A," 109, 110, 114, 115
"Schooner, The," 11, 92-3, 236, 248
Scott, Cecil, 127, 185, 240-2, 244
correspondence with, 168, 181-3, 223, 227-9
"Sea, The" ("Look At The Boats"), 86, 92-3, 114, 178
major themes, 10, 38, 49
description of, 90-2
"Sea Road," 116
Selected Writing, 116
Sheils, George, 2
short stories, 47, 67-8, 138
major themes, 30, 37-8, 43, 45, 49-50, 52-3, 64-5, 67
prototypes, 34, 35-7
influence on novels, 85-6
moving away from, 109, 116, 160-1

occasional, 168, 178, 180
return to, 195, 198-200, 241-2, 244
Sign, The, 198
Single Lady, A (Lavin), 180
"Six Weeks On and Two Ashore," 11-12, 22, 23, 133, 138, 248, 250, 255, 256
description of, 143-7
Southport Guardian, The, 83
Spectator, The, 115
Spring Sowing (O'Flaherty), 30
"Steeplejacks," 244-6, 248, 252, 255
"Stone," 10, 38, 49, 67, 90, 199, 248
description of, 86-9
Stories of the Forties, 74
Sun, 128
Sunday Times, The, 174
Sylvester, Harry, 84

Thérèse Desquéroux (Mauriac), 22, 170, 172
Thomas, Edward, 221
Thoreau, Henry, 110
Three Brothers, The, 30, 38, 178, 233
moral tone of, 19-20, 22, 24, 206-7, 234
characters, 34, 207, 211, 212
description of, 148-57
reviews of, 157-61
McLaverty favourite, 217
Time, 189
Time and Tide, 158
Times Dispatch, The, 148
Times Literary Supplement, 128, 190, 206
Tolstoy, Leo, 10, 216, 217, 247
influence of, 12
"Trout, The," 47, 49, 50, 58
Truth in the Night, 167, 178, 199, 205, 206, 216, 236
description of, 168-73
influence of Mauriac, 171-2, 176-8
reviews of, 173-6
"Turf Stack, The," 29, 35-7, 40, 58
Turgenev, Ivan, 142, 212
influence of, 232-3

Ulster Literary Theatre, 2
"Uprooted," 168, 195, 241-2, 248, 255
description of, 198-9

Vann, Fr Gerard, 235
"Vigil," 109-10
"Vision" (Corkery), 42, 216
Voice of the Irish, The, 175

Waste Ground, 6, 58, 77. see *Call My Brother Back*
West Australian, The, 83
"White Mare, The," 10, 67, 86, 91, 148, 248
   major themes, 37, 38, 40, 41, 49
   description of, 89-90
   anthologised, 114, 115
White Mare and Other Stories, The, 92, 109, 110, 113-15, 121-2
   reviews of, 114-15

"Wild Duck's Nest, The," 29, 50, 53, 55, 132, 153, 248, 256
   major themes, 37, 49, 58, 74, 89
   description of, 43-7
"Wild Goat's Kid, The" (O'Flaherty), 40
Wordsworth, William, 254
World War II, 120-2
   Belfast air raids, 14-15
"Wounded Cormorant, The" (O'Flaherty), 40

X, 217

"Young Girl, The" (Mansfield), 216
Young Ulster Society, 16

Zinnes, Harriet, 157

In Quiet Places

The Uncollected Stories, Letters and
Critical Prose of Michael McLaverty

Edited with an Introduction
by
Sophia Hillan King

POOLBEG

The Choice

by
Michael McLaverty

A fine subtle novel of human goodness and frailty

POOLBEG

School for Hope

by
Michael McLaverty

A novel of love, guilt, fear and forgiveness

POOLBEG